973.⁷   . B.
B189p   Pemberton
1991

Pemberton
A Biography

Pemberton

A Biography

Michael B. Ballard

University Press of Mississippi
Jackson & London

973.7
B189p
1991

Copyright © 1991 by University Press of Mississippi
All rights reserved
Manufactured in the United States of America

94   93   92   91   4   3   2   1

Library of Congress Cataloging-in-Publication Data

Ballard, Michael B.
    Pemberton : a biography / Michael B. Ballard.
        p.   cm.
    Includes bibliographical references and index.
    ISBN 0-87805-511-8 (alk. paper)
        1. Pemberton, John C. (John Clifford), 1814–1881.   2. Generals—
Confederate States of America—Biography.   3. Confederate States of
America. Army—Biography.   4. Vicksburg (Miss.)—History—Siege,
1863.   I. Title.
E467.1.P365B35   1991
973.7′13—dc20
[B]   91-19760
                                                                  CIP

British Library Cataloging-in-Publication data available

H F DAVIS MEMORIAL LIBRARY
COLBY COMMUNITY COLLEGE
1255 SOUTH RANGE
COLBY KS 67701

To the Memory of

Stephen H. King

1943–1982

Contents

Preface

During the winter of 1969–70, my cousin Steve King, to whose memory this book is dedicated, introduced me to the world of Civil War relic hunting. I quickly learned that successful relic hunting requires extensive research. From that point, fate led me down a road to a career in the history and archives professions. I owe Steve much for his invitation to roam a Civil War battlefield.

The dedication to Steve is appropriate, too, because most of the battle sites we walked over were scenes of major battles during the Vicksburg campaign. Our reading of the available books on that pivotal event convinced us that the Confederacy might have saved Vicksburg and won the war if only a competent commander had been on hand to lead Rebel defenders. We had a very low opinion of John C. Pemberton, that despicable Pennsylvania-born Confederate general whose incompetence lost Vicksburg. I am sure no one would be more surprised than Steve to see my name as author on the cover of a Pemberton biography.

Thankfully, an in-depth study of history, complemented by excellent graduate training, gave me the maturity to look beyond personal prejudices. Six years ago I had finished one research project and was looking for another. I had always wanted to do a study related to the Vicksburg campaign, and, after considerable thought, I decided to do a biography of Pemberton. After all, the only book ever written about him was published in 1942 and had been written by his namesake and grandson. That volume was more a history of the Vicksburg campaign, with Pemberton as the central character, than a true biography. I had read the book more than once, and I realized that I still knew very little about Pemberton the man. He had failed, but why had he failed? Was it truly incompetence? Did he have personality problems? What other factors may have been involved? His prewar and postwar years, as well as his war activities previous to and following his Vicksburg assignment, were discussed very little in the old book. Could those years provide some answers? The more questions I asked, the more I knew that I had found a good potential topic.

All that remained to be determined was the availability of sources. I was delighted to find a large cache of Pemberton papers in the Historical Society of Pennsylvania. These papers had not been consulted by his previous biographer. Not only were his papers there, but the Pemberton family papers also included correspondence of his parents, wife, and siblings. Unfortunately, there were no papers for the Civil War years, not did any personal papers for those years turn up elsewhere. This was not too surprising. Pemberton was not likely to be in touch with his Philadelphia family during the war, and his wife and children traveled with him to each of his war posts. I knew, then, that the nature of the sources would dictate a biography characterized by an intimate portrait of the general for the antebellum and postbellum periods and by a less personal Pemberton for the war years. There were also problems with large time gaps in the Pennsylvania papers and an absence of correspondence between Pemberton and his wife. But by using all the family papers these problems could be overcome to some extent. Most letters by other family members frequently referred to Pemberton and his family. Thus assured that sufficient material was available, I launched the project.

The final result is *Pemberton: A Biography,* the story of a military man to whom fate was not kind. Generally, historians have been just as unkind, many agreeing with the spirit of Steve's and my original analysis. But those who have passed negative judgments have done so without the full story of the man cast in a key role of one of the Civil War's most important dramas. The Pemberton that emerged from my research was a complex, contradictory individual, and the varied strains of his personality certainly affected his military career. Fate, too, played a significant role. Pemberton might have made positive contributions to the Confederate cause had his abilities, which did not include field command, been properly used. The intertwining of personality and fate explains the career of John Pemberton, a man who more than anything else was simply unfortunate.

Readers will not find in this volume a rehash of operations in South Carolina during Pemberton's tenure there, nor is there a minutely detailed account of the Vicksburg campaign. I have tried to keep the focus on Pemberton. What did he know, when did he know it, how did he react, and why did he react as he did? I have built the Pemberton story around these questions. The answers left me sympathetic with John Pemberton the general, and with higher regard toward Pemberton the man than I ever would have expected. There is something inherently likable about a man who freely admits his foibles and who, when not cloaked in the arrogance of military power, could be very congenial. I did not find Pemberton to be a great general; neither was he the totally mediocre officer so often portrayed in the past. He was a man who did his best under very difficult circumstances and who, like so many of his contemporaries, was very much a victim of the American Civil War.

I am most grateful to the American Philosophical Society for a grant that made possible an extensive research trip to the National Archives and the Historical Society of Pennsylvania. Without the society's support, the publication of this biography would have been greatly delayed.

I am also appreciative for the aid of numerous archivists and librarians. For fear of leaving out a name, I will not endeavor to list them, but I do want them all to know how invaluable their assistance has been. There are, however, three individuals I must mention: Martha Irby and her assistant, Tracy Byrd White, of the Interlibrary Loan Department, Mitchell Memorial Library, Mississippi State University, and John White, reference archivist in the Southern Historical Collection, University of North Carolina at Chapel Hill. These ladies and gentleman patiently and efficiently handled my numerous emergency requests for research material.

In addition, there is a special group of people that deserve individual mention. My former major professor and current colleague, John F. Marszalek, shared a wintry research journey to North Carolina, Washington, D.C., and Pennsylvania in December 1988 (he is working on a biography of William T. Sherman), and he read every page of every chapter of the first draft of this volume. As usual, he offered constructive comments and made invaluable suggestions. If forced to choose only one reader to evaluate my writing, my choice would be John Marszalek.

Terrence J. Winschel, historian at Vicksburg National Military Park, read and offered many helpful comments on the Vicksburg chapters. He also assisted my research at the park, and our lengthy discussions of Pemberton and the campaign were of tremendous help to my understanding of that complex event. Thanks, Terry, for your assistance and your friendship.

Reverend Larry J. Daniel of Memphis also read the Vicksburg chapters and offered valuable advice. In addition to his clerical duties, Larry is a talented Civil War historian whose research on various aspects of the Vicksburg campaign made him a noteworthy consultant.

Herman Hattaway, University of Missouri at Kansas City, and Gary Gallagher, Pennsylvania State University, both offered valuable assessments of the manuscript, including suggestions that significantly improved the final version. I thank both these outstanding historians for their thoughtful and scholarly analysis.

Trudie Calvert did her usual superb job of copy editing. Both from my own experience and from observing her work with other books, I long ago came to the conclusion that Trudie is one of the best there is at what she does.

Alan Whitehead of Greenwood, Mississippi, read none of the drafts, but he is the kind of friend every historian needs. A prominent amateur historian himself, Alan assisted my research in ways too numerous to mention here, but he knows, and I think he knows the depth of my appreciation. I have never been able to complete a conversation with Alan without his asking, "What can I do to help you?"

David Riggs, museum curator at the Colonial National Historical Park, Jamestown, Virginia, and his wife Susan, who is a librarian at the Swem Library, College of William and Mary, made an invaluable contribution to this study when they discovered letters of Pemberton's mother-in-law in one of the Swem Library manuscript collections. These letters helped fill gaps in the Pemberton prewar correspondence.

Special thanks are due to Becky Smith for her patience and expertise in putting together the various maps and to Fred Faulk for his photographic assistance. Both of these longtime friends are valued employees of the University Relations Department of Mississippi State University.

I must express my appreciation to Seetha Srinivasan, associate director and editor-in-chief of the University Press of Mississippi, for her interest in the Pemberton project from its earliest stages and her professional and efficient handling of this and my past publishing projects. She always seems to call with encouraging words just when they are most needed.

Frank Chressanthis of Roslyn, Pennsylvania, provided excellent photographs of the Pemberton grave site in Philadelphia's Laurel Hill Cemetery. I thank him for his promptness and diligence in answering my request, and I express my appreciation to his brother and sister-in-law and my MSU colleagues, George and June Chressanthis, for contacting Frank on my behalf and getting us together.

Finally, I pay special tribute to my assistant, Betty Self, and to my student assistants, Michelle Cade, Jo Ellen Allison, David Wells, and Patsy Mims. They all helped in various ways toward the completion of the book, and, in the process, learned more about John C. Pemberton than they ever wanted to know. I am sure that they, too, are delighted that I am finally able to let the general rest in peace.

Pemberton
A Biography

Chapter 1

Rending the Sober Veil

Roots and Youth

May days in Mississippi can be hot, and May 16, 1863, had been one of the hottest. When added to the caldron of battle, such days can exhaust the best of men. The drained, dusty, demoralized Confederate army that retreated down the steamy road toward Vicksburg had more than its share of good men, but they had been beaten after hours of hard fighting on ground dominated by Champion Hill, about halfway between Jackson and Vicksburg. This night they would dig in along the Big Black River; tomorrow they would be beaten again and would be forced to abandon Vicksburg or march into the city's considerable defenses.

The man who led this army, General John Clifford Pemberton, had no intention of giving up Vicksburg without a fight. He had promised Confederate President Jefferson Davis he would hold the hill city on the Mississippi River, and he would do his best to keep that promise. The general felt little confidence, though, as he rode wearily toward Vicksburg on May 17. His dark brown, almost black hair was graying rapidly. He had never been more depressed. He rode in silence, accompanied only by one staff officer. At last he spoke: "Just thirty years ago I began my military career by receiving my appointment to a cadetship at the U.S. Military Academy, and to-day—the same date—that career is ended in disaster and disgrace."[1] In his melancholy, Pemberton may have thought of his beloved home city, Philadelphia, Pennsylvania. He may have wondered, as his family back there had wondered, why fate had sent a Philadelphia boy with Quaker roots southward to rise to the rank of lieutenant general in a Rebel army.

John Pemberton's determination to follow his own star regardless of circumstances or consequences made him a Pemberton in the tradition of his ancestors, who were prominent in the settling of Philadelphia and nearby Bucks County. His direct paternal ancestor, Ralph Pemberton, son of William Pemberton of Lancaster County, England, came to Pennsylvania in 1682 with his son Phineas and family. The Pembertons, practitioners of the Quaker religion, traveled with William Penn and other adherents to the faith to escape British persecution.

Phineas Pemberton became one of Penn's most trusted lieutenants and rose to a position of power and wealth in the fledgling Pennsylvania colony. Phineas followed the strict Quaker tenets of simple dress, nonviolence, and communal discipline. He passed along these values to his only surviving son, Israel, the future General Pemberton's great-great-grandfather and the first American-born of his paternal lineage.

Israel left Grove Place, his father's Bucks County estate, and moved south to the thriving town of Philadelphia, where he had been educated. Israel enhanced his birthright by becoming a wealthy merchant and active civic leader, ascending to a position of prominence among local Quakers. In 1745, he purchased a mansion known as Clarke Hall, situated at the southwest corner of Third and Chestnut streets, and established gardens on the estate grounds that became a city showplace. The ostentatiousness of the place represented a trend among prominent Quaker families toward fashionable clothes and stylish dwellings that would have astonished their ancestors.

Israel Pemberton, Jr., born in 1715, carried on his father's business successes and was also an activist in the defense of Quaker rights. He stood in the forefront of Quaker efforts to establish peaceful relations with area Indians. Israel and others of his faith opposed to war suffered harassment, imprisonment, and exile from the state of Pennsylvania during the American Revolution. He survived these indignities and returned to live in Philadelphia, where he died in 1779.

Israel's third son, Joseph, born in 1745, and his wife, Sarah

Kirkbride, continued the family tendency toward a more liberal life-
style. They went so far as to take up social dancing, a radical departure
from their strict Quaker upbringing. Joseph and Sarah, grandparents
of the future general, produced eight children, the youngest, John,
arriving in 1783.[2]

John Pemberton had all the advantages of upper-class family life.
His future successes indicated a solid educational and business background as well as schooling in the game of power politics. Though a
Christian by faith and a Quaker by birth, he never embraced the
doctrines of his forebears. He had a stern manner but in fact was
congenial and made friends easily.

Unlike his grandfather Israel, John went to war, the War of 1812,
though he did not enlist until August 1814. He joined a company of
Pennsylvania volunteers that probably never left the state, the defense
of Pennsylvania being their top priority. John saw little action other
than mundane routines of camp life.[3]

About the time war erupted, John married Rebecca Clifford, the
only child of John and Anna Clifford. The Clifford family had British
and Dutch bloodlines and had been among the early settlers of Bucks
County. Thomas Clifford, Rebecca's grandfather, migrated to Philadelphia and succeeded in business while maintaining a farm retreat in
the country.[4] Rebecca was around twenty when she married twenty-
nine-year-old John. The match seemed a good one; both came from
respected families, and both had Quaker backgrounds. Though more
serious about religion than her husband, Rebecca had a decidedly
liberal attitude toward Quakerism.

The couple's second child, John Clifford Pemberton, was born on
August 10, 1814, fifteen months after the birth of his brother Israel.
The brothers, direct opposites in personality, were nevertheless close
from the very beginning. Black-eyed John was the active sibling, the
popular one, who often plunged ahead first and later regretted his
reckless actions. Blue-eyed Israel was the logical thinker, the reserved
one, perfectly happy with his own company. They would always be
there for each other; their mother noted that when John was less than
a month old, Israel began "to be fond of his little brother." At night
while their father was away soldiering, the Pemberton boys flanked
their mother: Israel in a crib by her bed and John on the bed sandwiched between Rebecca and the boys' nurse.[5]

To support his growing family after the war, John the elder traveled extensively, working as a commission merchant and speculating in land. His activities took him to the ports of Charleston and New Orleans and as far away as Havana. He dealt in land both in the United States and South America. During a journey through Tennessee and Alabama, John met and became fast friends with a future president, Andrew Jackson. Traveling together, the two shared campgrounds and beds when encountering families willing to take in overnight guests. The friendship would be a profitable one for Pemberton, who received many favors from President Jackson, including appointment as naval officer for the District of Philadelphia. Jackson's influence probably also helped him gain the position of port collector for the city. In return, Pemberton faithfully supported Jackson and even named one of his later sons after the Hero of New Orleans. The president would play a more significant role in the life of Pemberton's second son.[6]

By May 1820, young John Clifford and Israel had three sisters. Anna, born in May 1816, and Rebecca (known affectionately as Beck), who arrived in April 1820, would both become special favorites and confidants of John. The third sister, Mary, died in 1820 less than three years after her birth.[7]

Though the elder Pemberton's frequent absences from home were unsettling, his family managed quite well. He often had rambunctious son John on his mind. From long distance a concerned father tried gently to discipline his son in a letter to Rebecca: "Tell him I hope to hear every good account of him from you and all the family. I hope he keeps cleaner than when I left him." Perhaps feeling guilty for being away from his boys and fearing possible negative results, the father filled letters home with counsel and admonition. He urged his sons to find happiness through pursuit of knowledge and to be obedient, kind, and polite to everyone, especially their mother. They should read their Bibles and always be truthful. The affectionate lectures seemed to increase the boys' yearning for the papa they seldom saw. Israel moved John to tears when he read aloud one long, loving epistle enclosed in a letter to their mother. Rebecca then read her letter to the boys, who listened in attentive silence. She proudly wrote her husband, "They think and talk a great deal about you."[8]

John and Israel tried to live up to their papa's expectations. When Israel was nine and John eight, their mother noted that both had fulfilled their resolutions to be "*very* good." Father John learned that his boys were accepting more responsibilities, arriving on time, for example, to escort their mother home from a visit to a neighbor. They made such a positive impression with their gentlemanly appearance and manners that they were rewarded with "grapes, cake & apple & returned home much gratified." John Pemberton welcomed such news and was relieved that young John, who had been ill the last time he was home, felt good enough to join in the feast. Rebecca assured him: "John has improved in his appearance since you went, grown fatter & fresher couloured."[9]

In addition to working on their conduct, the boys pursued their studies as papa had instructed. In the midst of distractions, they spent evenings "writing their thoughts *aloud*" and letters to their father on slates, seemingly oblivious to sister Anna's "prattling," little Beck's fussing over a lost pencil, and nurse Eliza's pacing about with baby Mary in her arms. Rebecca sat at her parlor tea table, surrounded by noise and commotion, reveling in the sights and sounds of her young family.[10]

When the boys were of the proper age, Rebecca enrolled them in an acceptable school. She had shopped around and finally settled on a private academy run by a Mr. Eustace. She characterized Eustace as "mild yet very firm" and liked the way he took "great pains to elucidate every thing to his scholars." She agreed with his philosophy that students must "stand on their own feet" so they could learn to help themselves. Proudly clad in new sealskin capes, the boys went off to school and did well, though John complained about grammar and geography lessons. He did excel at his favorite subject, exposition, and probably showed skill in an area in which he was naturally talented, drawing. Eustace pleased Rebecca with his analysis of her sons' ability. They had the talent to be in the upper third of their class, he thought, but needed to work harder to get there. To raise their achievement level, Eustace assigned much work, resulting in a considerable loss of leisure time at home for the Pemberton boys. Their daily evaluation books almost always had marks of "good" or "very good" in conduct. Both learned quickly and became especially adept at linguistics, particularly Latin and French. Throughout their lives, the brothers would read, discuss, and translate works in both languages.[11]

When not in the classroom, John joined his siblings in adventures at mother Rebecca's heritage, Clifford Farm. John especially loved to visit the horses. In later years, far from home, he would often write and ask about his favorite steeds and express a longing to see them and go for a ride.[12]

For John the farm was a diversion rather than an escape from the city. He enjoyed growing up in lively Philadelphia. A typical seaport at the turn of the century, the town would become "the first major American industrial city" by the time Andrew Jackson's America blossomed. Philadelphia passionately pursued technology; the American Philosophical Society encouraged scientific inquiry among scientists and the professional classes. The arts also thrived, as evidenced in works by sculptors, engravers, and artists. Museums opened and theaters drew large audiences. Perhaps reflecting the days when the United States Congress met in the city, politics frequently dominated public attention. The city's politically oriented newspapers influenced the national scene. All in all, Philadelphia's multifaceted activities, plus good neighborhoods, solid pebblestone streets, and above average hotels, stores, and restaurants made the city seem almost self-contained.

Religion played a prominent role as it had since Philadelphia's founding. On Sundays, chains were stretched across streets to discourage horse and buggy traffic, assuring a more serene Sabbath. Yet by the 1830s, Philadelphia's progressive notions would have a noticeable effect on its early heritage. As Nicholas B. Wainwright put it, "The sober veil of Quaker origins had been rent to shreds."[13]

It was little wonder that an active youngster like John would love his hometown so much. During his first long periods away from the city, he longed for its sights, sounds, and society, for during his teen years he became quite active socially. Philadelphia's changing mores allowed all the young Pembertons to enjoy the parties, dances, and theater most of their ancestors had been denied. At age thirteen, John danced his first cotillion with eleven-year-old Anna as his partner. Israel thought his brother "made out very well for the first time."[14]

Another aspect of life in Philadelphia had a potentially profound though at the time no doubt very subtle influence on John, the future Confederate. The city had close ties with the South. To escape unhealthy conditions, South Carolinians and Virginians summered in the area, and many intermarried with locals. Strong business connections also existed; Southern entrepreneurs frequently dealt with Philadelphia commission merchants.[15]

In addition to occasional Southern accents, John was exposed to the glamour of the military. History dictated that the city be a hotbed of patriotism, and it was. Local militia dressed in colorful uniforms marched in commemorative parades. Fifteen thousand participants joined in a processional honoring the centennial of George Washington's birth. These spectacles, combined with Andrew Jackson's influence on the family, inspired John and his young friends to reenact battles.[16]

The Philadelphia of John's early years also had race problems. Until the War of 1812, the city had enjoyed racial harmony; more than seven thousand free blacks coexisted peaceably with the city's whites. The war brought a deluge of poor, untrained black labor, and racial tolerance in the white community plummeted. Though significant antislavery organizations originated in Philadelphia during the Jacksonian era, violent white resistance to abolitionism led to increased tension that resulted in the burning of an abolition headquarters building in the city in 1838.[17]

This milieu planted seeds in John's mind as he grew into young manhood, but none had any immediate visible effects. As he reached his late teen years he was faced with deciding what to do about continuing his education beyond preparatory studies.

John finally decided to try college, and he began preparing himself in the summer of 1830 for entry exams at the University of Pennsylvania. He immediately encountered difficulties. His tutor reported that John was failing some of his lessons and was apparently not studying properly at home. The tutor warned that unless he "studies harder for the seven weeks to come than he has studied of late he will not deserve to enter even as a freshman." He did study harder, and on July 27 his mentor wrote to the university that John C. Pemberton had been working under him for a year and "is offered for examination in all the studies preparatory for admission to the freshman class in the University of Pennsylvania." John was admitted to the university on the condition that he correct a deficiency in Greek.[18] Freshman Pemberton settled into the life of a college student, but after a time his thoughts began centering on another institution of higher learning.

Just when John decided to study civil engineering is unclear, but his desire to prepare himself for such a career at the United States Military Academy at West Point is easy to understand.[19] It involved more than simply a resolution to become an engineer. Andrew Jackson's military career certainly had an influence, as did growing up in Philadelphia. John's contact with things military had been of a romantic nature: the Hero in the White House, the gaudy military parades, and perhaps his own father's stories of 1812. West Point had much to recommend it as an engineering school, but John C. Pemberton surely had more on his mind.

Early in 1833, the Pemberton family began maneuvering to get John appointed to West Point. Influential friends wrote Secretary of War Lewis Cass urging him to consider this "young gentleman of excellent morals and fine attainments." Correspondents advised Cass that at nineteen, he felt he would be too old if forced to wait another year.[20]

Aware that his personal intervention might appear unethical in light of his close personal relationship with President Jackson, John Pemberton refused to intercede overtly on his son's behalf. Rebecca Pemberton decided after some hesitation to appeal directly to Jackson, restating the argument that "the delay of another year would leave . . . [John] too late for his outset in life." She confessed, "I am aware that it is an unusual thing for a Mother to make such a request, but I cannot prevail upon Mr. Pemberton to do it for me, though he will not oppose his Son's ardent wishes."[21]

John Clifford made his own direct appeals to the president. In his first letter, he introduced himself as "the son of one of your warmest friends." He reminded Jackson that he was attempting to gain an appointment without his father's aid and that, although his application was on file, it appeared he might not be considered before the summer of 1834. This would not do "as I am very anxious to relieve my father from the charge of one of his large family."[22]

The pressure worked; perhaps all President Jackson really needed to know was that the son of his old camp fire mate wanted to go to West Point. On May 15, 1833, John got his appointment directly from the president. The delighted youngster wrote Secretary of War Cass, who had provided the official notification, "I will use my best endeavors to assure myself worthy of the station." His father enclosed a statement assenting to John's commitment of five years "unless sooner discharged." John even had the heady experience of meeting with the president, probably during a visit by Jackson to Philadelphia, and receiving a pep talk from the commander in chief about the importance of doing well at the academy.[23]

The good news relieved the discomfort John had been suffering from a broken arm. On May 1, he and three friends had been riding in a carriage. The horse fell while making a turn, upsetting the vehicle and throwing its occupants to the ground. The accident left John with two broken bones in his left arm just above the wrist. He was recovering well and did not expect the mishap to keep him from entering West Point on time.[24]

All that remained was to withdraw from the University of Pennsylvania. When he completed his second year there, John ranked twelfth on the merit roll. The university "regularly and honorably dismissed" him, and Acting Provost W. H. Delancey added "an expression of my sense of the uniform excellence of Mr. Pemberton's character," as well as complimenting his study habits and deportment.[25] At West Point, John would find both academics and deportment a much greater challenge.

So the five-foot, ten-and-a-half-inch tall "handsome boy with black curly hair; genial, companionable . . . with a decided talent for drawing and painting" prepared to go to West Point.[26] As he stood on the threshold of a military career, John had in a sense culminated his own family's rending of the sober veil. From strict Quaker origins, the Pembertons and Cliffords were on the verge of producing a professional soldier. And John C. Pemberton was about to take the first step that would lead him to his destiny in Mississippi.

CHAPTER 2

A Peculiar Liking for the Life

West Point

Accompanied by his father, an excited John Clifford Pemberton traveled to New York City and caught a steamer up the Hudson River. He found West Point all he had hoped it would be. He breathlessly wrote his mother: "I am at West Point at last [and] it is a most beautiful place & the scenery is the most magnificent I have seen." Aware of the major reason why the academy appealed to his parents, he assured his mother that discipline was "extremely strict," so much so that even his stern father was impressed. He could not leave his barracks without permission, and if newcomers strayed to the nearby hotel, "we are gone chickens." Lights out came at 9:30 P.M., and everyone was expected to be in bed. His temporary roommate from Illinois was "a very industrious fellow." Pemberton deplored the school's temperate atmosphere, however; food was boring, consisting of a steady diet of corned beef and potatoes. He wished he could meet incoming steamboats, lifelines to the outside world, which were off-limits to would-be cadets. He wanted to mingle with visitors, but they were seen only rarely by novices who had not yet passed entrance exams. If he passed the tests, a better life awaited. He would be a cadet in fact and could immerse himself in the busy beehive that for the moment must be kept at arm's length.[1]

West Point in 1833 emphasized both discipline and engineering, legacies of Sylvanus Thayer, the thirty-one-year-old academy's third superintendent. Thayer's influence on the academic and administrative structure of the school earned him the title Father of the Military Academy. Political difficulties with President Andrew Jackson caused his resignation about the time John arrived. Major Rene De Russy, a more lax disciplinarian, took over West Point that summer, a fortuitous development for a carefree young Philadelphian.[2]

Pemberton answered two questions on fractions and read and wrote "a few words," and that easily, or so it seemed to him, passed the entrance exams. The academy surgeon examined his recently broken arm and announced that the bones could have been set better but he should have no trouble handling a musket. A relieved John wrote his father, "I was very glad of [that], as I like the place better every day I stay here." He was a cadet now, and all he had to fret over was a delay in getting his uniform.[3]

Cadet Pemberton stepped into army life in the form of summer camp, an annual ritual that packed drills in riding, tactics, musketry, artillery, fencing, and endless marching into an eleven-and-a-half-hour day. Then there was guard duty, which he and other first-year cadets, or plebes as they were derisively called, had the honor to draw every third day for eight to nine hours in the hot sun. Pemberton was officially admitted on July 1 and had his uniform by the second week of the month. He was enjoying camp life. His arm survived musketry drill, and he took great pride in the praise heaped on his five-man squad by a senior cadet. Despite all rigors, John wrote Israel that he was still "much pleased" with the Point, as all those who were part of the academy family affectionately called the school on the Hudson.[4]

From that first summer experience until his fourth and final camp, Pemberton looked forward to time away from academics. He thought it "a devilish pleasant life" even when marred by "blessed" drills and guard duty. He learned that "it is no trifle to stand post eight hours a day," and night duty meant little sleep "as we are turned out every hour almost to receive somebody." Yet "variety is the spice of life," he philosophized when he thought of the classroom. By his last summer, he viewed camp scenes with the smugness of a veteran: "Right-left shoulders square to the front—hail arms, one, two, three, heft! heft! heft! &c &c are all the time sounding in my ear [so] that I can scarcely think of anything to say. These plebes are a great deal of trouble."[5]

He needed the summer breaks from academic trials. Studying was not his long suit; he had the ability, but the spirit was unwilling. He never devoted the attention necessary to achieve a high academic standing. He maintained a slightly better than average overall record, but only with much difficulty.

During the fall of his freshman year, his knack for languages landed him in the first section of French class. Through three years of study, he maintained a 95 average (out of a possible 100 percent) in French. His success did not particularly impress him because he was aware of the lack of emphasis on classical studies at the Point.[6]

Math was another story, though he started out well enough. Before long, however, he complained to his parents that the instructor covered as much material in a month as previous teachers had in nine weeks. One recitation (the favorite academy teaching method in those days) required command of ten to thirteen pages of text, and cadets had to write problems on the blackboard and give detailed explanations of solutions. So far he had managed the highest possible marks, but he worried how long that would last. Not long as it turned out; by his second year he had sunk to the second math section. He characterized areas of math related to architecture as "rather disgusting," and he "could not make head nor tail of" descriptive geometry. His overall average in all math courses was about 68 percent, a less that sterling performance.[7]

Because of his problems with math, difficulties with engineering courses seemed inevitable, a troublesome situation for someone who wanted to be a civil engineer. His one year of engineering studies could fairly be called disastrous. He earned only 165.3 points out of a possible 300.[8]

With one exception, his performance in other academic fields ranged from average to poor. His marks in chemistry rivaled those in math. In ethics he scored about 80 percent; in natural philosophy, around 70; in tactics, 46; and in artillery, 52.[9]

Pemberton did best in drawing, exhibiting genuine talent. He missed having a perfect score for three years of study by less than three points. In addition to class work, he spent spare time sketching landscapes and individuals. He particularly enjoyed drawing scenic winter scenes around West Point. His work so impressed instructor Robert Weir that he kept the best of it to display at the academy. When John the elder learned of this, he fired off a letter accusing his progeny of ingratitude and caring so little for his parents that he gave his best work away. The cadet retorted that he had done nothing wrong, and the rift subsided when his father learned that the drawings were on display.[10]

Pemberton's drawing ability drew him into yet another clash with his father. A Philadelphia visitor to the academy saw a caricature he had sketched of his French teacher, Claudius Berard. The elder Pemberton berated his son for degrading a professor. John denied that such was his intent and sent the sketch home so his father could judge for himself. Typical of Pemberton family bickering, the whole business ended peacefully. The father accepted the son's explanation and offered friendly counsel: "I hope you will never allow yourself to put on an indifference of manner towards any of your Professors, or teachers, whatever may be your belief in their opinion of you. Remember dear John, that you are much in their power."[11]

Such advice hardly seemed necessary because the youth was indifferent rather than antagonistic toward most of his professors. He may have been referring to the eminent, brilliant, and not too well-liked engineering professor Dennis Hart Mahan when he commented on one class that "there is more sifting and straining here to make one good scholar than there is in a whole class at College." Otherwise, only Robert Weir made a solid impression on him. Weir's artistic skills so impressed Pemberton that he asked for private tutoring.[12]

The Philadelphia cadet also liked Superintendent De Russy. When Israel contemplated a visit during John's plebe year, his brother guaranteed him a personally guided tour of the place because De Russy was "very obliging & kind[;] he has never refused me anything yet." Pemberton often asked for time away from his duties "on account of the great number of acquaintances that I have seen since I have been here," and De Russy almost always obliged. Pemberton was among a large portion of the corps who attended the funeral of De Russy's wife in 1835, and he took pride in the character of the commandant's new bride two years later. Pemberton understandably was fond of De Russy but might have been better served by a more rigid commander.[13]

Had the cadet been instilled with a little more self-discipline, he no doubt could have avoided many strident exchanges with his parents, especially his father. Part of the problem was John Pemberton's refusal to let his sons go. He continued to give advice much as he had done during their childhood. He urged John to keep his class standing high and to keep his goal of graduation ever in mind. After all, an academy degree was a passport to the world. "Ever be polite," he urged, "study to your uttermost—and dear, dear John leave not the camp without leave, nor do anything from petulance or excited feelings—if anything unhappily should occur let me know it instantly. I may assist you, when it may be out of your power to redress yourself—avoid studiously chewing tobacco, smoking and above all, drinking anything that is not permitted to the cadets—it will be a sacrifice, not worthy of a thought, compared to the evil it may bring on you, and those you love!" The youth sometimes resented the advice but his years at the Point proved that his father knew him well.[14]

Chastisements from both parents were more specific and severe when John's grades faltered. Impatiently he tried to explain the intricacies of grading systems and class rankings, but his assurances that bad monthly reports did not affect rank at the end of the year usually fell on deaf ears. When his mother suggested that he consider resigning rather than settle for a poor class standing, the bitter response was "I would rather have my hand cut off tomorrow and I beg you will not speak to me of it again. I would not resign with my own will if you could give me twenty thousand dollars for doing so."[15]

A consistently high number of demerits plagued him and produced more unhappy letters from home. Again, he tried to explain that he was in no danger. Exasperated by continual inquiries from anxious parents, he finally blurted, "I have only again and again to assure you it [their concern] is groundless . . . do you suppose I am going to be ass enough to be dismissed after I have been here nearly three years— no I am not nor if you understood the subject would you think so yourself." His words settled nothing, for both the demerits and demands from home for explanations continued.[16]

Despite the sharp exchanges, Pemberton maintained a close relationship with his family. They worried over their cadet's myriad afflictions: colds, flu, eye infection, and a sprained foot. He in turn worried about his father's chronic asthma, an ailment that seemed to run in the family and, in his father's case, grow more serious with age. The bitter exchanges never altered John's strong affection for his father. He advised brother Israel to be guided by papa's advice in making important decisions. And he was particularly proud of the impression the elder John made during visits to West Point. The cadets "all speak of you as a friend," he wrote after one such visit. One who saw him at the theater commented that the *"old gentleman* (meaning you) shook hands with him although not being personally acquainted as if you had been old friends & wished to know if you were not a Southerner. . . . They say I am very like you . . . which you know has often been said before." Papa John wrote with equal pride regarding his son's relationship with other cadets: "They all think highly of you, your rogue!" The Pemberton family practiced bickering coated with a thick layer of love even at long distance.[17]

The parents worried and cajoled in vain. Pemberton's lack of studying and love of socializing remained constant during his West Point years. He looked forward to the occasional dances and concerts that broke the monotony of daily regimentation, rules, and regulations. Cadets risked demerits by visiting among themselves after hours, sharing stories, tobacco, and perhaps a taste of alcoholic beverages. John basked in such adventures, admitting to Anna, "I am not particularly pleased with quiet," and reminiscing about Israel's fastidious nature as opposed to his own trait of being "uncommonly rowdy." His freshman year he was rowdy enough to be arrested for throwing bread in the mess hall. Such trouble was mild compared to disciplinary problems that awaited him in his senior year.[18]

The few diversions at the Point never satisfied Cadet Pemberton. He longed for vibrant Philadelphia. When walking guard duty on a cold night, his mind often drifted back to the family parlor, a warm fire, and old girl friends. In his barracks bed he dreamed of girls from the "city of brotherly love." In one such dream loud voices singing the "Star Spangled Banner" suddenly accompanied his partying. One of the fairer sex suddenly stepped on his toe, waking him to the reality of several intoxicated, dissonant cadets, one of whom had tripped over Pemberton's foot that dangled from his bed.[19]

The excitement of the city clung in his memory. Each fall he pictured residents returning from summer homes and vacations. He recalled the streets, "very gay and full of life," and how the first chill of winter was "the jolliest time of the four seasons." Philadelphia parties, dances, and theater dominated his thoughts during slow times at West Point. He urged Anna to keep a daily journal of her activities and to report the results. He needed the news, for "no one knows the value of home and all its pleasures till he is away from it."[20]

Furloughs provided some relief, but Pemberton was careful not to ask for too many. He was wise enough not to test the limits of De Russy's good nature and willingness to stretch rules. Anyway, so many Philadelphians visited the academy that he must at times have felt the entire city had come to see him. During good weather, it seemed that scarcely a day passed without numerous chances to squire around acquaintances from home. Young women received his special attention.[21]

He especially longed for the company of Israel and Anna and did his best to keep up with their lives. He sent congratulations upon Israel's graduation from the University of Pennsylvania in 1833 and his obtaining a position as a railroad surveyor. He advised Israel to "do all in your power to make yourself independent of the exertions of any but yourself," predictable words from a cadet weary of regulations. He could not resist poking fun when his staid brother suddenly seemed to show an interest in Philadelphia parties. You "must be considerably changed from what you were formerly . . . if I were you I would make the best of my time . . . and file into the good graces of the young ladies well to do in the world—don't allow yourself to be put in the rear rank if you run any chance of getting into the front."[22]

Anna received gentler needling. During his first winter at the Point, John wrote that he had no doubt that she would "be very much altered" when he next saw her; she was, after all, changing from girl to woman. He took pride in her visits, for his sister had a winning personality and a spirit of adventure that impressed other cadets. On one occasion she journeyed up to the "Crow's Nest," a 1,418-foot-high peak in the Hudson highlands bordering West Point to the north. Anna frequently attended academy parties, and her presence always perked John's spirit.[23]

The winter months proved a particular challenge for isolated cadets who sought diversions. The weather had a depressing effect. "You have no idea," John wrote Anna, "how the wind blows here until you hear it once a continual whew, ew, ew, ew the whole night." The Hudson usually froze, shutting off steamboat traffic and, with it, visitors. Pemberton probably used slow winter days to catch up on reading; he liked to spend time with newspapers and books sent from home (he rarely visited the academy library). On occasion he played billiards or ventured outside to join in a favorite cold weather pastime, ice skating. That sport could be hazardous because cadets who wandered too far up or down the frozen river out of sight of the academy were periodically attacked by so-called river pirates (would-be muggers) though muscular cadets sometimes gave a good account of themselves.[24]

Christmas and New Year's were the best days of winter. De Russy relaxed rules to help young men cope with being away from home during the holidays. Eggnog flowed in abundance, and all had "a very merry though rather noisy time." One could get "as tipsy as any one thinks proper, so . . . [long as] he does not stand out on the plain & cut his anticks there." Those who tried to sleep often awakened to "the manifold discordant sounds which proceed from the Barracks." Pemberton no doubt contributed his part to the "infernal noises" of the jubilee.[25]

Winter holidays were not the only impetus that fueled sampling of alcohol. Peer pressure and natural curiosity led to drinking and to experimenting with tobacco. Pemberton began smoking a pipe during his first year at the Point. He later assured his father that he had given it up, though he eventually took up the habit of chewing tobacco. But his drinking, at least to excess, seemed confined to winter holiday revelry. He mentioned the famous tavern Benny Haven's, where many cadets imbibed, briefly in his letters, but he never admitted to going there.[26]

In addition to fun and games and vices, the cadets loved to talk politics. Andrew Jackson's battles with Congress held the attention of most; "we are politicians en masse, and pretty nearly all on one side," Pemberton reported home. Jackson's campaign against the Second Bank of the United States, however, did not produce unanimity. John observed, "There are some cadets here who are very hot against him but they are all nullifiers." For someone later characterized as having pro-Southern sentiments dating all the way back to West Point, this is a revealing statement.[27]

Pemberton kept a close eye on all elections that might reflect good or ill on Old Hickory. He supported Jackson on all major issues and was relieved when Jacksonian Martin Van Buren won the 1836 presidential election. He made bets with fellow cadets on state-by-state results of the election and, thanks to Van Buren's victory in Pennsylvania, almost broke even; overall he lost slightly more than he won.[28]

National politics directly affected the Point when several cadets left the academy to fight in the Texas revolution against Mexico. Except for his strong family ties, John Pemberton might have gone too; the thought crossed his mind. He strongly defended those classmates who did go against his parents' criticism. He considered their action anything but "disgraceful or dishonorable." After all, how could those educated to defend the country be dishonored for assisting others in a just cause? He remained at the academy not because he thought his departed friends wrong but because "I would not be doing my duty to my parents or properly returning their affection." These comments are interesting in light of the future that awaited him.[29]

The coming years would offer more opportunities for combat for Pemberton and others at the academy. Among them were George Meade, Lloyd Tilghman, Joseph Anderson, Montgomery Blair, P. G. T. Beauregard, Irwin McDowell, William J. Hardee, Henry Halleck, William Sooy Smith, E. R. S. Canby, George Thomas, Richard Ewell, William T. Sherman, Paul Hebert, and Bushrod Johnson. From Pemberton's class Braxton Bragg, William Mackall, Jubal Early, William French, John Sedgwick, Thomas Williams, Joseph Hooker and W. H. T. Walker would later become prominent. Another in his class, Lew Armistead, did not graduate but would be remembered, primarily because of the circumstances of his death at a great battle in a small Pennsylvania town. John's West Point letters do not mention most of these future Civil War soldiers. He did make general, prideful references to his class but only to extol its expertise at giving parties.[30]

Although Pemberton wrote little about his classmates, the available evidence disputes the myth that he preferred "affiliations with the young men of the South" to company with cadets from other areas. His best friend and onetime roommate was fellow Philadelphian George Meade. He rarely referred to other roommates, who over his

years at the academy came from all parts of the country. He liked most
of them, especially the adventurous, like the one who caught a squir-
rel, tamed it, and let it have the run of their room after inspection.
Aside from another pre–West Point acquaintance, Lloyd Tilghman,
Meade was the only cadet mentioned frequently in John's letters
home. He thought George a "very studious and a very clever fellow."
The two often did favors for each other and occasionally went on
furloughs together. Meade graduated in 1835, two years before John,
who never developed a comparable relationship thereafter. The first
four days of July 1863 would give an ironic twist to their friendship.[31]

Many cadets returned Pemberton's friendship; his lively personality
made him an academy favorite, as his father proudly noted. His infre-
quently used nickname Jack apparently originated at the Point,
though most acquaintances at the time and thereafter preferred John.
Other cadets enjoyed the girl-happy antics of the Philadelphian, one
summing him up as "a case."[32] As reader of one of the several academy
literary societies, Pemberton received from his friends the dubious
honor of reading to the society "A Short Dissertation on the History of
that Nondescript Lately Discovered Animal—the Plebe." Hardly a
literary masterpiece, it displayed a brand of humor that John practiced
at every opportunity:

> In sober truth I think the plebe is
> Fair subject for a lengthy treatise.
> One of a most elaborate nature
> might be composed upon the creature.
> But to conclude & be compendious
> the animal I'll style amphibious.
> Between two breeds the Brute doth vary
> half citizen half military.[33]

Pemberton received a more notable honor when in the spring of
1836 cadets elected him reader of the Declaration of Independence for
the Fourth of July celebration, the "major social event of the season."
He wrote Anna that he hoped his father could come hear him, though
he wondered how Papa would react to the party atmosphere. John
mused that "he must remember how seldom the opportunity occurs
here of making merry." Doubtless his son never missed one of them.[34]

As he launched his first class (senior) year at West Point, Pemberton had two experiences that led him to take a more serious view of his future. Given his personality, both events were predictable. One nearly cost him his chance of graduating. The other was an affair of the heart that might have changed the course of his life.

Sometime during the summer party season of 1836, he met and fell in love with Angeline Stebbins, a pretty sixteen-year-old from New York City. Neither family approved of the match, the Pembertons because they knew of John's record of gross immaturity regarding past girl friends, and the Stebbins family probably because of Angeline's youth. The two became practically engaged after "a three day acquaintance" that left Cadet Pemberton in love "up to the hub." Despite family protests, especially from Anna and his mother, John determined "in this matter to be Boss and follow my own inclinations." To his father he admitted his reputation of often "being momentarily taken by a pretty face." Yet this time "it may turn out earnest—certainly I feel very differently on this subject from what I have ever done before."[35]

The passionate attachment continued through the winter of 1836–37. John and Angeline exchanged letters frequently and maintained their determination to marry when John graduated. In the late spring of 1837, he met her family and was much pleased. Yet in a letter to Anna, he cautioned his sister against having "too extravagant an idea" of Angeline's physical appearance. "I think her very pretty perhaps a little more than pretty," he wrote, but Anna might not agree and might be disappointed. This curious comment was perhaps the first sign that John's ardor for his bride-to-be was fading. Stubborn pride kept him from admitting any such thing for some time to come.[36]

The threat to Pemberton's graduation occurred in November 1836, when he and some of his barracks buddies were arrested for breaking academy regulations. He faced several charges: (1) personal possession of liquor; (2) having liquor in his quarters; (3) causing liquor to be brought into his barracks; (4) bringing liquor into quarters; (5) drinking liquor; (6) though on duty as orderly, not reporting the presence of liquor in his quarters. Pemberton admitted guilt only to the last of the charges and told his father he would not report it "if it was to cause my dismissal & even in the eyes of many disgrace." He blamed the incident on "a jug which smelt of liquor." He thought it empty when he saw it and agreed it was convincing evidence that liquor had been in quarters. But he vehemently denied all charges except failure to report the presence of the jug.[37]

John Pemberton berated his son for not doing his duty. Cadet Pemberton continued to defend himself: "I am sorry, very sorry, you think me wrong—but I repeat that I would suffer any disgrace that a court martial could inflict on me before I would commit an action which has far more disgrace to it in my opinion than if I were twenty times dismissed from this Institution—and so would I believe the majority of fathers do, it is my misfortune that your opinion of right and wrong, differs so much from mine." The issue was hypocritical, he insisted. Liquor found its way into the barracks year-round as it no doubt did in every school and college in the country. As for the form cadets signed promising to obey all regulations, no one took such a pledge seriously. After all, boys will be boys. So went John's arguments, a mixture of common sense and the excuses of one backed into a corner.[38]

Although worried, Pemberton was convinced, and correctly so, that if he and his fellow accused refused to testify against one another, as they pledged, academy authorities could not convict. Still, his papa's consternation weighed heavily on his mind: "The fact is I do not know how to write. I am half ready to cry . . . [from] mere vexation—there is no more danger at this moment of my not graduating next June than there ever has been."[39]

The cadet's predicament dragged on for several weeks. Papa Pemberton offered legal help from a Philadelphia lawyer friend. John thought that unnecessary, but he did write for advice regarding several procedural questions. Again he tried to reassure his worried parent: "I feel and acknowledge Dear Father all your affection for me. Your very anxiety is the cause of my remarks as to yourself. You are *too* anxious. You do not look at things as others do. [B]ecause chance has placed me in a disagreeable situation you appear to think I am not acting rightly. The whole business is nothing more than an unlucky accident and what was just as likely to have happened to almost any room in Barracks as ours."[40]

Time crept on without any court being ordered to hear the case, and John became increasingly hopeful that the charges might be dropped. Angeline boosted his spirits by writing him letters of support, and he reveled in the good food and relaxed atmosphere of Mrs.

Alexander R. Thompson's boardinghouse, where he lived while under arrest. One of Mrs. Thompson's three daughters, Kate, made each meal an adventure with "the most ridiculous questions imaginable." On one occasion she asked a fellow cadet, Jubal Early, who was a guest for dinner: "Mr. Early, did you see the snow on the mountains last winter?" "Yes, Mamm," answered a cautious Early. "Warn't it white," Kate solemnly responded. Pemberton made a somewhat futile attempt not to explode with laughter at the bewildered look on Early's face.[41]

The suspended cadet continued to discuss his case with his father via the mail. He rejected the lawyer's advice to admit charges that were true and throw himself on the mercy of the court. He had witnessed too many courts-martial at the Point to anticipate any bene-fit from pleading guilty on any count. Besides, "I do not in the least fear any thing they can do—if they act justly."[42]

Pemberton turned out to be right. The entire class signed a pledge not to drink during the remaining days at the academy. Colonel De Russy accepted the petition and recommended that charges against all the accused be dropped. By February 1837, it was over, and John Pemberton had survived his greatest West Point scare. Perhaps he had subconsciously reached some conclusions about the value of discipline and strict adherence to regulations. Time would tell.[43]

John graduated twenty-seventh (out of fifty) in his class, having accumulated 163 demerits. Despite the academic and disciplinary problems of his years there, he never lost his affection for West Point. As a plebe, he argued that there was "not a finer place in the world." Two years later he commented that the longer he stayed the better he liked it, and he wrote Anna, "I still think it a *very very* agreeable life." Occasionally he grew tired of the routine, and certainly his arrest during his senior year cast a shadow over his positive attitude. Still, the prospect of graduation saddened him, for he had come to realize that he had developed "a peculiar liking for the life."[44] Or perhaps he had actually developed a sincere liking for the life. His persistent affection for the Point might have stemmed from his strong affinity for the comradeship and occasional revelry there. And perhaps he feared leaving a known and understood life for the outside world.

As its members prepared to leave West Point, the big question facing the Class of '37 was the branch and location of future regular army service. Pemberton's poor academic standing prevented him from going to the elite U.S. Army Corps of Engineers, an assignment reserved for those with the highest standing. He faced the possibility of being sent to the infantry or cavalry, the least desired branches. His influential father pulled a few strings to make sure his son wound up in the artillery, the best spot next to the engineer corps. John himself wrote to the adjutant general's office in Washington requesting a specific assignment to the Fourth Artillery Regiment. He received word that his request would be granted if "it can be done consistently with the interests of the service and the just rights of other graduates." As it turned out, most of the upper two-thirds of the class, including Pemberton, were assigned to the artillery. He joined several classmates in the ranks of the Fourth Regiment. The elder Pemberton's political clout resulted in his son's being initially stationed in New York, father and son's preferred option after Philadelphia.[45]

He did not remain in New York very long. Before receiving his diploma, he had written Israel that he would probably wind up fighting Indians in Florida, where the Second Seminole War was raging. Likely he would either "get scalped by those damned Indians or die a natural death in some of the swamps."[46]

Pemberton would go to Florida, but he would not be scalped or die in the swamps. He would get in trouble. His most disturbing problems in Florida resulted from a continuation of his fickle history with women. The faults of Cadet Pemberton seemed destined to haunt Lieutenant Pemberton as he moved on to the second stage of his military career.

CHAPTER 3

Heartily Tired of the Life

Love, Seminoles, Michigan, Love

Second Lieutenant John C. Pemberton spent his first days in the regular army with his Fourth Artillery comrades in forts guarding New York Harbor. Apparently he was first assigned to Fort Hamilton on the Brooklyn end of Long Island. Hamilton and Fort Lafayette, across the way on the mainland, guarded the narrow section of harbor connecting the upper and lower bays. Completed in 1831, but in need of much repair, Hamilton was no great bastion of defense and not an appealing home for a military garrison.[1] But having Angeline close by certainly eased the transition from West Point for one John Pemberton.

Before reporting for duty, he took a room in a New York hotel, though he first established personal headquarters at Angeline's house. "She is here and all is exactly as it should be," he wrote home. Members of the Pemberton and Stebbins families began to get acquainted, and all seemed to go well. Anna and one of John's aunts visited New York and were favorably impressed with his lady love. They thought her handsome with a "most sylph like form" and quite shy. Angeline's brother Henry came to Philadelphia and made a good impression on the Pembertons. Angeline did not do so well. John's opinionated mother liked Angeline's black eyes, but the young woman's face reminded her of George Meade. Angeline's singing ability and guitar-playing skill did redeem her somewhat in Rebecca's eyes.[2]

Meanwhile, John received orders, mostly involving administrative duties that included taking recruits down the Atlantic seaboard to Fort Monroe near Norfolk, Virginia. He returned to Fort Hamilton as often as possible and visited Angeline, on one occasion taking her and her family to a West Point ball. He continued to have sharp differences with his mother over his choice of girl friends. Rebecca had concluded that Angeline was unfit to be a poor man's wife on one hand and not suited for John on the other. John's sharp rejoinders were usually followed by an apology, but, as usual, he was too stubborn to give an inch when convinced he was right. The whole business was put aside when John was ordered to the wilds of Florida, where the United States government was trying to subdue Seminole Indians.[3]

The Second Seminole War had broken out in 1835 and was in the main a result of Seminole resistance to Andrew Jackson's policy of removing southeastern Indian tribes across the Mississippi River. When the war started, most of the geography of Florida "was scarcely better known than Africa" to the army or anyone else except the Seminoles. The soldiers sent there to fight had to contend with expansive swamps, high humidity, heavy rains, bitter winter cold in the north section of the state, swarms of insects, and much ignorance about trails and roads over which military operations must be conducted.[4]

By 1837 the Seminoles had succeeded in stalemating the army's efforts to dislodge them from their strongholds on the Florida peninsula. Commanders found it difficult to make the Indians fight. The Seminoles usually gave battle only if one of their villages was threatened. On such occasions they proved vulnerable to the army's preferred tactics of massed assaults. Like most Indian tribes, the Seminoles did not post sentries around their camps so the army accomplished several successful dawn attacks. But this was primarily a cat-and-mouse, run-and-shoot, guerrilla-style war in which the Seminoles, more familiar with the terrain of their homeland, had a decided advantage.[5]

When John Pemberton went south in the late fall of 1837, he landed in the midst of a war against an enemy that depended on

Pemberton's Florida

maneuver, speed, surprise, and elusiveness. He did not learn well from the experience, for the same characteristics in a future enemy would plague his performance as a commander.

Pemberton drew initial duty at several posts along the northern neck of the Florida peninsula. In January 1838, he joined part of a regiment from the Fourth Artillery at Jupiter Inlet to the south on the Atlantic side of the peninsula a few miles above the Everglades. On January 24 he participated in a battle against the Seminoles at Loxahatchee. The Indians retreated, and the army went in hot pursuit. Pemberton noted about forty Seminole casualties. Looking forward to more action, he hurriedly wrote his family the warning that lack of writing paper would force him to be out of touch for a while. His baptism of fire did not seem to overwhelm him. He reported the fight matter-of-factly to his family, perhaps because he did not wish to worry them, or perhaps his terse battle summary reflected West Point train-ing.[6]

A few weeks later, he expanded a bit on his south Florida experi-ences. He recounted pushing boats through mud and water for fifteen miles to chase Seminoles from an island in the New River area of the Everglades. In their hurry to escape, the Indians left powder, lead, packs, boats, potatoes, and alligator meat behind, most of which the army confiscated. Weary troops feasted on grapes, bananas, limes, lemons, and coconuts that grew abundantly in the area. During the operation, Pemberton befriended a colonel; he hoped he would be-come the colonel's adjutant. The job meant extra horses and money, rewards that might partially alleviate fighting a war in the Everglade jungle.[7] He had not forgotten one West Point lesson learned in dealing with Colonel De Russy: making friends with the right people could improve one's situation. Superior officers were the right people, and though his tactics did not work immediately, they would pay off in the future.

By April 1838, Pemberton had moved back up the peninsula to Newnansville, a hamlet just west of St. Augustine. For weeks he had been "in almost constant motion," and he looked forward to a respite. Some of his comrades in arms hoped all the artillery regiments would soon be sent back to New York and other points north, but he was not optimistic. He made the best of the situation. Small as it was, New-nansville pleased him. The place had adequate stores, and since cam-paigning virtually ceased in the summer because of disease threats, "I shall be perfectly at ease in a remarkably healthy and pleasant place."[8]

The rest gave Pemberton a chance to catch up on news from home. He sympathized with his father over the elder Pemberton's loss of his job as Philadelphia naval officer, but he was delighted that the family was attempting to purchase land in Virginia.[9] He had seen enough of the state during his trips to Fort Monroe to know that with adequate financial circumstances, he would not mind resigning from the army and settling there. His attachment to Virginia at this early date is notable considering the fateful decision he would make years later in 1861.

Pemberton did not spend the summer in Newnansville as he had hoped. He was ordered to the northwest and arrived in the Cherokee Indian country of western North Carolina, "a beautiful mountainous country with the purest water in the world," by the middle of June. Here he could enjoy the sights because no state of war existed. But army detachments were being sent to the mountains to flush out Cherokees hiding to avoid removal to the west. The Cherokees he encountered impressed him. They seemed "equally civilized with their white neighbors, living by the cultivation of their ground & their stocks."[10]

The delightful change in scenery and more peaceful Indians lifted Pemberton's spirits only slightly. He longed for Philadelphia and the Clifford farm. Recalling the farm created "a great passion for chickens," which he hoped were as numerous "as in auld lang syne." He also longed for an Indian pony left behind in Florida, "much to my chagrin." Many miles of campaigning had renewed his love of riding. "I have become a great rider of late and more fond of . . . [it] than ever." Lack of mail from home compounded feelings of isolation; he especially missed news of Israel, now doing survey work for railroads, and Anna. If Angeline dominated his thoughts as she had in the recent past, he made no mention of her in his letters home. His correspondence with her had been dwindling, and, whether he yet realized it or not, so were his feelings.[11]

Word finally came that Pemberton's unit would be heading back north, but not to New York or Philadelphia. In early September 1838, he and his fellow artillerymen arrived in northern Maine, scene of the bloodless Aroostook War, a border dispute between the United States and British Canada. The Fourth would help keep an uneasy peace while diplomats negotiated.[12]

The Maine duty was brief, and soon Pemberton was back in New York, assigned to Fort Columbus on Governor's Island. This place had the usual comforts soldiers expected. A man Pemberton would get to know well in the future, Ulysses Simpson Grant, described quarters at Columbus as consisting of "a chest and trunk for seats and a bunk to sleep." Israel came to visit his favorite brother and was most impressed with John's appearance in a dress parade. He thought John "was without prejudice by far the most military and best looking officer on the Island."[13]

Orders soon came for Pemberton to return to Florida, making his time close to Angeline short and bittersweet. The sweethearts were disappointed, but there was more to it than that. John's family and friends continued to discourage him about the relationship. Mother Rebecca remained adamant in her opposition, despite Angeline's attempts to win her over. Angeline was too immature to realize that letters to Rebecca containing such statements as "I am sure John sent some of these sweet and balmy South winds [from Florida]—don't you think it a reasonable supposition?" would not have the intended effect. John's continual stubbornness exacerbated the situation. When he left for Florida once more, he said his good-byes to the home folks without any "celebration in his manner." Israel was glad to see him go, thinking that "it may retard if not prevent his foolish marriage." Angeline had tried to make him stay; she was tired of his frequent absences and begged him to resign from the army. John refused, for no matter what his feelings, "resigning is impossible. The army is my profession & I can not leave it."[14]

With a somewhat troubled heart, John Pemberton returned to war in the Florida tropics. From Philadelphia, he carried with him blankets and comforters, silver teaspoons, knives, and forks. This time he would make the best of this uncivilized part of the world. He steamed south on October 5 on the *Westchester,* a "noble vessel with a fine commander, good fare & everything we wished." A welcome stopover at Savannah, Georgia, quickly had him wishing he could stay there for a while. "Savannah I think a delightful place & I would have been much pleased to have remained there a week but . . . we were obliged to depart to the land of Flowers." If the artillery were to be split up and sent to different posts as rumored, Pemberton hoped he would end up in St. Augustine, a town with perhaps more culture, parties, and pretty girls than any other in Florida. He got his wish, at least temporarily.[15]

En route to St. Augustine, Pemberton thought about the Virginia property his family was considering. While at sea on the *Westchester,* he had written his father all sorts of questions about the land. The possibility of living there remained much in his mind, and he wanted to know all the details of his father's recent visits to the area. If he ever seriously considered resigning from the army to live in Virginia, his feelings for that state must have been stronger than those for Angeline.[16]

In St. Augustine, Pemberton assumed command of the ordnance depot. He and a fellow officer rented a cottage, furnished it, and hired a woman to do their cooking. Rebecca Pemberton reckoned gleefully that a certain young woman in New York would not sleep well knowing that her fiancé had living arrangements that enabled him to socialize with guests.[17]

As in his West Point days, Pemberton continued long-distance bickering with his parents, especially with Rebecca, this time over the lack of letters he wrote home. He tried to assure her: "There is not a day that passes over my head, but that thoughts of home & you all arise in my mind, & no one I am sure can be more pleased at receiving letters from their own family than I am." Indeed, "I dislike writing, but I am sure I have written more frequently [than] I have received letters."[18]

Pemberton forgot about the bickering when he received a report from his father on the Virginia land. He urged his mother and Anna for lengthy descriptions from their observations of the place. Not only did it sound like a good investment, but the Warrenton, Virginia, area where the property was located sounded like a good place to live. "I should like to become a Virginian by adoption," he wrote home, unaware that, though he could adopt Virginia, the future and his place of birth would make it impossible for Virginia to adopt him.[19]

Out of the combat zone in Florida, Pemberton proceeded with an entrepreneurial idea of his own, the mulberry tree. Offered land by a local former army man, Pemberton figured that an investment of $1,000 for the planting and cultivation of the trees would yield a fortune. Usual ideal weather meant an extended growing season, and it seemed like a great opportunity. But he came to his senses. He was still in the army, a war was still going on, and with Indians raiding closer and closer to St. Augustine, money-making schemes would have to wait. After all, there were women to meet and balls to attend. That was the part of army life he had always liked best, and Florida combat had convinced him that it indeed was the best part.[20]

Pemberton spent New Year's Day 1839 drinking eggnog and champagne with friends. The new year and St. Augustine presented him with a new girl friend, and he decided to break his engagement to Angeline. In one of the most humble letters he would ever write, he appealed to his father: "You have asked me to make you my friend and confidant, at no period of my life have I so much needed a sincere and true one as now." Recalling parental and other opposition to the relationship with Angeline, he admitted that he had acted rashly after

knowing her for only three days at West Point. His first letters to her
after that were rooted "in boyish fancy which I then thought the most
devoted love, it [their correspondence] was continued when imagina-
tion replaced reality & finally when I knew my feelings for her were
not all that a husband should feel for a wife, my ideas of right and
wrong would not allow me to manifest it to her." Now with a new love
interest, he could pretend no longer, "but at the same time it is my
desire that she should have the opportunity to discard me, as I have
long since determined that such is the only proper course I can pursue." The letter seemed to indicate that John Pemberton was becoming a man. He had, after all, admitted his mistake, and he was willing
to do the right thing to escape from an uncomfortable situation. Yet
his real motive in writing home was to ask his father to explain the
situation to Angeline on his behalf. Worse, he planned to become
engaged to his new sweetheart, daughter of an army captain, regardless of how the situation with Angeline was resolved. Although
able to admit that his first serious relationship had been a mistake, he
obviously had learned nothing from it.[21]

Eventually Pemberton did dissolve his relationship with Angeline,
but not without traveling a bumpy road. His father was too ill to come
to his rescue so John wrote to her himself and suggested that she annul
the engagement for reasons other than his lack of affection, for "prin-
cipally pecuniary matters." Angeline's brother and head of the Stebbins household, Henry, felt so shamed by this turn of events that he
almost challenged John to a duel. Fortunately for both, he decided
that his family responsibilities precluded such a rash act. A letter from
John filled with profuse apologies soothed Henry somewhat, though
he made it clear that henceforth John would be considered a stranger
to the Stebbins family.[22]

The family of Pemberton's new flame had decided meanwhile that
even if his first engagement was settled honorably, their daughter must
not see him again. Her father threatened to disown her. The young
woman disobeyed, and Rebecca wrote a stinging letter to her son
condemning the couple's behavior. John replied in kind, demanding
that whatever anyone might think of him, his new love must be spared
harsh judgment. As for himself, "I can not always bear reproach, even
should I deserve it."[23] Eventually the affair fizzled, and a sadder and
hopefully wiser Lieutenant Pemberton found himself completely unat-

tached. He had at least stood on his own two feet, admitted error, and survived the tragicomic events without any violence. But his hesitancy to act and inability to learn from his past mistakes did not bode well for a young officer who might someday be leading an army.

As for his immediate military career, Pemberton thought he needed a change, so early in 1839 he applied for a transfer to the Topographical Engineer Corps. Aware of a rumored United States Senate sanction against officers currently in the army applying for the engineers, John asked his father to use his influential friends to overcome such a roadblock. John also wrote to several friends, asking for recommendations. His frustrated love life no doubt contributed to his restlessness, but he had grown weary of Florida and the seemingly endless Seminole conflict.[24]

While waiting for his transfer efforts to run their bureaucratic course, Pemberton managed a transfer to Fort Butler, several miles up the St. Johns River from St. Augustine. At his new post, he had better duties and more responsibilities, which slightly increased his pay. Just as things had taken a turn for the better, he received news from home that his father had had a life-threatening asthma attack. Aside from the natural worry over the elder Pemberton's condition, John felt much remorse for having bothered him with his girl troubles. He longed to be home and blurted to Anna, "I wish[,] with all my soul I wish that I had never gone to West Point or entered the Army." The sad and frustrating reality that his profession was controlled by faceless Washington officials, even in a time of family emergency, left him feeling "most wretched."[25]

Three weeks later came welcome news that his father had rallied and appeared to have passed the crisis. Even so, John emotionally reassured his mother of his concern for all the family. Even though "I am not fond of writing . . . I am quick tempered and as Papa used to say as head strong as a mule," his loved ones should know that no circumstances, including past disagreements over women in his life, could affect his affection for his parents and his siblings.[26]

Pemberton needed similar assurances from his family, for Fort Butler had not turned out to be the panacea he had expected. He found it "about as pleasant as solitary confinement in a state penitentiary. . . . I am more than half my time entirely alone, and have more business & responsibility on my hands than I have ever had before and at the most should receive but 14 dollars a month extra for it." On top of that, at least a thousand wolves hung around the place. Those who had never experienced the howling could not imagine "a more hideous and at the same time mournful sound than those legions of fiends emit." Indian threats added to the perverse fun of Fort Butler, and he almost always had captive Seminoles under guard. On the brighter side, fishing and hunting were good, and so were rumors that his regiment might be sent back to the Canadian border area. He would miss the mild Florida climate, but otherwise the news pleased him.[27]

On April 17, 1839, John's service in the Second Seminole War came to an end (the war would last until 1842 and the Seminoles would continue to give the United States government headaches right up to the eve of the Civil War). He sailed for Fort Columbus. The war had been of some value to him in that he had earned an excellent reputation as an administrative officer, primarily because of his work at St. Augustine and Fort Butler. There is little indication that he learned or cared much about the strategies and tactics of waging war. He had had limited combat experience, though certainly he had been exposed to valuable lessons about guerrilla warfare. He never mentioned such subjects in his letters home. Nor did he mention slavery, which became somewhat of a war issue because of the presence of escaped slaves among the Seminoles. To most soldiers, war was just a dirty part of the job, and that is most likely how John Pemberton viewed his time in Florida.[28]

Conflict entered Pemberton's mind as he left the war behind only as a possible confrontation in New York with Henry Stebbins. He also worried because he had heard nothing regarding his attempt to transfer to the engineer corps. He had no trouble with Henry, and his transfer request was rejected, so he settled back into the routine of Fort Columbus duties. He also expanded his wardrobe, caught up with Philadelphia news, and tried to boost the morale of Israel, who was between jobs. Finally orders came sending him to a job he wanted, instructor at an army camp. He packed and left for Camp Washington near Trenton, New Jersey, just a few miles from home.[29]

Located on the Delaware River above Philadelphia, Camp Washington proved to be just the medicine for a homesick native of the city of brotherly love. The site was picturesque, the Trenton race course was about a mile from the Delaware, and an abundance of shade trees bordered a sea of army tents. Pemberton relished the new duty.[30]

For the first time in a long while, John had a chance to get reacquainted with his family. He had grown up with Israel, Anna, and Beck but had not spent much time with Mary, aged seventeen, Henry, fifteen, Frances (Fanny), twelve, Sarah, ten, Andrew, eight, and Clifford, four. While stationed at the camp, John enjoyed family visits and balls and even found a new lady friend, though he took care not to get too involved this time. General Winfield Scott visited the camp, but rainy weather prevented a review of troops. Most days passed routinely; "Everything goes on as heretofore no news—no nothing." He did learn that his former girl friend in Florida had eloped with a lieutenant. Mostly he anxiously awaited a lengthy furlough, which finally came. He enjoyed several weeks of leisure before rejoining his regiment. This time he would be traveling to the northwestern frontier town of Detroit, Michigan, to assist in securing the United States–Canadian border.[31]

Shortly after Christmas 1839, Pemberton departed for Detroit. After nine days on the road from Philadelphia, he had only reached Pittsburgh, thanks to numerous delays. Exhausted and not yet halfway to his destination, he secured passage for Cleveland and a more direct route to Detroit. He was not impressed with his new post. His letters indicate that he never developed any affection for the frontier settlement on Lake Michigan. He may have ventured from Detroit to visit his mother's relatives down south in Lexington, Kentucky. Few of his letters from that time period survived, and little is known of his initial duties on the frontier.[32]

In May 1840, Pemberton learned to his sorrow that he was being ordered to Fort Mackinac on Mackinac Island off the northern tip of the lower Michigan peninsula. This fort, built by the British during the American Revolution, consisted of a complex of solidly constructed buildings that had been kept in reasonably adequate condition after passing into victorious American hands. Detroit had not been paradise, but Pemberton dreaded the prospect of being in another location rumored to be sprinkled with Indians and half-breeds. True, the place was supposed to be scenic, "but what is that unless some pretty girl is to enjoy it with you."[33]

After a few months at Mackinac, Pemberton truly relished trips to

Detroit. On one occasion he attended a wedding and the round of parties that followed, "in all of which I fully participated." In a letter to Israel he confessed, "I rather despised Detroit when stationed there, but in comparison with this place [Mackinac], it stands forth in bold relief." Winter was the worst time, surpassing his worst memories. "The wind blows as twould [sic] blow its last." Sleigh rides had to be postponed so horses could haul firewood. To eat, it was often necessary to trudge a quarter of a mile through waist-deep snow and then negotiate a slippery hill. On the plus side, he found a good supply of reading material, though soon he had read all the best volumes. Gossip provided some entertainment. He observed that all small places are full of scandals, "hot beds that find plenty of gardiners [sic]." An occasional cigar provided pleasure, but mostly routine work never varied; life was the same, he complained, day after day and hour after hour.[34]

At one party, Pemberton added to the local gossip. A brother officer "undertook to repeat some remarks of women, in an insolent manner to me, which our acquaintance did not warrant." Pemberton asked the officer and his wife plus one or two others to step into a separate room. "I then informed him he was a liar—and pulled his nose." Nose pulling was part of challenging an antagonist regarding an affair of honor and was rooted in white male Southern tradition, which no doubt was brought to West Point by Southern-born cadets and sometimes adopted by sons of the North. Naturally a row ensued, news of the event spread as far south as Detroit, the offended officer considered prosecution under civil law, and Pemberton was placed under military arrest. Fortunately, the commotion faded away.[35] The nose-pulling incident says something about the effect of service on men in an isolated post and perhaps something about the effect of military service in general on John Pemberton. At West Point, he had been a popular socialite who got along with most everybody. True, his personality had a hard side. He freely admitted that he was opinionated, slow to admit mistakes, quick-tempered, and stubborn. The Mackinac incident suggested that this side of his character was beginning to dominate. His abrasiveness and general conduct in that particular situation was foolish, as he later admitted. But as time passed, those around him began to see more and more of his negative personality traits.

To Pemberton, the nose pulling was probably indicative of the unpleasant experience in Michigan. He had never liked frontier areas, and Detroit and Mackinac reinforced his instincts. Thinking of Philadelphia made matters worse. Nothing in his present surroundings remotely compared to the pleasures of his birthplace. He even tired of drifting from girl to girl; some of his liaisons, particularly those with the fiancees of others, left him astonished at his conduct in retrospect. Such flings did little to relieve monotony because "stolen sweets can not be had often."[36]

Mackinac's only redeeming quality was that it was better than Fort Brady, Pemberton's new post as of August 1841. Brady had been constructed at Sault Sainte Marie on the eastern tip of the upper Michigan peninsula in 1833. It was farther north than Mackinac and winter weather was even worse, a prospect that reduced his already low morale. One redeeming feature of the new post was its excellent library with "a most choice selection of books." "I am *studying*," he wrote sarcastically to his mother, "the anatomy of *melancholy* at present." He dismissed the fort and surrounding area as "a miserable place." That anyone chose to be permanent residents there amazed him. He compared them to vegetables, oysters, or anything but creatures created in God's image. The slow mail, nonexistent during the heart of winter, the boredom, the large cowbell that substituted for a church bell, his failed love life, and his experiences in the wilds of Florida and other areas of Michigan left him exasperated and in need of relief. "I am heartily tired of the life I lead. Any change would be most acceptable."[37]

Change finally came with a move to Fort Porter in Buffalo, New York, but the new location did little to change his melancholy disposition. He judged Buffalo depressing and "vulgar." The local populace was "polite to us, so far as they know how to be." But he had to admit that he had "not much gloss myself—a white man will become an Indian if he lives with them entirely. I myself feel changed from what I was when last in Philadelphia. I wish I could see into the future, were it possible I would surely break the seal." His unhappiness was so great that refuge seemed to lie only in the future.[38]

Few improvements were forthcoming. One of Pemberton's longtime problems, mismanagement of money, continued to plague him. He had to renege on a promise to send funds home for payment of bills he owed in Philadelphia. Shamed by his fiscal irresponsibility, he confessed to his mother: "I am extravagant to excess, even when I know I

ought not to spend a cent beyond the absolute necessities I require, &
yet at this moment I have not even a decent suit of clothes to show for
my money. I throw away in a moment without thinking all that I owe
& should send to you. I am disgusted with myself."[39]

The series of shallow love affairs also disgusted him. Rejecting sister
Beck's playful insistence that he surely could not remain a bachelor
too much longer, he retorted, "I shall probably die an old batchelor
[sic], the more I see of women generally, the less I think of them.
Marriage seems to be the sole object of their thoughts, & they play so
many fantastick [sic] tricks to accomplish it, it makes me & others
laugh." He had learned how to avoid job trouble, too, he claimed. "I
have been long enough in the service to have learnt something on
that score."[40]

An acquaintance would maintain many years later that during his
and Pemberton's service on "the Niagara frontier" (Buffalo), the latter
often espoused "State-rights" views. Richard Taylor, a future Confederate general, maintained in his memoirs published in 1879 that Pemberton "imbibed the tenets of the Calhoun school" regarding nul-
lification and that he discussed these views with much conviction
while stationed at Buffalo. This allegation clashes with the fact that
John Pemberton was a Jacksonian who had commented with disgust
about nullifiers at West Point during his academy years. Furthermore,
Taylor prefaced his assertions with the false statement that Pemberton's first stop in his military career had been in South Carolina and
that while there he had formed friendships that led to his pro-Calhoun
views. Pemberton never served in South Carolina during the antebellum years. Taylor's comments are absurd and indicate that he was
joining with Jubal Early in a failed attempt to salvage Pemberton's
reputation in the post–Civil War South.[41]

Pemberton probably talked at length about transferring to another
post while in Buffalo. He would have one fond memory of the place:
his promotion to first lieutenant, effective March 19, 1842. New
orders came on the heels of the promotion, and he departed for Fort
Monroe, Virginia. He would now be in his adopted state and would
often visit his home state. For the next three years he served alter-
nately at Monroe and Carlisle Barracks, Pennsylvania; the latter was
in easy commuting distance of Philadelphia. This was a happy time for
Pemberton, especially when he managed a four-month leave of ab-

sence. At last he had emerged from the dark tunnel of frontier service.[42]

Philadelphia always would be his preferred home, and his time in Carlisle Barracks soon made Norfolk less appealing. He tried to make the best of the situation, focusing again on the local women. Coming back east seemed to have raised his opinion of the fairer sex. Yet when sitting on guard duty in a Fort Monroe casemate with small windows offering "an admirable view of a wet ditch," even a cigar and thoughts of pretty faces did little to lift his spirits. Other diversions offered varying satisfaction. On one occasion, Pemberton and other officers attended a navy commander's funeral. On an otherwise sad day, he enjoyed reunions with old friends attending the service. He would always remember an incident when the casket was moved from the dead man's home. A black woman on the second floor of the house "began to howl and moan most singularly. 'Oh Lord, oh Lord dey's taken away my poor old massa.'" His recording of the moment certainly had no abolitionist overtones.[43]

Aside from such funeral excursions or rare trips to Norfolk, service at Fort Monroe was monotonous. Pemberton detested the "everlasting drum beating," enjoyed occasional good weather and band concerts in the moonlight, did a lot of reading, drank more than "a *little* whiskey and water," and figured he needed only a lovely maid to make the place at least bearable. Such things composed "the enjoyments [of] my present highly praiseworthy life." His sarcasm revealed how trips to Philadelphia spoiled him. "Oh, for the pleasant nights passed in the dining room." Home, "be it ever so humble there really is no place like it, with all my wanderings I feel it yet."[44]

His ability to make friends with the right officers almost secured a permanent transfer to Carlisle Barracks. Two officers from Fort Monroe were to be picked and attached to the light cavalry there, and Pemberton's friends in high places chose him as one of the two. Washington red tape delayed the transfers for several months, but somewhere up the ladder of command his appointment was denied.[45]

A chance encounter soon had him forgetting all about wanting to get away from Monroe. He met Martha Thompson (nicknamed Pattie) in late 1844 or early 1845. Born on May 17, 1827, and a native of Norfolk, Pattie was the daughter of William Henry and Mary Sawyer

Thompson. The family had a thriving shipping business in Norfolk and a variety of other business interests. Pattie was of Irish ancestry, attractive, petite, just an inch or two over five feet tall, a brownette with gray-brown eyes, and the possessor of a dry sense of humor. Her entry into Pemberton's life was both fortunate and fateful. She would settle him down, keep him out of financial trouble, and give a solidity to his existence that he might never have had without her. And given his love for Virginia (if not for Fort Monroe), being smitten by a Virginia girl would be a deciding factor in steering him onto the road to Vicksburg.[46]

From the beginning of their relationship, John could never say enough good things about Pattie, and he said them with a mature sincerity that had been lacking in past comments about girl friends. "She is a dear little lady," he wrote his mother, and Pattie obviously had similar feelings about her soldier. She convinced her father to allow John to "present her most affectionately" to Rebecca Pemberton in one of his letters home. Pattie knew of his past dalliances with women and treated them with good humor. John quoted her comments in a letter to his family: "Don't you think they [Pembertons] are trembling for me, you must let them know how tyrannical is your present Pattie. . . . She is not to be trifled with. Present me affectionately to them. I hope at some future date to have their love."[47]

The relationship quickly developed to the point of marriage plans, which had to be delayed when John was ordered to Texas because of troubles with Mexico. John desperately wanted to marry Pattie before he left, lest something unforeseen destroy their plans. He feared her parents would object, "but she does not tho' she would not without their consent." For this and perhaps other reasons, the wedding was postponed.[48]

As the time for his departure for Texas neared, Pemberton spent as much time as possible with Pattie. For most of a week before he sailed, she doted on him, helped him pack, and convinced him that he had found a woman who cared as much for him as his own mother. At age thirty-one Pemberton had learned some hard lessons, and he would not, he assured Rebecca, forget his engagement on this tour of duty. For the first time in his life he was truly, maturely, in love, and he urged his family to write to Pattie to make her feel one of the family.

"She has the most winning manner in the world when she pleases & that she usually does, for she has great ideas of propriety." He was sure that "you & Papa will love her."[49]

Despite the many valleys he had experienced since leaving West Point, John Pemberton sailed for Texas in an upbeat mood. He had at last, he thought, met *the* wonderful woman, and he could look forward to marrying her as soon as he returned. He expected that to be in a few weeks. But he was not heading for minor border troubles this time. War clouds loomed on the horizon.

CHAPTER 4

Would Not Have Missed It

for the World:

The Mexican War

Pemberton would not have enjoyed the trip to Corpus Christi, Texas, under any circumstances. His beloved Pattie was back in Norfolk, and miserable weather in the Gulf of Mexico compounded his depression at having to leave her behind. Battling contrary winds, his vessel took thirty-two days to complete the voyage. Pemberton initially liked the place he would call home for the next several months, but he quickly tired of if.[1]

Corpus Christi, located at the mouth of the Nueces River along the Texas Gulf of Mexico coastline, was in 1845 a tiny settlement that had sprouted around Kinney's Fort, a trading post built in 1839 and a fortress in the sense that it offered protection to locals against area bandits. The village had a Mexican-American flavor that typified southwestern border towns. Both adobe and wooden houses dotted the landscape.[2]

To meet the potential crisis with Mexico over the boundary of the west Texas border, some four thousand men traveled toward Corpus Christi, where they would be organized into an army under the command of General Zachary Taylor. The hot spot of the boundary dispute was the extreme southwest area of Texas. Rooted in the successful

Texas revolt against Mexico in 1835–36, the controversy centered around Mexican attempts to minimize the loss of Texas by keeping the Nueces River as Texas's west-southwest boundary. Texans considered the Rio Grande their natural boundary, and when Texas became a state in 1845, the United States government pressured Mexico to accept the Rio Grande line.

If the boundary problem had been the only one, war might have been prevented. But Mexico owed the United States millions in compensation for American property and other losses incurred during frequent past Mexican internal revolutions. Further, United States President James K. Polk wanted more than the Rio Grande line. Embracing the philosophy of Manifest Destiny (the United States was destined by divine providence to encompass western lands all the way to the Pacific Ocean), Polk desired the New Mexico and California territories. He offered to purchase these territories and to cancel compensation claims if Mexico would accept the Rio Grande boundary. But Mexico was experiencing its normal internal political turmoil, and no leader wanted to do anything that might seem to favor the Americans. After receiving the diplomatic cold shoulder, Polk's emissary to Mexico gave up trying to sell the president's deal, returned to Washington, and advised Polk to teach the Mexicans a lesson. War was getting closer.[3]

The maneuvering between the two governments meant little to a lovesick John Pemberton. Images of his beloved Pattie continually raced through his mind. He had determined that if war could be avoided, and he believed it could, he would ask for leave in the spring of 1846 and travel back to Norfolk to marry his Virginia belle. Pattie's father had promised financial help. "He is very well off, tho' not exceedingly rich[,] worth quite a hundred thousand I hear." Pattie stood to inherit property that might produce income up to four hundred dollars annually. Pemberton believed that he could afford a wife and family. Lest his mother get the wrong idea, however, he hastened to assure her that he would choose Pattie even if she had no money and would "think myself exceedingly fortunate."[4]

He could do nothing but play a waiting game along with the rest of Taylor's men. They all grew weary of the Corpus Christi camp, named Camp Marcy in honor of Secretary of War William Marcy. The camp was spread out along the water's edge at the junction of the Nueces and Corpus Christi bays. There was adequate water from wells dug in the beaches, but it was "slightly salty," according to Pemberton's Philadelphia and West Point friend George Meade, and it had "an awful effect on the bowels of a newcomer." Gulf breezes made the fall weather pleasant enough, but winter brought cold winds, sleet, and rain, and local prairies provided little firewood. Gathering parties had to comb neighboring hills and prairies, sometimes hauling wood from as far away as six miles.[5]

Corpus Christi was changing along with the weather. Both legitimate and unsavory entrepreneurs flocked in, drawn by the presence of bored soldiers seeking diversion. Gambling, billiards, bowling, and prostitution flourished. The atmosphere of excitement and money even brought a theatrical company down from Galveston. The mostly transient population of the once lazy hamlet zoomed from a few hundred to several thousand before Taylor finally marched his army into war.[6]

Pemberton enjoyed and even participated in theater productions. He played one character fittingly named Dick Dashall. Otherwise he rode, hunted, and fished. Mustang ponies were plentiful and cheap so he purchased "a strong pleasant little fellow for which I gave only six dollars." He often mounted his mustang and took extended tours of the countryside. He and his five messmates lived comfortably for about fifteen dollars a month. They managed to get fresh venison and other game just about every other day. The war threat had produced a West Point reunion of sorts, and Pemberton enjoyed seeing old friends, though he found Marcy "the most quiet camp I have ever been [in]."[7]

He cherished most any word from Philadelphia. He rejoiced in the birth of Beck's first child. She had married Charles Newbold in November 1844, the first of his siblings to take a mate. He longed to see his new niece and her mother and suggested that the baby be named after their mother, as it was—Rebecca Clifford Newbold. He sent his congratulations to Beck and Charlie and his condolences to the child, knowing "how it must want to meet its uncle." All was not well back home, however; John's father continued to have chronic asthma problems, and his condition seemed to be deteriorating. In letters home, John tried to be optimistic about his father's health, but the possibility of never seeing him again was a great worry.[8]

Weeks rolled by. Christmas came and went peacefully, and still they waited. Pemberton persisted in his belief that there would be no war. He was sick to death of the camp and desperately wanted to get leave so he could marry Pattie. As if afraid she might lose interest during his absence, John repeatedly urged his mother and Anna to write her. He assured Anna that this time he was truly serious and intended to take Pattie to the altar. To demonstrate his devotion, he even bragged about what a wonderful correspondent his future mother-in-law was.[9]

Pemberton began maneuvering for a recruiting assignment in New York. If successful, he could certainly wangle a trip to Norfolk for a wedding. But while he worked on the details of his plan, General Taylor ordered the army to move toward Mexico in early March 1846. Pemberton's artillery company occupied Point Isabel, a high bluff at the southern end of Madre Lagune between the mouths of the Nueces and the Rio Grande which served as Taylor's supply depot. Undaunted in his optimism, Pemberton saw little significance in the advance. He dismissed the "thousand ridiculous rumors, about Mexican troops being here, there and every where." Meanwhile, he and the rest of the Point Isabel detachment entrenched and waited for news of Taylor and the main column.[10]

President Polk had ordered Taylor to the Rio Grande, and regardless of the accuracy of rumors of Mexican troops, Taylor had good reason to be apprehensive about his action. Polk's orders indicated that Taylor should not treat the Mexicans as enemies but could take the offensive if faced with hostilities and could ask the Texas state militia for help if needed. In effect, Polk had left to Taylor the decision to make war. At the same time, by encouraging use of state troops on foreign soil, Polk had set up Taylor to violate the United States Constitution, which forbade such use of state militia. The former part of the order did not trouble Taylor. John Pemberton was not the only soldier disgusted with the weeks of inactivity; the army needed to move to boost morale. If his army met resistance, he would fight. He would solve the constitutional problem by requesting Texas volunteers if needed and ignore the state militia.[11]

The main body of Taylor's army marched west-southwest toward Matamoras on the Rio Grande. Though challenged briefly by Mexican cavalry at a stream called the Arroyo Colorado, the Americans crossed without a shot being fired. Taylor moved his men from camp at

Palo Alto on toward Matamoras. Here wars of words ensued between the invaders and angry Mexican forces across the Rio Grande in Matamoras. Such dialogue settled nothing. Mounting morale and desertion problems and an ultimatum to withdraw or else left Taylor in an angry and frustrated mood. Finally he concluded that the ultimatum meant war, and he ordered the mouth of the Rio Grande blockaded and sent troops to cut other Mexican supply routes.[12]

Before he could attack Matamoras, Taylor had to resolve the problem of having his main supply base several miles away at potentially vulnerable Point Isabel. With war imminent, he could no longer be sure of the base's safety. A regular escort for his wagon supply train might not be sufficient, and rumors that Point Isabel was already under attack fueled his anxiety. So Taylor left a small detachment of infantry in a defensive position called Fort Texas on the north bank of the Rio Grande and on May 1, 1846, led his army back to Isabel. Two days later, Fort Texas received a storm of Mexican artillery shells, but the garrison held firm. On May 7, Taylor's resupplied force left Isabel for Matamoras with at least one additional man: John C. Pemberton.[13]

While the rest of the army was camped before Matamoras, Pemberton and his fellow soldiers at Isabel endured gossip that the Mexicans might attack their position at any time. Rumors became "so much a matter of course" that he wearied of them and decided that "no attack would be made on that place," which he considered impregnable. When the army returned to Isabel for supplies, Pemberton had made up his mind that it would not march back to war without him. He wanted to be where the action was, especially since this action promised to be a departure from the guerrilla war in the Florida swamps. "So after a great deal of exertion I succeeded in getting transferred to one of the companies of my rgt that was to march."[14]

For Pemberton and the rest of Taylor's force the march back to Matamoras across the hot, dry, "incredibly flat plain" was exhausting. Near Palo Alto, Taylor's advance scouts and lead elements discovered the Mexican army of Mariano Arista. American engineers, including Pemberton's old friend Lloyd Tilghman, found the Mexican line strongly anchored on both flanks by a swamp and a knoll. In the center lay chaparral thickets, nearly impenetrable growths of oaks and thorns that masked artillery batteries and troop dispositions. Taylor detached a small force to guard his supply wagons. Outnumbered three to one, the American army of some three thousand waited for Arista to make a move.[15]

Pemberton watched anxiously as Mexican big guns opened up, inaugurating an artillery duel lasting nearly three hours. Taylor had superior firepower so Arista tried a flank attack, but his men could not get through the chaparral. While the artillery fight continued, American infantry repulsed a Mexican cavalry charge. The repulse ended the battle. Infantry had finished it off, but the spotlight at Palo Alto was on the artillery. Artilleryman John Pemberton enjoyed the show. He later wrote Israel: "Beautifully was it used. Theirs was well directed but not to compare with ours." But the results were dangerous, for the "balls and grape flew like hail, many a man had the narrowest possible escape."[16]

More than any experience in Florida, this battle introduced him to the horrors of war. General Arista retreated toward Matamoras during the night, leaving several hundred dead behind, many burned to death in grass fires ignited by artillery and musket fire. Under the dark sky, Pemberton listened to the groans of Mexican wounded being removed from the battlefield, and the next day he helped bury what seemed to him several hundred enemy bodies. Taylor's army lost four killed.[17]

Despite heavy casualties and being forced to retreat, Arista's army could still fight. The Mexican general led his army about six miles to a dry lake bed called Resaca de la Palma. This was a good position, fringed with extensive chaparral that would help negate Taylor's artillery advantage.

The Battle of Resaca de la Palma began when Taylor's army arrived and quickly evolved into a series of small clashes. John Pemberton was in the thickest of the fighting. He went into battle as part of an advance skirmish line composed of four companies led by Captain George A. McCall. With McCall in command, Pemberton led the captain's company. George Meade later confided to Israel that when he saw John and the rest of McCall's men march out ahead of the army, he feared that "many would never return" from the "gallant little band" that would be so severely exposed to enemy fire.[18]

McCall's detachment practically bumped into Arista's well-concealed line and received a heavy dose of artillery fire that cut down five of its number. Pemberton and the other survivors retreated slowly,

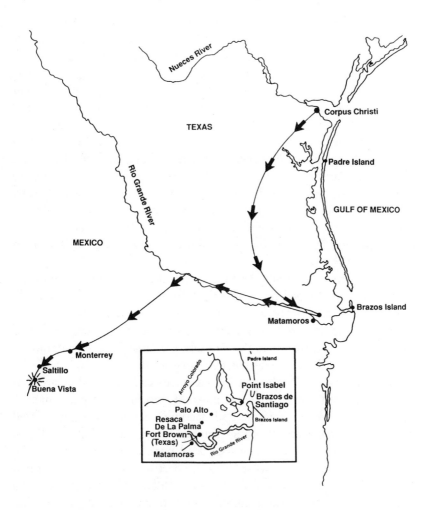

Mexican War: Zachary Taylor's Campaign

forming a rough square to meet expected Mexican charges. He would remember that "the Mexicans might easily have cut up our small command had they not feared to get between us" and the rest of Taylor's army that was rushing toward the fight. Though keeping up a constant fire, the Mexicans never attacked the isolated "gallant band"; but McCall and his soldiers spent long, anxious moments waiting for Taylor.[19]

When the main column came up, there was little relief; McCall was ordered to lead the assault. Pemberton took his company into a very hot enemy fire that cut foliage "as with a scythe." The air grew thick with flying lead; a musket ball passed through Pemberton's straw hat, fortunately leaving the owner's head unscathed. Six men fell near where he stood. A soldier close at hand dropped mortally wounded to the ground, grabbing one of Pemberton's pants legs as he went down. He continued to cling to Pemberton, who helped pull the man away from the firing line. He never forgot the soldier, and he also would always remember three others who fell when he ordered his company to shift position. One died instantly, but the other two were so badly mangled they begged the lieutenant to kill them. That he "could not do, though it certainly would have been merciful." He made them as comfortable as he could and wrote a letter to one's parents. Both men died during the night.[20]

Taylor's army eventually broke through the center of Arista's line. The Americans staged the final attack from the area where McCall's men had so stubbornly and bravely held the Mexicans at bay. A gallant charge captured enemy artillery on the Matamoras road, and Arista had to retreat across the Rio Grande, abandoning Matamoras. The beleaguered Fort Texas garrison was saved.[21]

After the battle, Pemberton toured the Resaca de la Palma area. In the heat of battle it had been a place of "nothing but excitement." When the smoke cleared, it had become "a horrible sight." Dead bodies lay everywhere, some so thickly congregated that the living could scarcely find room to walk. Dead horses and mules had to be pulled aside to open the road. And the destruction was not confined to the battlefield. Arista's panic-stricken soldiers left a trail typical of a wrecked army. Baggage and ammunition littered the road, and the Rio Grande was dotted with the bodies of drowned Mexicans.[22]

Pemberton saw it all, and, despite the horror of the human wreckage, he felt exhilarated by the experience. He could appreciate the anxiety of his loved ones in Philadelphia, but, as he commented in a letter to his father, "I really like this part of my profession better than any other. I would not have missed the two fights for the world, nor will I any more that are to come if I can help it."[23]

As the dust of battle settled, soldiers reflected on their adventure, wondering how friends, relatives, and politicians back in the states might react to their exploits. For the professionals, like Pemberton, the volunteer soldier was a problem. The press preferred volunteers; they made good copy. Pemberton and his professional soldier colleagues, the regular army, resented sharing, or as seemed more likely, giving up the glory spotlight to undisciplined, untrained would-be heroes. The professionals depended on official reports by commanders to give them their just due. Usually they did, though politically ambitious generals knew the value of praising volunteers. In any event, the idea of sharing laurels spurred the resolve of the regulars, who composed just about all of Taylor's army at the time. If they could win this war quickly, volunteers already en route to the front would simply have a long trip home.[24]

John Pemberton settled into camp on the edge of Matamoras and wrote accounts of his experiences. In one letter home, he admitted as usual that he did not write as often as he should. He understood his mother's "*kind* reproaches" on the subject and insisted that his problem was laziness, not lack of affection. He also made the valid argument that some of his letters had probably been lost in the mail. Certainly, he claimed, he had written more than the three letters that had arrived in Philadelphia.[25]

During the postvictory lull, Pemberton relaxed and enjoyed the quiet, puffed cigars abandoned by Mexicans, and looked at pretty Hispanic women. His heart belonged to Pattie, but his eyes still wandered. Unless the generals should decide to launch a campaign into southern Mexico, and he did not believe they would, he felt that the war was over. Very soon he expected to be in Virginia, celebrating the death of his bachelorhood.[26]

In reality, the occupation of Matamoras had only ended the first phase of the fighting; the war was just beginning. President Polk wanted his army to conquer more territory, especially in northern Mexico, to strengthen his hand for future peace negotiations. The president and his advisers also realized the advantages of a southern campaign; taking the capital, Mexico City, would surely force a Mexican surrender. As a first step, Polk ordered Taylor to push westward from Matamoras toward Monterrey. As diversions, Stephen Kearny would lead a separate column into New Mexico territory and John Wool would take another detachment from San Antonio into Mexico just north of Taylor's route. These plans should accomplish both of

Polk's goals. More northern territory would be under American control, and Mexico City would be threatened and, if necessary, ultimately captured.[27]

While the planning and expansion of armies went forward, Pemberton managed to do what he had done so well in the past—get the favorable attention of a higher-ranking officer. In August 1846, he became aide-de-camp to Brevet Brigadier General William Jenkins Worth. In a huff arising from a dispute with Washington over his rank, Worth had left Taylor's army after the initial advance to the Rio Grande. He returned when hostilities began, and Taylor welcomed him back. Though Worth had never been a personal favorite, Taylor respected his military abilities.[28]

Pemberton had indeed chosen a solid military man to work for. A native New Yorker, Worth was "above medium height . . . erect, well-built . . . with dark hair and very dark eyes, and with an engaging and decisive manner marked by quickness of apprehension. He was called the most handsome man in the army and was generally acknowledged as its finest horseman." He had had a long military career, fighting in the War of 1812, serving as commandant of cadets at West Point, participating in the Black Hawk War, and helping suppress Nat Turner and remove the Cherokee Indians from Georgia. In 1840, he had been ordered to take command of United States forces in the Florida Seminole conflict. A confident fighter in battle, Worth had vanity problems in dealing with those around him. He had a Quaker background, and this factor plus his superb horsemanship and his experience in Florida may all have worked to draw young John Pemberton to his flame. Whether an opinionated, self-assured Pemberton could coexist with a commander described variously as "rash and impetuous," "intense and narrow," and "self-centered" remained to be seen.[29]

Pemberton joined Worth's inner circle after General Taylor moved his army up the Rio Grande about a hundred miles to a place called Camargo on the San Juan River. Camargo was much closer by land to Monterrey than was Matamoras. Unfortunately, it also proved to be a death camp for many Americans; poor sanitation and heat produced disease that was much more devastating than enemy bullets.[30]

In his lone surviving letter from Camargo, Pemberton did not complain about camp conditions. He focused on news accounts of recent battles, disagreeing with his mother's inclination to blame his superior officers for the lack of publicity McCall's advance had received for successes at Resaca de la Palma. Names of all participating officers had been mentioned in official reports, but decisions about what to publish from those reports lay in the hands of higher-ups. Pemberton especially defended his own company commander, Captain C. F. Smith: "We are *great friends.* I like him as much as any officer in the army." Professionals shielded professionals, even in letters home. Pemberton also promised to send money as soon as possible to take care of Philadelphia debts. His new job with Worth meant a few extra dollars per month. He wrote lovingly of Pattie's letters, of wanting to go north (the excitement of battle apparently had faded), and of being "heartily tired and sick of this life."[31]

On August 19, 1846, Pemberton left Camargo with Worth's designated Second Division, which marched some sixty miles to Cerravalo. The rest of the army, excepting some unacceptable volunteers whom Taylor felt must be left behind, would follow. On September 14, Worth's division moved forward again, this time sandwiched between David Twiggs's First Division, which had taken the lead, and William Butler's Field Division, bringing up the rear. The army camped at Marin on September 17, moving on the next day. Finally, on Saturday, September 19, Pemberton and his comrades stood before Monterrey.[32]

Most of Monterrey's buildings were constructed of stone, and the Mexican army of General Pedro de Ampudia, which occupied the town, could turn any number of dwellings into useful defensive fortifications. To the south and east of town, the Santa Catarina River was a natural impediment. Also to the south stood Federation Hill, a spur of the Sierra Madre, and to the west rose Independence Hill from which Ampudia could protect his supply line along the Saltillo road. Taylor's army approached from the northeast, where Ampudia had two forts, the Tannery and Fort Diablo (Devil's Fort). Then there was the Citadel (called Black Fort by the Americans), a great stone quadrangle on the north side of Monterrey. The Citadel had high walls, space for several hundred occupying troops, and a large number of cannon. These formidable defenses had one weakness; they were so far apart that Ampudia would have problems moving men around to the points where they would be most needed.

Since the Citadel stood in the path of a direct assault from the north, Taylor decided to split his army and hit Monterrey from the east and west. On the west side, the most imposing target on Independence Hill was a structure called Bishop's Palace. If Taylor's forces could take this spot, they could cut the Mexican supply line. The mission required a lengthy flank march, and Taylor chose Worth's division to do the job.

As an aide to Worth, John Pemberton was undoubtedly kept busy writing and delivering orders and attending to other details necessary to coordinate the march. The division moved on Sunday afternoon, September 20; the initial advance was slow and tedious, and the column covered only ten miles before halting for the night. At first light on Monday, the division pushed on, brushing aside a Mexican force in a bloody fight that cleared the Saltillo road. Worth ended a fruitful day with a successful attack that gave his division possession of Federation Hill.

Next day, Worth occupied Independence Hill and assaulted Bishop's Palace. Mexican resistance gave way to superior artillery, and Worth had another victory. While Worth enjoyed successes, Ampudia had checked Taylor's attack to the east, but the loss of the palace forced a Mexican retreat to the city's inner defenses.

On September 23, while Taylor kept up a slow, steady pressure on Ampudia, Worth grew tired of waiting for further orders and sent his division charging into Monterrey. During this action, Lieutenant John Pemberton received a brevet promotion to captain for unspecified gallant conduct, probably carrying messages or performing other staff duties under fire. Worth's aggressive action broke Mexican resistance and led to a truce. Taylor allowed Ampudia and the survivors of his army to leave the city minus most of their weapons. Taylor recognized Worth's contribution to another successful campaign by naming his impetuous subordinate temporary governor of Monterrey. Worth also participated in surrender negotiations, as did Jefferson Davis, commander of a Mississippi volunteer regiment. Worth probably used the services of his aides to help handle peace talk paperwork so John Pemberton must have met this man who would have a profound effect on his future.[33]

A proud General Worth had Pemberton deliver a message to his men. Worth proclaimed that "this noble division has given an exhibition of courage, constancy, and discipline above all praise." And to "Lieuts. Pemberton and Wood . . . special thanks are due, for the alacrity, zeal and gallantry with which they have performed every service." The press applauded Worth and his soldiers, the *Charleston* (South Carolina) *Mercury* noting, "No one has pretended to deny that everything [at Monterrey] was affected by Worth's regulars." Monterrey would indeed prove to be the crowning achievement of Worth's long career. But he and his division were not done yet.[34]

While President Polk and his advisers pondered future strategy in Washington, General Taylor decided to probe further into the Mexican interior. In early November he ordered Worth to march his men to Saltillo, which they reached without incident, to keep watch for any Mexican military activity. Taylor, who had accompanied the expedition, returned to Monterrey.

In Saltillo, Pemberton and the division spent several quiet weeks. He wrote home three weeks before Christmas and told of one scare involving Mexican General Antonio Lopez de Santa Anna. Santa Anna knew that Worth was isolated from the rest of Taylor's army and decided to move north from San Luis Potosi and attack Saltillo. Worth's scouts learned of Santa Anna's plan, and Taylor began concentrating his forces to meet the threat. Mexican scouts sent news of this development, and Santa Anna canceled his plans. Pemberton thought the whole business a Mexican fabrication to begin with and was not surprised when the Mexicans never appeared.[35]

Pemberton did believe the persistent rumors of peace. He hoped "most heartily" that hostilities would end soon, for "like all others here I'm tired enough of the war." But the war in Saltillo had a different face than Monterrey and the Matamoras campaign. A few days before Christmas, he was assigned to take the division band around town to serenade local citizens. All went peacefully, yet his homesickness, lack of mail, and the time of year made him feel miserable. In battle or between battles did not matter; he had to spend Christmas in a country he had long since expected to leave. This might have been his and Pattie's first Christmas as husband and wife. Another Christmas was to pass before that happened.[36]

During the first month of 1847, he received word from Israel that their father's ill health had continued to deteriorate and death seemed imminent. The news left Pemberton shaken. He knew that his papa had had a bad winter, but he had not realized the severity of his condition. He longed to rush home. Leaving now would require resignation from the army, however, and, as much as he loved his father, Pemberton refused to entertain any thought of giving up his military career.[37]

Pemberton did not know when he responded to Israel's letter in late January that his father had been dead for over two weeks. In February a lengthy letter from Anna arrived detailing the elder John's last days of severe suffering with consumption. Anna thought his going out in raw Philadelphia winter weather had brought on the final, fatal illness. To soothe the news, Anna related how much their father had been impressed with Pattie's letters, that he wanted John to have a small brown pitcher that he greatly valued, and how he "wished his Dear John was safe at home" to be with him during those final hours.[38]

Pemberton did not have time to dwell on this devastating news. The names of both Zachary Taylor and Winfield Scott were being bandied about as future presidential candidates, and neither Scott, a Whig, nor President Polk, a Democrat, wanted Taylor, the potential Whig party nominee, to steal all the battlefield glory. So with Polk's blessing, Scott came to Mexico to launch a spring 1847 campaign against Mexico City from Veracruz, situated on the Gulf of Mexico almost due east of the Mexican capital. For his campaign, Scott took almost all of Taylor's army, including Worth's division. Though he tried to keep the war going on the Monterrey front, Taylor realized he could not function with so small a force, and he returned in frustration to the United States. He would get sweet revenge on Polk and Scott by winning the presidential election of 1848.[39]

The change of battle fronts put increased responsibility on staff officers, and Pemberton worked hard to get Worth's men ready for the new campaign. From the beginning, he and the general had had occasional flare-ups, and the pressure of the current situation increased tension. Pemberton mentioned problems with the general in letters home, and when weeks sometimes passed with no word from the front, his family feared he was under arrest. After one particularly heated exchange, Pemberton had resigned, but Worth smoothed things over and he withdrew the resignation. Rebecca Pemberton understood the potential for friction between the vainglorious general and her opinionated son. She knew that in spite of John's military

training, he tended to lash back when criticized. To Israel she suggested that "perhaps he [Worth] knows John has a little of his own
mettle & therefore avoids speaking in that way."[40]

The increased duties involved in shifting the army made Pemberton
complain that he was more adjutant general than aide-de-camp.
Worth wanted his staff to be constantly in motion, even if they were
performing useless tasks. Despite their conflicts, Pemberton gradually
began to like Worth, admitted that he was usually polite and kind in
their relationship, and admired him as a soldier in spite of his tenden-
cies toward recklessness and belligerence. Although developing a
close relationship with the general may have eased his life in Mexico,
Pemberton might have been better served for the future if he had been
influenced by a different role model. Worth had an inflexible, sometimes abrupt nature. Colleagues would someday describe Confederate
General Pemberton as having the same characteristic.[41]

Worth's division plus other elements of Taylor's command concentrated first at Tampico on the Gulf shore, then helped transfer the
remainder of Scott's army to Lobos Island above Veracruz. Scott's
force, including Taylor's veterans plus reinforcements brought in for
the Mexico City campaign, landed at Collada Beach just below
Veracruz in early March. Scott decided to besiege the city, and Pemberton moved with his division to the right flank of a line that ran
west to northwest on the land side of Veracruz. He and fellow veterans
encountered familiar chaparral as they dug in and positioned artillery.
After a severe bombardment of several days, Veracruz was surrendered
on March 27. Scott now had a secure beachhead from which to
launch his campaign against the Mexican capital.[42]

In April, Worth, now a brevet major general, became temporary
governor of Veracruz. Though Worth's success undoubtedly resulted in
more duties for Pemberton, he did find time to send a quick note to his
mother with George Meade, who had been granted leave to return
home. He assured her that Meade would tell her all about the Veracruz
operation. He also wrote a hurried note to Pattie but decided not to
send it because he was afraid she could not read his messy handwrit-
ing.[43]

As General Scott prepared to march his army inland, he chose to
move via the Mexican National Highway and ordered David Twiggs's
division to take the lead. Scott's choice infuriated Worth, who would

never forgive his old friend for the slight. On April 8, Twiggs marched out of Veracruz, the rest of the army close behind. The first significant resistance encountered by the Americans occurred at Cerro Gordo, where they defeated Santa Anna's army.

After his victory, Scott lost about three thousand volunteers whose year of service was up. Almost all chose not to reenlist. Undaunted, Scott pushed on, sending Worth's division on ahead to Puebla. By May 25 the entire army was concentrated at Puebla, where it would remain for three months until reinforcements arrived. On August 7, with his force built up to some fourteen thousand, Scott pushed on toward Mexico City.

It may have been during this period, though the exact time is uncertain, that a young soldier named Ulysses Simpson Grant noted an anecdote involving an aide to General Worth named John Pemberton. Of Pemberton in Mexico, Grant wrote in later years, "A more conscientious, honorable man never lived. I remember when a general order was issued that none of the junior officers should be allowed horses during the marches. Mexico is not an easy country to march in. Young officers not accustomed to it soon got foot-sore. This was quickly discovered, and they were found lagging behind. But the order was not revoked, yet a verbal permit was accepted, and nearly all of them remounted. Pemberton alone said, 'No,' he would walk, as the order was still extant not to ride, and he did walk, though suffering intensely the while." The event was another illustration of how professional soldiering had changed the West Point youth from a cadet who would have been the first to leap into the saddle to a stubborn, hard-bitten military man. Grant claimed that his recollection of the incident in later years convinced him that his opponent at Vicksburg would not yield that city easily.[44]

Twenty miles from Mexico City, another future Civil War hero, Robert Edward Lee, and the rest of General Scott's scouts reported that a direct approach to the city was impracticable because the Mexicans held a strong defensive position called El Penon. On August 13, Pemberton rode with Worth's division, which led a flank march toward San Agustin. Scott's other three divisions followed. On August 18, Worth marched north from San Agustin and ran into a roadblock at San Antonio, but the remainder of the army moved on southwest and west of the city to pressure San Antonio and Churubusco. Santa

Anna's right flank gave way, and Worth was able to get by San Antonio and pursue the retreating Mexicans northward.

At Churubusco, Worth's men and other portions of Scott's army ran into two exceptionally strong defensive positions, one at the Churubusco River bridge and the other at a convent to the southwest. Pemberton and other staffers worked to coordinate the main attack against the bridge by Worth's and Gideon J. Pillow's divisions, while Scott ordered other portions of the army to attack the convent and flank the bridge. Worth and Pillow achieved their objective first, and Worth immediately had his artillery open on the convent, which soon surrendered. He then ordered his victorious men to pursue retreating Mexicans.

Santa Anna had had enough, or at least he wanted Scott to think so. The wily general needed a truce to regroup and redeploy his forces. Scott granted the truce, and peace talks began that lasted several days. Numerous violations of the truce and the obvious fact that peace discussions were going nowhere led to a renewal of war in early September.

During the lull in peace talks, Pemberton dashed off a letter to his mother assuring her that he was well and that she need have no further apprehension for his safety. He believed that peace was at hand. He casually referred to Churubusco as just another battle with the usual result that the American army swept everything before it. He estimated Scott's losses at eleven hundred men. He thought Mexico City could be taken in an hour so the Mexicans had no choice but to surrender. Anticipating a quick end to hostilities, he planned to leave Mexico as soon as possible and rush to Pattie. He was careful not to promise anything to the family because he knew there was always a chance that negotiations would break down. Events proved him correct.[45]

To begin the final phases of his campaign against Mexico City, General Scott decided to assault Molino del Rey, a group of stone buildings used as a mill and a foundry and currently occupied by Mexican troops. Worth's division was closest and was chosen to make the attack. Pemberton and his companions charged into battle on September 8. First the division took Molino, one of two strong positions in the area, then the Casa Mata, a much tougher bastion. The persistent bombardment by Worth's artillery finally forced the Mex-

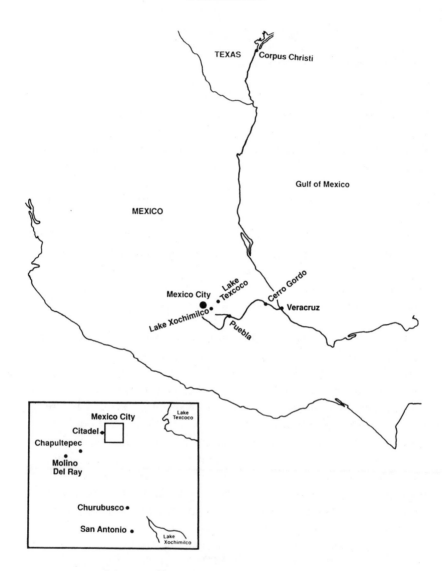

Mexican War: Winfield Scott's Campaign

icans to evacuate Molino del Rey. Victory came at a high price. Worth lost 120 killed and nearly 700 wounded. During the action at Molino del Rey, John Pemberton was promoted to brevet major for "gallant and meritorious conduct," again presumably for staff work under fire.[46]

Now Scott consulted with his officers and ordered a feint from the south in the area of San Antonio. His actual target would be a strongly fortified hill called Chapultepec, located west of Mexico City and to the east of Molino del Rey. In this operation, Worth would support Gideon Pillow's division as it assaulted the western face of the hill.

American artillery punished Chapultepec on September 12, and the infantry attack began the next day. Pillow fell wounded early, and Worth took over command in the western sector. During the fighting a soldier who would become all too familiar to John Pemberton in later years, Joseph E. Johnston, led a regiment. The battle grew fierce as men from three attacking divisions gathered and attempted to scale the walls of the fortress gallantly held by young Mexican cadets and some of Santa Anna's regulars. Superior numbers made the difference. Chapultepec fell, and the surrender of Mexico City soon followed. Detachments from Scott's army, which included U. S. Grant, used artillery to knock out a well-defended gate beyond Chapultepec, and the last of the capital city's perimeter defenses was breached. Worth sent his aide Brevet Major Pemberton to fetch Grant and bring him to headquarters, where the general offered a personal word of congratulations. The irony of the moment was not lost on Grant and probably not on Pemberton, though Grant was the one who recorded it for posterity.[47]

After the fall of Mexico City, Pemberton anxiously awaited permission to leave Mexico. Worth agreed to facilitate a transfer to recruiting service, which would get him back to the East Coast more quickly. But General Scott issued an order that every physically able officer was to remain on current duty. Grudgingly, Pemberton agreed that Scott's position was sound, given the loss of so many officers during the campaign. Reinforcements might get to the city quickly and allow the general to rescind his order.[48]

Compounding his disappointment was news that his youngest sister, Sarah, had passed away on July 17, little more than a month short of her eighteenth birthday. She fell victim to consumption and asthma, the same diseases that had killed their father. Pemberton became so depressed that he even began to fear that the string of American victories in Mexico might ultimately prove meaningless. Perhaps Santa Anna would try to continue the war. The situation in Mexico City gave him good reason to be apprehensive. During the first days of American occupation, chaos had reigned, and citizens sometimes were abusive and violent. Martial law helped calm the situation, but occasionally shots rang out. Gradually peace returned, and Pemberton enjoyed some quiet times. Like other soldiers, he awaited action on peace terms by the United States Congress and hoped for an official end to this "far sojourn of ours."[49]

In a letter home, Pemberton warned his family not to pay any attention to General Worth's mention of his being wounded during the Mexico City battles. The hand wound did not "hurt in the least, a ball passed across . . . [it], just raising the skin, but not giving any inconvenience, not even making a scar." He had tried unsuccessfully to get Worth not to mention the incident. Apparently Pemberton's desire to get home was making him uncharacteristically humble.[50]

He had a long wait. Feuding within the inner circles of the Mexican government delayed completion of the peace process until February 1848. Meanwhile, in the usual American manner following a war, officers began feuding over who should get credit for what. Gideon Pillow, who would be a miserable failure in the future Civil War, ignited the process by sending out unsigned press releases lauding his own exploits at the expense of others. Worth and Twiggs were drawn into the debate, and Scott finally had all three arrested. Nothing came of it, though the wrangling probably damaged Scott's and Worth's political aspirations. His role as one of Worth's chief letter writers gave Pemberton a firsthand view of the controversy. He would be drawn into similar controversies during the Civil War as a participant, and the arguments would be over who took the blame, not the credit. Pillow, Worth, and Twiggs were eventually released, and a court of inquiry adjourned without settling anything.[51]

At last in December 1847 Pemberton obtained leave. He would eventually assume recruiting duties in the East but for the present would remain attached to Worth's staff. He had been in a position to learn much from the Mexican War. He had fought, he had led, and he had observed on a daily basis the activities of a first-rate combat general. He had enhanced his credentials as a career officer, and he had gained honors. In May 1849 the Pennsylvania legislature recognized him and other native sons for their war exploits. He also received a sword from the city of Philadelphia on which were inscribed words of praise for his gallant conduct during the Monterrey campaign. His and the swords of others so honored were placed in a Philadelphia store window under the caption "Honor to the Brave."[52]

None of these experiences or honors guaranteed that he would excel as a leader. An impartial perusal of his record might indicate that he would one day be a good general. All things being equal, the next big war should give him a chance to prove his mettle as a commander. He had proved that he was a good operations manager. When the next war came, he would demonstrate that such was his special skill. Circumstances of that war and his own personality would work against his proving his ability to lead men in combat. For the present, his only desire was to step ashore in Virginia and make Pattie Thompson his wife.

CHAPTER 5

Parade Grounds

Florida, New Orleans, New York, the West

John Clifford Pemberton and Martha "Pattie" Thompson were married on Tuesday, January 18, 1848, in the Norfolk, Virginia, Episcopal Christ Church. Rector George Cummins officiated. None of John's family came to the wedding. The newlyweds' granddaughter would say years afterward that she believed the Philadelphia Pembertons were hesitant about accepting John's choice of a mate from a small Southern town. Another factor could have been an August 1847 visit to Philadelphia by one of Pemberton's great mistakes, Angeline Stebbins, now Mrs. Angeline Fleming and mother of a one-year-old child. Angeline's presence no doubt stirred unpleasant memories of John's record with women. Perhaps the Pembertons feared he was on the verge of another mistake in judgment. But if her in-laws did suffer a bit from Northern urban prejudice or were apprehensive about history repeating itself, Pattie would quickly win them over.[1]

Settling into married life was the first order of business, and John and Pattie had little time for it. Soon after the wedding, the couple arrived in Washington, where John continued his campaign for a permanent reassignment to recruiting service. He feared that remaining on Worth's staff in absentia could cause future complications.

Worth was still in Mexico, whereas Pemberton had visions of a Philadelphia assignment. His early, idealistic dedication to the army had been on the wane for some time. He had developed a military mindset, but two wars and frontier service had him thinking of settling into an easy assignment that would complement a quiet married life. Instead he was in a state of limbo. The War Department wanted to send him to a new command in Mexico. To avoid that possibility, he reminded those in authority that technically he was still on Worth's staff. Since a recruiting job seemed more and more out of the question, he turned to his old mentor for help. Worth sent word that he should do nothing until hearing from the general. While he marked time, Pemberton continued to lobby for a favorable assignment. Finally, he requested and received a leave of absence that would enable him to set aside his career uncertainties and enjoy being with Pattie.[2]

Marriage proved beneficial to John Pemberton, even in the area of personal economic affairs, which he had always managed so badly. Pattie insisted that the family money be budgeted so as to eliminate her husband's debts. His great affection for his bride made him accept her advice and generally eased his domestication. Rebecca Pemberton was both surprised and pleased at the positive effect her new daughter-in-law had on John. "She is the very woman for him," she wrote Israel, "and we all love her more every time we have her here." Pattie had indeed changed the Pembertons' opinion of her in short order. They found themselves "agreeably disappointed" by John's attentiveness and thoughtfulness when around Pattie and by his respect for her judgment and discretion.[3]

The newlyweds' first few months together were spent in Philadelphia, Norfolk, and Washington. By the summer of 1848, Pemberton's old regiment, the Fourth Artillery, had returned from the Mexican War to Old Point near Norfolk, but he still waited for instructions from Worth. He had to decide whether to remain with the general or return to his regiment. Pattie liked the idea of living close to her hometown; yet she knew John would enjoy more benefits as a general's aide. While they waited, a near tragedy struck. The house they temporarily occupied in Norfolk caught fire one June night, and they barely awoke in time to escape with their lives.[4]

The fire seemed to emphasize the frustration and uncertainty that engulfed Pemberton. Weeks passed with no message of instruction from Worth. John and Pattie visited Philadelphia in July. He relaxed with his favorite cigars, except in the presence of his bride, who hated the smell. His resolve at West Point to give up the habit had long since disappeared, but he would not let any vice interfere with his new marriage. In addition to being a proud husband, he was already a father-to-be. Pattie's condition made him happy but increased his anxiety about his next assignment.[5]

Finally, General Worth called Pemberton to Washington for a meeting. Worth "received him like a son," assured him that he wanted to keep him as an aide, and begged bride and groom to come live with the Worth family in Washington. Flattering as the offer was, it did not solve the Pembertons' future. Worth was waiting for a new assignment himself, and John did not want to make a blind commitment. Pattie's pregnancy forced him to think more seriously about rejoining his regiment, which was still at Old Point, close enough that Pattie's mother would be available to help as the pregnancy progressed. Beyond this practicality, Pemberton had been upset when his name was struck, accidentally it turned out, from Worth's roster as an aide-de-camp. The clerical error created a misunderstanding. Worth thought that Pemberton had voluntarily resigned, which explained why he had had to wait so long for word from the general. Worth smoothed things over and reinstated him, but Pemberton had to forfeit some of the extra pay received while technically off the staff. Though the issue was settled, Pemberton continued to think about going back to the Fourth Artillery.[6]

In late August, the Worth family visited Philadelphia. The Pembertons, including Pattie, came to town from the country estate to pay their respects. Worth's affection for Pemberton was never more evident as when he assured Pattie that her husband could be with her as much as necessary during the coming months. Worth expected a military buildup in the West to control the plains Indians and convinced Pemberton that his life would be more predictable if he remained a general's aide. Worth hoped to get duty in San Antonio, Texas, which, though not ideal for an expectant mother, would be better for both John and Pattie than an assignment in the far West. Rumor had it that some units might be sent as far away as California.[7]

Pemberton decided to stay with Worth, at least temporarily. The decision drained him financially. Worth traveled to and fro in the

Northeast; Pemberton trailed after him, paying his own way because he was under Worth's, not the government's, orders. He did manage to spend occasional days in Philadelphia. He played so much with Beck's young son that the child cried whenever Uncle John had to leave. In early October, he gave Anna away at her wedding to a physician, Sam Hollingsworth. But the happy times soon passed.[8]

Pattie had not had an easy pregnancy, experiencing much swelling in her feet and knees. She often did not sleep well. Traveling back to Norfolk after Anna's wedding to be with her mother, Pattie had caught a severe cold and developed an "incessant cough," which kept her awake for several nights. Her condition worsened right up to the time her baby boy was born, and for a good many hours thereafter she lay unconscious. Finally waking, she experienced prolonged periods of delirium. Pattie's mother thought it a miracle that her daughter survived. The baby did not, and Pattie's critical condition prevented her from even seeing her firstborn.[9]

Pemberton handled the tragedy and Pattie's illness very well. Mrs. Thompson thought that he "throughout exhibited all the sensibility of a woman." She knew he suffered more than he allowed others to see. To a friend, Mrs. Thompson confided, "We love him more than ever. His whole behavior during these trying times has been so feeling, and so proper." John wrote his mother a few days after the birth to assure her that Pattie was improving. Most of her hair had been cut so as to treat her fever by direct applications of compresses to her head. The fever subsided, and recovery seemed certain. John did not have long to dwell on the ordeal. He would have to leave Pattie in the capable hands of her mother. Orders had finally come; he was to join Worth in San Antonio.[10]

On December 1, Pemberton left for Texas. At a stopover in Galveston, he was given a letter from Anna with news of the death of his unmarried sister Mary. He accepted it calmly and matter-of-factly. Mary had been ill a long time. His emotions were probably drained by his own recent ordeal. In a letter to his mother, John counseled, "It is better not I think to converse on such sad subjects after they have once been spoken of. It grieves without benefitting."[11]

A delay in Galveston gave Pemberton time to set about trying to straighten out his financial affairs. Without Pattie at his elbow he had spent himself back into debt and was trying with some success to

COLBY COMMUNITY COLLEGE LIBRARY

struggle back toward solvency. He paid a large tailor bill and sent Pattie one hundred dollars to cover her doctor bills. [12]

The next leg of his trip left him wondering why he had decided to rejoin Worth. Houses along the stage route were primitive at best. Windows had no glass or shutters, and floors were uncovered clay. Not only did travelers face the absence of luxuries; basic necessities of existence were missing. By the time the stage rolled into San Antonio, Pemberton had decided that he could not bring Pattie to such an uncivilized land. Nothing about San Antonio changed his mind. He thought the town was "decidedly worse than the poorest Mexican town I have ever been in." He got a room at the best boardinghouse in town, a dilapidated structure. This "miserably uncomfortable" location, so far from Norfolk, ended his long vacillation about whether to remain on Worth's staff. He made a written request for a transfer back to the Fourth Artillery, another indication that he was seeking the more convenient route along the road of his military career. When John Pemberton was unhappy, he always tried to move on to another assignment. [13]

Within a few weeks, John and Pattie were together again in Norfolk. He applied for extended leave and contemplated where new orders might send him, hoping it would be a place he could bring Pattie. He anticipated returning to Florida, which, though trouble with Seminole Indians had flared up once more, had better housing than San Antonio. The Indian trouble seemed isolated so security for Pattie and other members of soldiers' families should not be a problem. The killing of a white man by a small group of drunken Indians had led to white demands for removal of remaining Seminoles not already sent west under Andrew Jackson's old policy. The resulting tension had forced Washington to build up U.S. troop strength in the area. John and Pattie began preparing for the trip, wherever the destination might be. They put together a semblance of household furnishings, trying not to strain their limited budget. Her parents provided "table linens" and silverware. They looked forward to being settled somewhere. Pattie complained that "our drab life since we have been married is not exactly to the taste of either of us." [14]

Finally, they received word that they would move to Florida, the Pensacola area. Pemberton also received upsetting news that General Worth had died of cholera in Texas. He did not regret having left

Worth; had they been there, he and Pattie might have fallen victim to the epidemic. He summed up his feelings in a letter to Israel: "His death was a great loss to the country & to me, [but] had I continued with him, I should have taken my wife there, and in such a place and at such a time you can imagine what she would have been compelled to go through." Marriage "changes one's *feelings,* quite as much as circumstances."[15]

John and Pattie spent several days in Philadelphia before departing for Florida. The trip was tedious. From Philadelphia, they traveled by steamer to Charleston. The rest of the way was overland by stage and rail. Rebecca Pemberton hoped her son would continue to assume the responsibilities of married life. She remembered his past high living, consisting mainly of spicy food and strong drink, and worried that despite Pattie's influence, he might backslide. If he did, Rebecca would place the blame where it belonged, on John, not his "excellent" wife.[16]

The trip took two weeks and was just as rigorous as anticipated. Pattie suffered from severe seasickness, which caused them to delay an extra day in Charleston. At Savannah a misplaced trunk resulted in another day's delay. Then, while they were having dinner, John and Pattie were victimized by a thief who broke into their hotel room and stole Pattie's watch, chain, and gold pencil. At journey's end they were forced to share quarters with another officer's family while waiting for their furniture to arrive from Philadelphia. Their own quarters in Fort Pickens proved pleasant enough. The freshly painted living area offered ample space, and the Gulf climate was "delicious."[17]

During their Florida sojourn, the Pembertons moved several times as the Indian trouble ebbed and flowed. At Fort Pickens routine duties occupied John while Pattie coped with the monotony of garrison life. She gave dinner parties, made new friends, and enjoyed "parades, fine music, boats & a lovely view of the navy yard." A couple of months later they experienced a rainy, stormy sea en route to their next home, Fort Brooke in Tampa Bay. In November 1849, they moved again, once more in the company of a rainstorm, to the Manatee River, still in the Tampa area. At the dock, John noticed with disdain "a crowd of lazy, plantation negroes, males & females, gaping at us with eyes & mouths stretched to their ample capacity."[18]

Occasionally, Pemberton got to explore the outer reaches of their always temporary locations. While on patrols, he lived in tents in the piney woods, read books, and enjoyed the scenery. While out on these forays, he always tried to return to Pattie on weekends. Soon it was confirmed that within a few months she would once again be "in her room" as Pemberton delicately phrased it.[19]

Because of Pattie's first experience, they decided to accept the offer of a brother officer's wife at Fort Brooke that she attend Pattie at delivery time. So Pattie went from the Manatee to the fort, where the local doctor subjected her to "a copious bleeding" and prescribed a tonic to help her through the last weeks. The Pembertons' baby daughter Martha (to be called Pattie like her mother) came into the world on January 14, 1850, at Fort Brooke. A week later the proud father reported to grandmother Rebecca that mother and child were doing fine. A delighted Pemberton wrote that "it is a lovely little thing" and confessed his worry over his daughter's occasional colic attacks.[20]

Little Pattie's arrival coincided with talk of peace in Florida. The new year also brought a visit from Pemberton's old friend George Meade, who was working as a surveyor in Florida, and good news from the Philadelphia Pembertons. Anna had had her first child, a boy, and Beck had given birth to her second daughter and third child. Pattie was flattered at the description of Beck's progeny as a miniature of Aunt Pattie.[21]

Despite the joy, Pemberton could not rid himself of fears that the government's insistence on sending the rest of the Indians west could bring on another war. If that happened, he would have to spend too much time away from his two Patties and would be delayed in seeing his new niece and nephew. He was beginning to suffer from his usual restlessness, ready to find better duty somewhere regardless of whatever military necessities might arise. He still wanted an assignment close to Philadelphia or in St. Louis, where he might have been anyway if not for the Seminole trouble. But Winfield Scott stepped in, as he had in Mexico City, to cancel his potential transfer to St. Louis. Scott did not feel that Florida was yet ready to be demilitarized. So Pemberton relaxed and reveled in fatherhood, watching his baby grow. He smiled when others complimented her nice features and frowned when they said she resembled him. Finally, he came to a painful decision; mother and daughter would be better off in Norfolk. The baby especially needed a more settled life.[22]

Fortunately, the family was able to stay together. Pemberton's next orders sent him to New Orleans, a suitable place. Their new home would be a militia post on the east bank of the Mississippi River at the southern end of New Orleans. Pemberton probably traveled there in the steamer *Fashion,* which carried sixty Seminoles on the first leg of their trip west.[23]

Known during and after the Civil War as Jackson Barracks, the New Orleans barracks had its origins in the 1815 Battle of New Orleans, when General Andrew Jackson wanted a place where he could keep his victorious troops away from temptation. Shaped like a parallelogram, the post had an expansive parade ground and was enclosed by a high brick wall. From the end of the Mexican War through the mid-1850s, batteries of the First, Third, and Fourth U.S. Artillery regiments periodically occupied the fort. Company commanders included names that would become well-known in the Civil War, including George Thomas, Isaac Patton, James Ricketts, and John C. Pemberton.[24]

Pemberton's first days in New Orleans were busy, attending to numerous administrative details. As officers came and went, he at one point found himself in command of the entire post, and he spent many hours supervising building repairs.[25]

The move to south Louisiana greatly pleased Pattie, who felt that they were "again in a civilized portion of the world." The new home offered much variety. The barracks complex reached almost to the Mississippi's edge; steamers and all manner of other vessels plied the muddy waters. The harbor of New Orleans lay visible in the distance. Scenic trees, green grass, and white clover dominated the barracks grounds. Supplies were much more plentiful than the Pembertons had been used to. The fort had good cistern water, the weather was pleasant, Pattie had two servant women to help out, and all in all, New Orleans proved to be a paradise compared to the "wilds and wastes of Florida."[26]

As time passed, the Pembertons confined their lives mostly within the barracks walls. John spent spare time "playing nurse to his wonderful daughter." Baby Pattie grew rapidly and to her doting parents was the "smartest, funniest little thing you ever saw." They appreciated the child's good health, interrupted only by infrequent dysentery.[27]

Little Pattie's Uncle Israel caused a bit of a stir when he indirectly chided her mother for not producing a male Pemberton. He made his tongue-in-cheek remarks in a letter to Philadelphia, knowing full well that they would be passed on to Pattie in New Orleans. Pattie, no doubt recalling the loss of her firstborn, a boy, berated Israel with scathing humor, informing him that he was being soundly verbally abused in Louisiana. Thoroughly enjoying the affair, John wrote Israel that though his niece was "very charming," she would grow up like her mother, small but certainly not diminutive. Pattie assured Israel that once he saw their little one he would change his mind and concluded her remarks, "in the 'bliss' of 'ignorance' she [little Pattie] sends her love."[28]

Pattie also used the occasion to take a shot at Israel's bachelorhood. His brother had become "the pattern of a good husband." "I often wonder," she wrote, "at the change which has come over him since our acquaintance began," for "'tis funny to witness the little chats, plays, etc. which take place between him and little Pattie. Indeed he would convince you silently that 'tis not good for men to be alone."[29]

Certainly the presence of his daughter removed whatever rough edges remained on the brash, womanizing West Pointer Pemberton had once been. He fussed over her, helped Pattie take care of her when his duties permitted, and flatly refused his mother's request to call her Mary in memory of his deceased sister. Perhaps the fate of his firstborn still haunted him. He did promise, however, to give his mother the privilege of naming their next female child. Further to appease her, he sent a daguerreotype of the baby that had been made at the request of her other grandmother.[30]

In July 1850, the Pembertons packed up and left with the rest of barracks personnel for Pascagoula on the Mississippi Gulf Coast. The move was a routine military exercise because Pascagoula was considered healthier than New Orleans from midsummer through early fall. Pemberton had a bathhouse built close by their quarters so Pattie could enjoy the luxury of salt bathing, "which has been of decided benefit to me I think."[31]

By the time the family returned to New Orleans, Pemberton had been promoted to captain, to rank from September 27, 1850. His previous promotions to captain and major during the Mexican War had been by brevet, or nominal, honorary ranks. Orders awaited him in New Orleans to report to Fort Hamilton in New York Harbor. Once more the Pembertons were on the move, John traveling on ahead to the fort, while his wife and daughter visited the Thompsons in Norfolk.[32]

The two Patties stayed in Norfolk longer than planned. Pattie waited until her father's New Year's birthday before moving to New York. The delay gave her and the baby time to get adjusted to the harsh northern clime. Their time in the North, however, proved shorter than expected. Pemberton had managed to get assigned to Fort Washington, a post on the Potomac River a few miles downstream from Washington, D.C. He probably made enemies by using his seniority to get the transfer; transfers often forced others to move. But he cared only that he was pleasing his wife by getting her closer to Norfolk. She was not pleased, for she had been looking forward to the excitement of New York City, but she soon became reconciled to being "perfectly in the country" in this rural fort, high on the Potomac banks almost directly opposite George Washington's estate of Mount Vernon.[33]

Fort Washington also lay within easy traveling distance of Philadelphia. John and Pattie tried hard to persuade the Pemberton clan to come for a visit, especially John's mother and his unmarried sister Fanny (Frances). John even arranged to have his friend Bill Mackall, a future Confederate officer, meet his mother and sister in Baltimore and arrange for their transportation to the fort. Persistent persuasion worked, and both Rebecca and Fanny made several visits.[34]

Rebecca Pemberton never liked Fort Washington. She found it "the most tiresome life in the world; so much monotony, and so shut out from society. The neighborhood is wild and desolate, but one road on which they can ride or walk, and that a bad one." Nevertheless, "the scenery from the ramparts is beautiful looking up and down a noble river from a great elevation, with a distant view of Alexandria, and even the white buildings of Wash[ington] can be discerned on a clear day, which are nearly 20 miles off."[35]

Rebecca also had opinions and observations about the day-to-day life of her son. His attentiveness to his wife and child and his attitude were "so domestic, so *nice* in his house, and altogether so changed," that "I am struck with astonishment." He smoked a pipe to save the expense of cigars, kept wine and brandy, and had ample food on the table and sufficient servants "belonging" to Pattie. Pattie's black cook was a gift from her father; two white women also worked in the household under her supervision. Rebecca also was taken with her grandchild, every inch a Pemberton with her dark eyes close together like her father's, the long Pemberton face and chin, and light hair. The grandmother naturally saw mostly paternal features in her son's little girl.[36]

The isolation of the Pembertons' new home promoted socializing within the fort. Other married officers and their wives were frequent dinner guests. Sometimes dinners were preceded or followed by cruises on the river, a welcome respite from routine garrison life. Pattie welcomed trips on the river and any other diversions that got her away from the parade ground world. She attended church when John could baby-sit and occasionally went horseback riding along the river with her husband. But because of the burdens of motherhood and her nature as a homebody, she rarely ventured to Washington and the outside world with him.[37]

Pattie was pregnant again, and again Uncle Israel would be disappointed. Her pregnancy prevented the John C. Pembertons from attending Henry's wedding. John sent his regrets, admitting to his mother that he had always thought more of Henry than himself, "*vain* as I may be." The new baby, who was named Mary, arrived on August 9, 1851, the day before her father's thirty-seventh birthday. Pattie hoped Israel would not be told right away; she knew he would be disgusted. Before he knew the results, he had commented, "It is folly to go through so much pain and trouble for the sake of a brat of a girl, that will only remain with her a few years if it is worth looking at." Humorous sarcasm aside, Israel did encourage Pattie after the birth, saying perhaps she would do better next time.[38]

For the first months of Mary's life her family was close by. The fort was snowed and iced in during the particularly bad winter of 1851–52. The Potomac froze, snow fell continuously, and the Pembertons saw and heard nothing from the outside world for weeks. Rare mail and a butcher's cart that appeared every five days were the sole links to the outside world. Only horses could negotiate the frozen, icy roads. Pattie's and John's fourth wedding anniversary passed quietly on January 18, 1852. Pattie reflected that the years had brought her to the point of being a "*stern matron* superintending the nursery education of two daughters."³⁹

Being so close to Washington, John learned something of national affairs in spite of the weather. The United States tour of Hungarian patriot Louis Kossuth prompted him to comment to Israel, "I have never been more disgusted in my life with the impudence of this country than I have since his presence in it." Pemberton considered Kossuth a traitor to Hungary's legitimate government. Had he known what his future held, even he would have appreciated the irony of his opinion.⁴⁰

At last spring came and with it trips to Philadelphia. John's ability to obtain leaves made Israel envious. He needled John: "Necessity is a sterner master than Uncle Sam, and allows his nephews but few holidays." John took little Pattie for rides on the city's omnibus, causing Rebecca to remember when her son disdained such transportation, much preferring to ride horseback. "Truly marriage performs wonders," she mused.⁴¹

Pattie also took the children on tours of Mount Vernon and on extended trips to Norfolk. She was pregnant again and had to get about while she could. Once while the family was away, John surprised Pattie by moving the household into larger quarters. His efforts caused her to comment to Rebecca: "John you know is blest with a full and entire appreciation of all the *good* that is in him, and when I am *slow* in applauding I find that he is always his own commender."⁴²

In addition to household chores and military duties, Pemberton rekindled his relationship with Israel during his time at Fort Washington. In preceding years their correspondence had been sporadic at best. He begged his brother to come for a visit. "Is, we scarcely know each other," he complained in one letter, "so long have we been apart." He worried about his brother's financial affairs and social ups and downs just as Israel had worried about him in earlier times. He was determined to make Israel more communicative and used every excuse to write to him. When an act of the United States Congress entitled servicemen to 160 acres of bounty land in the Midwest, John asked Israel for advice on the disposition of his share. They discussed other areas, but, except for John's joy that General Worth's old nemesis Winfield Scott was defeated in the 1852 presidential election by Franklin Pierce, rarely talked politics. Although the subject is absent from their surviving letters, they probably discussed the hot issue of the day: slavery. No doubt their views were similar. Both had spent extensive periods in the South. Once Israel wrote his mother, "The more I see of slavery, the better I think of it." He liked the affection he saw between slaves and masters and noticed with special pleasure that slaves seemed to be more interested in their owners' welfare than were free servants in the North. John had a more personal view of the peculiar institution through contact with slaves in Pattie's family. He once decided not to take little Pattie with him on a trip to Philadelphia because her nurse was a slave. He feared that problems might arise from taking her into the free state of Pennsylvania, but he never considered freeing her. If a choice should have to be made, there was little doubt that John would side with Pattie on the slavery issue, and headstrong Pattie would never turn her back on her family or Virginia.[43]

In mid-November 1852, Pemberton was ordered to report to Fort Hamilton. The move had to be delayed because of Pattie's ill health. During a visit to Philadelphia, she developed a cough similar to the one that had decimated her and doomed her first child. Pemberton arranged for her to stay in a Philadelphia boardinghouse while she recuperated. Cancellation of court-martial hearings at West Point in December relieved him of that duty and allowed him to spend Christmas with his family. His brother Henry had already seen to it that little Pattie's sick mother and absent father did not ruin this special time of year. He presented her with a remarkable doll that opened and shut its eyes.[44]

Because of Pattie's condition, Pemberton obtained twenty days leave but still was responsible for court-martial assignments. He commuted to various points and then hurried back to Pattie's bedside. When her condition stabilized, he decided to take the children to Fort Hamilton. He would bring her on as soon as her condition allowed.[45]

John Clifford Pemberton, Jr., entered the world on January 31, 1853, weighing in at a robust ten pounds, eight ounces. His father just missed the event, having returned to New York the day before. Pattie immediately wrote to Israel, demanding the respect he had promised on delivery of a nephew. Israel manfully responded that she had indeed redeemed herself and that she was "a perfect little captain of a woman." Hurrying back to Philadelphia, John beamed with pride at the sight of his son. Each birth had been so nerve-racking for him that he usually wound up on his knees in prayer. Like his father, he never cared much for organized religion, but he had a strong belief in a supreme being. The birth left Pattie with a slight fever, not as severe as the first time, and she recovered nicely but remained for several weeks in Philadelphia. Fanny returned to Hamilton with John and took care of housekeeping and child care until Pattie could travel.[46]

Fanny enjoyed her time in New York; she was especially fond of John and was eager to help out. She purchased French white china vegetable dishes for him during one shopping trip to the city. She disliked Fort Hamilton, the "place of winds," as she called it. But she settled in and even stayed on for a while after Pattie arrived with young John.[47]

Not long after Pattie's return, Pemberton survived a threat on his own life. Corporal John White passed Pemberton by without giving a salute. He dutifully reported the incident, and White was confined to quarters. After three days, Pemberton decided the corporal should have learned his lesson and withdrew the charge. On Tuesday, March 22, 1853, Pemberton sat reading and smoking in another officer's room. All the officers but one were busy drilling the garrison. When a light knock sounded at the door, Pemberton responded, "Come in." Corporal White stepped inside, saluted smartly, and said politely, "I wish to say a few words to the major." Pemberton waited and finally responded impatiently, "Well, White?" The corporal continued, "It is owing to my being arrested a few days ago major, that I am upon guard [duty] today, and I wanted to tell you so the day you released me, but you would not let me speak." Pemberton rejoined, "No, you know I told you at the time that I did not want anything more said on the subject, but now you may say whatever you wish to." White thanked Pemberton for withdrawing the charges, and then very calmly and deliberately pulled out a pistol, cocked it, and pointed it at Pemberton's chest. Barely two feet separated the two men. Pemberton quickly seized White, who had a size advantage, grabbed his throat with one hand, and tried to disarm him with the other. A terrific fight ensued in which Pemberton kept the pistol barrel pushed away from his body. Finally, he shoved his assailant to the floor, keeping his grip on White's throat and pushing his gun hand down. Pemberton had been yelling "murderer" at White for some time during the struggle and a passing band member heard the noise and rushed in, followed closely by an officer. Together they pushed the gun to the floor and disarmed the desperate corporal. White was put in irons and taken away; Pemberton emerged relatively unscathed, though he would be stiff and sore for several days.[48]

A general court-martial found White guilty of "drawing a weapon upon and offering violence to his superior officer, he being in the execution of his office." White was sentenced to be shot, but President Franklin Pierce, acting on the recommendation of Secretary of War Jefferson Davis, commuted the sentence to "solitary confinement at hard labor, with a ball and chain, for the remainder of the term of his enlistment, and to suspension of pay and allowances except the necessary clothing and subsistence." Though harsh, Pierce's decision did not please the Pembertons. John's reaction is not recorded; Pattie blamed the easy access to liquor outside the walls of the fort for White's behavior. He did not appear drunk at the time of the attack, but witnesses had seen him drinking heavily after Pemberton dropped the initial charges.[49]

Tragic news of the severe illness and death on the same day, April 20, of Anna's two children, Clifford and Samuel, pushed the White incident into the background. Anna had become Pattie's favorite of John's family, and she feared her sister-in-law might never recover from such a blow. The tragedy devastated John. "How terrible, my dearest Mother," he wrote home, "seems this dispensation of Almighty God—that he will temper the affliction to the bereaved parents that they may be able to bear it, and that He will support them under so terrible a trial is the heartfelt prayer of their sympathizing and affectionate brother—let them know when it can be done, how truly and deeply I mourn with them."[50]

Anna's trial seemed to set off a chain of deaths among Pemberton children. Henry and Caroline's firstborn, a four-month-old son named John, died on July 19, 1853. John's and Pattie's two-year-old Mary was claimed by illness in September. The string of debacles strained the family, especially Rebecca, who somehow always had the strength to see her progeny through tragedies.[51]

Pemberton himself suffered a variety of illnesses that fateful summer. A mountain lake trip gave him a severe case of bilious fever that resulted in "total prostration of his system." He lay bedridden, debilitated and depressed, for several weeks. A glass of port three times a day plus heavy does of quinine helped dissipate a hacking cough and finally put him on the road to recovery. Pattie had problems, too, suffering from an inflamed eye and the flu. The Pembertons would remember the summer of 1853 as one of the family's darkest times.[52]

While he recovered, Pemberton fantasized about getting an assignment as a bearer of dispatches that would take him and the family away from Fort Hamilton, possibly to Europe. He thought the move would improve his health. Pattie would have welcomed a change; she was tired of "band box" quarters in which she had to entertain guests. Life in which the main diversions were inspections and band music grew tiresome indeed. Europe never beckoned, however. The best Pemberton could achieve was a brief furlough.[53]

The leave of absence returned him to good health, but Pemberton soon found himself entangled in another incident at Fort Hamilton. He and the other officers despised the garrison commander, Major W. W. Morris, for his officious and spiteful manner, which had once forced him to apologize to his subordinates for his behavior. In March 1854, he had John Pemberton arrested over a very trivial procedural violation.

Pemberton's trouble with Morris stemmed from the former's arrest of a soldier who played in the post band. Regulations required that an arrest be reported to the arrested party's immediate commander "as soon as practicable." Morris considered himself the commander of the band; a questionable assumption unknown to Pemberton. When Pemberton did find it out, he proceeded to write his report. As he wrote, Morris's adjutant approached and informed Pemberton that the major was upset because the matter had not already been reported. Furious, Pemberton explained, in writing, that he had not had an opportunity to report earlier. Furthermore, he could not have reported any sooner unless he had done so in person, which he refused to do. Morris considered Pemberton's letter "insubordinate and disrespectful" and ordered his arrest. A court-martial threw out the charge.

Pemberton's sometimes arrogant manner showed through in his comments to his brother. He would always get the best of Morris, he wrote, "because I know I am always right, and he is known throughout the army to be an infernal scoundrel." The two would be enemies ever after, occasionally clashing over other trivial matters.[54]

The joy of the ever-growing Pemberton family made trouble with Morris seem trivial indeed. On December 15, 1853, they welcomed another son, named William, born at the fort. William's arrival added to the pride of a father already glowing at his eldest son's imitation of soldiers marching about the post. William would be followed by yet another brother, Francis Rawle Pemberton, also born at Fort Hamilton. Francis was born on May 3, 1856, weighing in at an impressive twelve and a half pounds.[55]

Before the end of 1856, Pemberton had to leave his growing family for Florida, where the seemingly endless problems with Seminole Indians had cropped up again. Small bands of Seminoles continued to resist forced removal to the West, and the federal government once more had to build up its military forces in Florida. Pemberton's orders took him to Fort Meyers on the west coast of the peninsula, southwest of Lake Okeechobee in the Everglade region. His voyage around the tip of southern Florida carried him close to Israel, who was doing survey work in Cuba.[56]

Pemberton remained in Florida through the summer of 1857, suffering from the heat and worrying over Fanny's ill health. He went out on several patrols, operating from Forts Center and Kissimmee west and north of Okeechobee. One particularly strenuous march carried him over a hundred miles from Kissimmee to the southeast by Okeechobee through the Everglades to Fort Dallas on the Atlantic side of Florida near the southern tip. The patrol struggled through saw grass, cypress, and swamps, living on horse and alligator meat when rations were used up. The humid summer brought floods and mosquitoes, and Pemberton complained to Pattie about living conditions and hoped for a new assignment. The duty seemed even more tedious and depressing when the news came of Fanny's death in July.[57]

His tour in Florida ended when Pemberton and other elements of the Fourth Artillery were ordered west to Fort Leavenworth, Kansas. From this base, he participated in the Utah expedition, which consisted of a military force sent by President James Buchanan to remedy problems the federal government was having with Mormons.[58]

Pemberton's family went with him to Kansas, and young Pattie came back from the west with memories of the nice parade ground and good post band at Fort Leavenworth. She remembered in later years that her mother had opinions to the contrary and longed to come back east. The elder Pattie quickly tired of Pemberton's endless patrols and expeditions and thought it silly that artillery batteries were stationed in areas more suited to cavalry and infantry. She was upset at her husband's participation in the Utah business, even though he managed to get her and the children sent east to Jefferson Barracks near St. Louis. Her seventh child was on the way, and she hated being away from her husband, Norfolk, and Philadelphia. Anna was born in September after Pattie's return to Leavenworth.[59]

Pemberton came back from the Utah expedition unscathed and was granted a brief furlough in the early winter of 1858. Leaving the family in Kansas, he made a quick trip to Philadelphia and Norfolk, purchasing a sewing machine for Pattie along the way. The Thompsons were pleased to see their son-in-law in fine health. Mrs. Thompson thought his part in the march to Fort Kearney, New Mexico, the first leg of the Utah campaign, "had agreed with his physique. I never saw him so cheerful, or in such perfect" condition.[60]

In 1859 the Pembertons left Leavenworth and traveled by covered wagon and steamboat to Fort Ridgely, established in 1853 on the left bank of the Minnesota River at the junction of the Rock River and the Minnesota in the south-central part of the state. Pemberton had to endure serving under the command of his old nemesis Major Morris at Ridgely for most of his time there. En route to the fort, the Pembertons lost their milk cow in an otherwise uneventful trip. The fort itself had little to offer other than a library, which the Pembertons no doubt frequented. Mail was slow and newspapers were extremely old when they finally arrived. Cold winters, isolation, limited social activities, and music limited to fife and drum made excessive drinking and boredom major problems for the garrison. Area Indians, colorfully costumed, probably made the soldiers nervous, but post children found them fascinating. The place was not conducive to having offspring; Pattie relived her past experiences when she helped deliver a stillborn son to a sergeant's wife.[61]

Fate and Pemberton's restlessness had taken him and his family on a lengthy odyssey through the 1850s. No longer the enthusiastic West Pointer, John Pemberton the veteran soldier had been persistent, if not always successful, in his search for comfortable duty. Like life revolving around other parade grounds, the Pembertons' years at Ridgely were consumed by daily, mostly ordinary routine. Elsewhere, the family had had its share of routine, struggles, tragedy, and triumph during the decade that was about to end.

The United States was undergoing a struggle to overcome traumatic events that seemed inexorably leading to civil war. Debates over slavery had grown increasingly strident. Massachusetts Senator Charles Sumner had been beaten senseless by a South Carolina congressman over the issue. Fanatical John Brown had been hanged as a result of his conspiracy to incite a slave rebellion. Always in tune with public events, John Pemberton was no doubt aware of these and other symptoms of the growing crisis. If his thoughts were recorded, they are lost to history or hidden away in an unknown attic. Like most Americans, he must have wished for a peaceful solution. There appeared to be no doubt where he would stand if forced to choose sides. He had adopted Virginia as his home state before he met Pattie, although that alone might not have been a critical factor. William T. Sherman had lived in and loved the South, and he would fight for the Union. George Thomas was a native of Virginia, and he would fight for the Union. Pemberton had to consider his Philadelphia family's feelings, but he also had to think of his beloved Pattie. When his regiment was recalled to Washington in early 1861, Pemberton's emotions must have been thoroughly tangled between memories of long years of service to his country and mixed loyalties of family ties.

CHAPTER 6

The Weight of Responsibility

Going South, South Carolina

John Pemberton was assigned to duty in Washington, D.C., during the Fort Sumter crisis. He decided to remain with the North unless Virginia seceded. His brother Israel welcomed this stand, particularly in the face of the escalation of anti-Southern feelings in Philadelphia. Mobs roamed the streets there looking for Southern sympathizers, giving suspects the choice of flying the United States flag or having their homes burned. Israel reasoned with John: "I think if you were here a little while, you would feel that you and your ancestors were Pennyslvanians, and that your destiny, in case of a dissolution of the general government should be with Penn. Governments may change but to our country we owe I think a never swerving allegiance."[1]

The same day Israel wrote that letter, April 15, 1861, Abraham Lincoln reacted to the Confederate attack on Fort Sumter by declaring the South to be in a state of insurrection and issued a call for seventy-five thousand volunteers to put it down. Israel attended a party that evening and heard a rumor that John had already resigned or was about to. The next morning he penciled a postscript to the letter urging John to remain loyal to his country and Pennsylvania. If the rumor about his resignation was true, wrote Israel, then he would surely never be able to come home again, for all his friends would consider him a traitor. "You wouldn't even have the poor apology of your state going out of the union for forsaking the government and laws you've sworn to protect."[2] On Wednesday, April 17, the day after Israel mailed his letter, Virginia left the Union. Israel hurried to Washington.

Virginia's secession did not lead immediately to Pemberton's resignation, as he had said it would. In Washington he received orders on April 19 to take his artillery company and "seize and hold possession, in the name of the President of the United States . . . all the steamers plying between Washington City and Aquia Creek" along the Potomac River. He carried out the order, all the while torn between his love for Pattie and Virginia and his devotion to his Philadelphia family.[3]

Israel went to Washington and temporarily swayed his brother; he "begged and pleaded" with John, "telling him how . . . all [the Pembertons would] suffer if he did it [resigned]." Finally, Israel concluded that John's "ideas of duty & honor are all the other way," but his "affection & feeling for us, prevents him from resigning." John continued to delay his decision.[4]

Pattie and the children had gone to Norfolk, and she expected him to arrive in Virginia at any moment. When he did not come, she wrote impatiently: "My darling husband why are you not with us? Why do you stay?" She assured him that Confederate President Jefferson Davis had a position for him, but Davis was still in Montgomery, Alabama, the first capital of the new Confederacy. In her desperation, Pattie was obviously dropping names. John, Israel, and their mother all wrote to Pattie trying to explain his difficult position to her. Afraid of the effect his resignation would have in Philadelphia, John procrastinated, attended to his Washington duties, and worried. If he should be ordered to participate in an attack on Norfolk, he would resign at once, he told Israel.[5]

Finally, on April 24, John Pemberton made his fateful decision and resigned from the United States Army. According to one account, his resignation was held up until General Winfield Scott could talk with him. The story may be true; certainly Scott could be expected to try to convince all his veteran officers to stay with the Union. John's memories of Scott were less than fond, and he had already made up his mind. He left for Richmond. In Philadelphia, the Pembertons were disappointed but also probably somewhat relieved that the suspense was over. Rebecca commented, "I have been more wretched in this horrid state than words can tell." But the decision had been made; "I must accept it . . . we have done all we can."[6]

Pemberton's defection to the Confederacy has been cloaked in unsubstantiated myths rooted in the writings of Jubal Early, Richard Taylor, and John Pemberton, Jr. The general's son added to the states'-rights, pro-Southern myth put forth by Early and Taylor in an 1882 biographical sketch of his father. The article asserted that Pemberton "was, from earliest manhood until the close of his life, a firm believer in the doctrine of State sovereignty, and was at no time in harmony with the advocates of a 'paternal government.' " Not believing in a paternal government did not make Pemberton a believer in state sovereignty to the point of wishing to see the Union broken up. Though he may have been sympathetic to such a view in the 1850s as the storms of war approached, and there is no known evidence either way, he certainly did not always hold to such a tenet. His delay in joining the Confederacy once Virginia had seceded did not support his supposed strong Southern, pro-states' rights sentiments. Available historical evidence proves otherwise. The only documentation of his attitudes on matters involving state versus federal power was reflected in antinullification statements written while he was at West Point. Nowhere in his surviving antebellum writings is there any advocacy of states' rights as a doctrine.[7]

The mythological explanations of Pemberton's decision, all but one of which (Early's) were written after his death, appear to be an attempt to prove that he was totally committed to the Southern cause before the war. A man who follows long-held convictions is usually respected, no matter which side of an issue he is on. If Southerners, and other Americans for that matter, understood anything, it was devotion to a cause. Pemberton's performance during the war led many to question his devotion. Hence Early and others undertook a campaign to enhance his image.

Why, then, did Pemberton fight for the Confederacy? He had strong feelings for Virginia, which predated his meeting and marrying

Pattie. Though his affection for the Old Dominion may have been a factor, standing alone it probably would not have been decisive, as it proved not to be for William T. Sherman and George Thomas.

The only reasonable conclusion is that Pemberton left the Union because of his marriage. His documented political views indicate that had his wife been a Northern woman, he would never have joined the Confederacy. His choice ultimately came down to fighting for the North or for Pattie, and for John Pemberton that was no choice at all. It is hardly coincidental that his resignation came close on the heels of her letter urging him to come to Virginia, to come join "us." Pattie had made clear where her heart lay, and he would never have turned against her. His political orientation had no doubt been influenced during their years of marriage so there could be some small credence to the myths of his antebellum views. But he was never as dogmatic as his apologists claimed. He wore gray because of Pattie; that is the only feasible explanation.

When Pemberton arrived in Richmond, Governor John Letcher nominated him to be a lieutenant colonel of volunteer state troops. In one of the many ironies of the Civil War, Pemberton was one of three officers who reported for duty to General Joseph E. Johnston, with whom he would carry on a bitter debate following the Vicksburg campaign. Johnston's immediate assignment was to set up a series of instructional camps around Virginia, and Pemberton supervised one such camp in the Norfolk area. In later years, he claimed that Johnston arranged his rank and assignment to Johnston's command. If true, it is not clear why Johnston wanted Pemberton. Their paths may have crossed before, in Mexico perhaps, but more likely Johnston simply wanted a regular army artillery veteran to train the volunteers.[8]

Johnston's advocacy may have assisted in Pemberton's continual upward movement in rank. On May 8, 1861, he became lieutenant colonel of artillery in the Provisional Army of Virginia. On June 15 he was designated a major in the artillery corps of the of the Confederate States Army; two days later he was promoted to brigadier general, bypassing the intermediate ranks of lieutenant colonel and colonel. On June 28, he was named a colonel of artillery in the Virginia army. The profusion of ranks illustrates the confusion that occurred in transferring men from state to Confederate service. There is no clear answer to why Pemberton moved up in rank so rapidly. Perhaps he played the game of military politics well; he had a history of doing so. There is no question that he was a favorite of Confederate President Jefferson Davis. Pattie's family also may have had an influence, and Johnston apparently favored him. But the results were not positive for Pemberton's future. His seemingly unwarranted advancements would provoke jealousy among his fellow officers and place him in highly pressured situations.[9]

A more significant reason for negative reactions to his rank was his Northern nativity. Since there is no known record of his personal impressions of the early days in Confederate Virginia, any verbal abuse he may have encountered because he was a Yankee is not documented. But the Richmond papers were vocal and vicious in their assaults on everything Northern. An *Examiner* editorial, for example, said that cowardice was "inculcated on the Yankee from his birth." The *Enquirer* also spoke pointedly about Pennsylvanians and Ohioans living in Virginia who allegedly had Unionist sentiments: "These men are not of us, nor with us. . . . They are illegitimate Virginians."[10] Pemberton probably read these papers, and their venomous attitude toward the North must have made him feel awkward. As long as he stayed out of the spotlight, however, his birthplace was not an issue.

Pemberton remained in the Norfolk vicinity through November 1861. The Confederate capital had been moved to Richmond during the summer, and he had cast a vote for Virginia's secession, supposedly the first vote he ever cast. Otherwise times were quiet. While Pattie and the children settled in Smithfield, John's artillery brigade operated in the Smithfield-Suffolk region just west of Norfolk. He was working to get shore batteries in place along the James River when the first great battle of the war occurred at Manassas on July 21, 1861. During this period, Pemberton may very well have encountered William Wing Loring, who briefly commanded at Suffolk and would later be a thorn in his side at Vicksburg.[11]

The Confederate career of John Pemberton took a fateful turn in November 1861, when Robert E. Lee received orders to take command of the South Carolina coastal defenses. Though Lee was destined to become the Confederacy's greatest hero, his only Civil War adventure thus far had been an unsuccessful campaign in western Virginia. But Jefferson Davis had faith in Lee and chose him to meet Federal threats to the Charleston area.[12]

On November 29, mainly in reaction to an insistent request from
South Carolina's volatile governor, Francis Pickens, that Lee lacked
brigadier generals, Davis ordered N. G. Evans and John C. Pemberton
to Charleston.[13] Pemberton's experience with the Norfolk and James
River defenses no doubt influenced Davis's decision. Because he and
Pattie were conveniently located near her home area, it is not likely
he would have asked for a transfer. Again the Pembertons gathered
their belongings and moved to South Carolina.

Lee placed Pemberton in command of District Four, a coastal area
south of Charleston extending from the Ashepoo River to the Port
Royal Sound area. He established his headquarters at Coosawatchie, a
stop on the Charleston and Savannah Railroad about halfway between
the two cities. Defense of this rail line and the two cities it connected
was Lee's primary objective.[14]

Pemberton had an opportunity to observe, implement, and learn
about Lee's strategic concepts in defending the coast against Yankee
gunboats. Lee decided to withdraw all artillery and garrisons from
minor outlying positions and to strengthen more important defenses,
especially those around Charleston and Savannah. Finally, he had his
army construct a deep interior line, far enough inland to protect the
railroad but out of range of Federal boats. One of Lee's innovations was
the idea of moving troops from place to place by train to take advantage of his interior lines.[15]

From his district, Pemberton watched Lee in action, unaware that
the mantel of overall leadership of the Confederate coastal army
would fall on his shoulders within a few months. He kept his men busy
and alert. On New Year's Day 1862, his men beat back a Union
incursion up the Coosaw River. Pemberton heard sounds of battle,
started for the front, and learned that Yankee infantry was landing
along the banks of the Coosaw. He managed to save one big gun, but
heavy gunboat fire made resistance difficult. The skirmish was one of
many incidents that convinced Pemberton of the futility of stopping
gunboats with outlying forts and batteries. It was a conviction that
would eventually cause him much trouble with South Carolina authorities and superior officers.[16]

With the dawn of 1862, Confederate lines in South Carolina remained largely intact despite occasional Yankee forays. But trouble of
another nature arose. A rift between Lee and one of his brigadiers,

Roswell Ripley, portended the problems Pemberton would face. Ripley was the sort who seldom got along with superior officers. Moreover, he was a native of the North, an Ohioan, though he had lived in Charleston for several years before the war. Governor Pickens defended Lee in a message to Jefferson Davis: "General Lee is a perfect head, quiet and retiring. I find him all that a gentleman should be, and all that ought to be expected of a thorough and scientific officer."[17] Pickens's comments about the traits he admired in an officer are significant in view of his future relationship with Pemberton, who was anything but quiet and retiring and lacked Lee's engineering skills. Like Lee, Pemberton would have problems with Ripley; unlike Lee, he never won Pickens's approval.

For the moment, however, he had only his own district to worry about, and most of that worry proved groundless. Almost all Union activities were either reconnaissances or simple diversions to keep the Confederates guessing about Yankee intentions. Pemberton frequently had to alert his troops or prepare to move to the aid of other districts on his flanks. Lee pointed out to his subordinates that holding their lines was more important than trying to save any particular area in their front. Pemberton learned that lesson, and it, too, would cause him future problems.[18]

Though he had actually done very little and certainly nothing spectacular during his brief time in South Carolina, Pemberton's performance had obviously pleased someone. On February 13, Secretary of War Judah P. Benjamin signed an order promoting him to major general dating from January 14.[19] Civil War historians have universally questioned why he received this and a later promotion to lieutenant general. Certainly his performance had not justified Richmond's action. That he was a favorite of Jefferson Davis is certainly part of the answer. Another factor may have been more decisive. If Davis was already thinking of calling Lee back to Richmond before he finally did in early March, then he needed a replacement, someone familiar with the Charleston area. The date of his rank gave Pemberton seniority over the other brigadiers under Lee so he would have been a logical choice to assume command. But if he did assume Lee's position, he would need a promotion to distinguish him from other brigadiers. Lee must have had some say in the process; if so, one can only assume that he endorsed Pemberton.

Lee left for Richmond when the massive Union Army of the Potomac began operations that would culminate in the Seven Days' campaign. On March 4, John Pemberton was assigned to temporary command of the Department of South Carolina and Georgia; on March 14
the assignment became permanent.[20] It had been almost a year since
the fall of Forth Sumter, and Pemberton was embarking on his first
independent command. From Washington he had gone to a position
of relative anonymity in the Virginia tidewater. Now he had been
swept into the mainstream of Confederate command.

When he took command of the Department of South Carolina and
Georgia, Pemberton began an inexplicable reorganization of Robert E.
Lee's district plan that blossomed into an unnecessarily complex bureaucracy. District Four was divided in two. The First and Second
districts were combined. The Georgia coastal area became the Second
Division, District of Georgia. Troops in the Third and Sixth districts
operated under the entity of Brigade Headquarters, Fourth Military
District of South Carolina, while men of the Fourth and Fifth districts
were designated as Brigade Headquarters, Third Military District of
South Carolina.[21] Perhaps the changes simply demonstrated Pemberton's penchant for managerial manipulation. He was a bureaucrat at
heart and may well have reorganized for no other reason than the
challenge of doing it.

Whatever his motives, circumstances within his domain further
complicated administrative changes. In March, the east Florida coast
had become the Department of Middle and Eastern Florida by order of
the War Department. In early April, eastern and middle Florida as far
west as the Choctawhatchie River were placed under Pemberton's
control, though the region still existed as a separate department.
Pemberton, like Lee, would devote little time to the Florida coast.
Other than an early inspection tour, he mostly ignored the area.[22]
The Federals, and consequently the Confederates, were more concerned with the Savannah-Charleston line. But the Florida situation
typified confusing aspects of Pemberton's command structure.

Pemberton's style as chief administrator of the department complemented his command structure. He became bogged down in minute
details. He paid too much attention to matters that were normally
taken care of by a general's staff. Pemberton approached the job as if
he were still doing staff work in Florida, for Worth in Mexico, and in

his other prewar posts. The lack of a cohesive staff compounded the problem. Most of Lee's aides had followed him to Virginia so Pemberton had to put together a new team, which did not begin to show signs of functioning well until the end of his South Carolina tenure. Several of his staff officers, including Adjutant John R. Waddy, Assistant Adjutant Robert W. Memminger, and aides-de-camp James H. Morrison and John C. Taylor, would accompany him to Vicksburg. Of this group, only Waddy had served with Pemberton before he came to South Carolina.[23]

The myriad of details such as getting lumber for construction of boats, iron for building railroad rails and other structures, and small arms and large caliber artillery to equip men and fortifications would have tested the most seasoned of staffs. Pemberton considered impressment as a means of obtaining supplies. He asked Richmond for permission to impress lead, powder, and other essentials that periodically arrived aboard blockade runners. The War Department decreed that Pemberton might "exercise the right of impressment in case of great extortion [by suppliers] and emergency, but as a general rule, you will avoid a resort to that measure."[24] He could and sometimes did use the "emergency" loophole, especially when absence of funds kept him from purchasing what he needed.

Lack of money proved to be a persistent problem, and not only in obtaining supplies. Pemberton frequently had to cajole Richmond into supplying funds to pay his soldiers. Too often he had to make a choice between supplies and salaries, and the government usually stepped in to insist that supplies be the top priority. When his balance of funds descended to zero, he resorted to impressing supplies and using certificates as promises to pay. Money also had to be found to pay the owners of his slave labor force, though money in fact was the least of his labor problems.[25]

While still acting commander of the department, Pemberton received word from Lee's old nemesis General Ripley that there was not enough labor on hand to strengthen the defensive works on James Island which protected Charleston's southern flank. This situation set the tone for Pemberton's tenure as commander; there was never enough labor available to accomplish any job. Just before he officially took over the department, the South Carolina Executive Council had authorized him to requisition and impress slaves for labor as needed.

The council, consisting of the governor, lieutenant governor, and three members elected by the state's secession convention, was a war measure creation of that convention. As the major governing body of South Carolina, the council was unpopular and was eventually abolished after Pemberton had left the state.[26] He quickly learned how difficult the council could be to work with.

The council, or more particularly, I. W. Hayne, chief of the South Carolina Department of Justice and Police and a council member, tried to renege on its slave labor policy. Hayne notified Pemberton that greater impressment power had been given than had been intended. Because no new fortifications were being planned at the time and impressed labor was not the most reliable, Pemberton promised that he would not use the power. He did point out that defensive works already begun were mostly incomplete because of insufficient numbers of workers and that owners had recalled most of his current labor force.[27] In short, he was willing to cooperate with the council, but he expected its help.

The situation worsened, and Pemberton pressured the council into setting up an intertwined system of impressment and payment of funds to slaveowners. A rotation schedule kept plantation and fortification work going simultaneously, at least on paper. Even after the new system was in place, Pemberton did not let up. If the rotation schedule interfered with a critical stage of building earthworks, he asked for workers to fill in until the next group of slaves rotated in from the plantations. The council generally cooperated and promised in August 1862 to provide at least three thousand slaves per month through the end of the year.[28]

Cooperation was not unanimous. Lieutenant Governor W. W. Harllee opposed the whole process. He did not like the idea of bringing slaves from other parts of the state to work in an unfamiliar coastal climate. Harllee argued that sufficient slave labor was available locally but that it was not being properly used. He bitterly criticized Pemberton's "utter want of system and management that has . . . characterized the employment of negro labor." The general, Harllee complained, had "neither a defined nor digested" plan "for the supervision and management of negroes . . . which is so important to the interests of the owner and the well being of the slave." Undaunted, Pemberton ignored Harllee and continued lobbying for more labor.[29]

The labor issue no doubt strained Pemberton's relations with the council, which, though mostly cordial, were never warm. Evidence shows that the council made a genuine effort to meet Pemberton's demands. The large number of incomplete fortifications he later left behind in South Carolina suggested that there was merit in Harllee's criticism. The labor problem was exacerbated by mismanagement, lack of money, lack of material to get the job done, resistance to impressment, and a shortage of slaves when needed most. Logical strategic positions and Federal threats dictated locations of fortifications. In some cases old earthworks were modified or abandoned. These factors, plus the rotation system, created spot shortages in areas where, as Harllee argued, local slave labor should have been sufficient. The labor issue was illustrative of the administrative and political problems Pemberton faced, and too often created, in South Carolina.[30]

Labor problems were aggravated by a lack of engineering expertise. Pemberton had little knowledge in the field and had little faith in his staff engineers. For difficult assignments, he borrowed Colonel W. R. Boggs, state engineer of Georgia. Pemberton's concern was justified. When General P. G. T. Beauregard replaced him in September 1862, the two toured the department, and Beauregard, who was more skilled in engineering, found much to criticize. Redoubts, redans, and other fortifications had been built in a faulty manner. Beauregard noted that he glazed over the problems in his report to Richmond but tried to be understanding, acknowledging that Pemberton did not have a suitable engineering background and had been provided very little assistance.[31]

Aside from labor and engineering, Pemberton's most pressing concern was strengthening his army. Richmond viewed his department as a reinforcement pool for other parts of the Confederacy. In the aftermath of the battle at Shiloh, Tennessee (April 6–7, 1862), Pemberton had to send several regiments to Corinth, Mississippi, where the defeated Confederate army was regrouping. Such losses from his own army forced him to constrict defenses, making South Carolinians nervous and unsure of his ability to defend the state.[32]

The Seven Days' campaign near Richmond (June 25–July 1, 1862) further drained Pemberton's manpower. In mid-June he wired Richmond requesting that newly arrived conscripts from South Carolina be sent back to their home state to fill his depleted regiments. He also suggested that since Union naval successes along the Mississippi River had thrown some Confederate sailors out of work, these men be given to him to help man his shore batteries. Navy Secretary Stephen Mallory refused the request and Pemberton found little sympathy in his numerous pleas to Richmond for more men. Incessant demands on his department reduced his "present for duty" strength from 23,000 in June to 18,700 in July. He sometimes legitimately used Federal threats to excuse refusals to send men elsewhere. But since most threats proved to be diversions designed to keep Pemberton from reinforcing Richmond, he usually had to send off more men anyway. Like constricted defenses, this situation kept state officials uneasy and weighed heavily on Pemberton, who had insufficient resources to defend an extensive coastline.[33]

In addition to the long coastline, Georgia presented other strategic problems. It bordered western South Carolina and therefore was logistically significant to defense of the coast. Georgia's governor, Joseph Brown, frequently placed his state's interests above those of the Confederacy, but he was initially cooperative toward Pemberton. Georgia state troops were needed to help defend Savannah, and Brown did his best to provide adequate numbers. This was a stopgap measure at best, but Pemberton's pleadings with Richmond for help brought only the retort that the new conscription law might help.[34]

Governor Brown considered the conscription bill another example of Richmond's encroachment on states' rights. He informed Pemberton that he would supply militia rolls and facilities, but the Confederacy would have to enforce the law. The expirations of state militia enlistment periods and other complications might require that the Georgia troops be disbanded, enlisted as conscripts, and reorganized. Pemberton knew that this process would take valuable time, but he had to accept Brown's conditions.[35]

Though Brown resisted conscription, he was most anxious to have Pemberton and the regular army defend his coastline. He cooperated with the placing of obstructions in the Savannah and Chattahoochee rivers to keep out Yankee vessels. More important, Brown readily, agreed to Pemberton's plan to connect interior railroads via Augusta. The connections would provide vital alternative routes in case the Charleston-Savannah line was cut.[36]

Linking the rail lines required completion of plans originally proposed by Robert E. Lee. Top priority was connecting the Augusta and Savannah road to the South Carolina line via Augusta. Charleston and Savannah would then be connected by an arc of rail lines. Other projects included linking the line between Augusta and Charleston with the road that connected Charleston with North Carolina and Virginia. These two lines came into northwest Charleston, and a bridge over the Ashley River would connect them with the Charleston and Savannah. Shortages of funds, labor, and iron delayed the work, adding to the frustrations of Pemberton's administration.[37]

A more sensitive issue that affected Pemberton's realm beyond the coastal area was martial law, which involved the suspension of most civil authority and the establishment of military rule. Military emergencies usually led to martial law, and Pemberton first considered instituting the measure when Fort Pulaski, near Savannah, fell to Union troops on April 11, 1862. Fearing penetration of his lines via the Savannah River, he proposed a declaration of martial law inland all the way to Augusta. President Davis and the War Department chose to ignore his request. Davis knew that martial law usually caused a negative reaction and refused to proclaim it except in extreme circumstances. Matters in Pemberton's department did not seem sufficiently extreme yet.[38]

Increased Federal activity along the coast and perceived threats to Charleston instigated a request from the Executive Council for Pemberton's opinion on martial law. He replied that he wanted to establish martial law from the Santee River north-northwest of the city down to the Edisto River to the south-southwest. Armed with the council's inquiry, Pemberton wired Richmond about the matter. Davis deferred to the council arguing that that body had the power to declare martial law within the boundaries of South Carolina. If the council acted, Davis would issue a proclamation giving Pemberton power to enforce the measure as the representative of the central government. The council declared martial law within a ten-mile radius of Charleston, far less territory than Pemberton wanted included. Once Davis had issued his order, however, Pemberton used it to extend the territory covered to the boundaries he had originally proposed.[39]

Seeking to build on this success, Pemberton again turned his attention to the Savannah-Augusta area. He contacted the War Department, Lee wired Governor Brown, and Brown agreed to accept martial law if city officials had no objection. Savannah officials did object, and Pemberton protested to Lee in vain. Lee reminded him that Davis still held firm to the policy that martial law required a local emergency and local support. Neither stipulation applied to Savannah. Pemberton relented, knowing that without a declaration in Savannah, pursuing one in Augusta would be pointless, although he advised Savannah's mayor that plans should be made for the evacuation of noncombatants in case of enemy attack.[40] This was an obvious hint that if trouble came, city officials and not John Pemberton would be responsible for Savannah's citizens.

Rebuffed in Georgia, Pemberton held firm to martial law in South Carolina. Though Federal threats fluctuated in intensity, the proclamation was not revoked until near the end of his tenure there. In late July 1862, Governor Pickens and the council complained to Davis that martial law was no longer necessary. The president responded that he had agreed to the council's request "reluctantly," then wired Pemberton for his opinion. Pemberton assented to the request that the area covered by the proclamation be limited to military encampments, and afterward martial law was confined to fortified islands adjacent to Charleston and a one-mile perimeter around the city. Pickens was appreciative, but he took the occasion to criticize Pemberton for extending the area of the council's original intent. By overly expanding the covered territory, Pemberton had in effect left interior sections in a state of anarchy. There were no military officials on hand, and local authorities had no power.[41]

The martial law issue had made Pemberton seem insensitive to the effect of the war on citizens in his department. He seemingly learned nothing from Davis, who clearly understood the potential political ramifications of martial law proclamations. This was not the first time Pemberton had shown such insensitivity. During his earlier tour of Florida, he had recommended evacuation of sparsely settled regions to avoid tying troops down in guerrilla war situations.[42] Some commanders could promulgate unpopular policies and still retain public trust. John Pemberton could not, for he failed to understand the nuances of public relations in a command that influenced the lives of civilians and the operations of civilian governments. The result was that the strict, officious military man he had become through his long years in the antebellum army had trouble building public support for anything he did or wanted to do.

Pemberton's nativity also contributed to his lack of success in dealing with the nonmilitary sector. Francis Pickens was a politician of the sort a Southerner like Robert E. Lee did not necessarily like but certainly understood. Pemberton never understood Pickens and rarely had good relations with the governor. A recent biographer commented, "Like so many other members of the Carolina gentry, Pickens possessed a complex temperament. Living by the chivalric code of honor to which aristocratic Carolinians subscribed and possessing a romantic, moody disposition," the veteran politician could be gracious and kind. "On the other hand, he was often overbearing, proud, envious, and stubborn. Intelligence and abundant knowledge he possessed, but he was also a romantic dreamer who often appeared insincere." Pickens resented the council because he thought it usurped his power. Even though he supported many of the council's actions, he was not associated with that body's decline in popularity. Its very existence made him aggressive and, combined with his "complex temperament," made him difficult for Pemberton to deal with. The Pennsylvanian and the South Carolinian were bound to clash, and they did on martial law and many other issues.[43]

They disagreed, for example, on distribution of salt. Pickens thought there was enough salt in Charleston to provide much of the state's needs. Pemberton argued that there was barely enough to meet the demands of the city's population. Both retreated. Pemberton agreed to withdraw his order impounding Charleston's salt as long as large amounts were not taken out of the city. Pickens set aside state funds to stimulate salt manufacture and wrote with a touch of sarcasm that he hoped Pemberton would allow salt manufactured "under the patronage of the State . . . to be sent into the country."[44]

Morale problems at Fort Sumter produced yet another confrontation. Pickens was sensitive about the fort, more for its symbolic value than its military necessity. When reports of mutiny among enlisted men and rivalry among officers leaked to the mainland, Pickens called on Pemberton for assistance. When Pemberton did not act quickly enough, Pickens contacted Lee, suggesting that South Carolina–born artillerists be placed in the fort to guard enlistees "who are strangers." Lee wired Pemberton, who responded that he had found no major

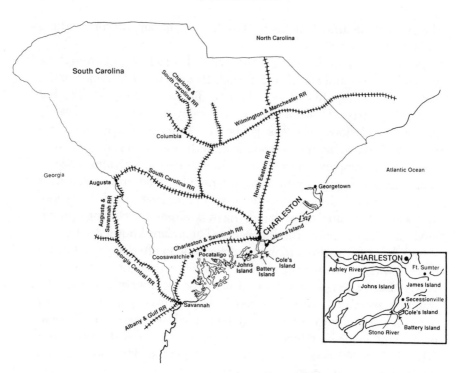

South Carolina Theater

problems in the fort other than those that normally occurred when
men were confined together over an extended period of time, and they
involved only a small portion of the garrison. Lee accepted Pemberton's report, and Pickens dropped the issue.[45]

The most severe strain between governor and general resulted from
Pickens's objections to Pemberton's general strategy in defending the
coastline, especially the immediate Charleston area. The root of the
debate was Pemberton's decision to abandon two prominent defensive
positions shortly after he took command.

On March 27, 1862, Pemberton notified Confederate Adjutant and
Inspector General Samuel Cooper that he was abandoning batteries
on Cole's Island. Later he included guns on Battery Island. These
positions defended the entrance to the mouth of the Stono River
southwest of Charleston. Federal gunboats would have an easy route to
attack James Island if these outer batteries were removed. Pemberton

also took steps to have cannon removed from Georgetown, a coastal town halfway between Charleston and the North Carolina border to the northeast. He left sixteen hundred troops to guard the Georgetown area, but this small detachment could do little to combat Federal gunboats and would be vulnerable to attack by Union infantry. Also, gunboats getting by Georgetown would have access to inland waterways, especially the Black and Pee Dee rivers, thereby allowing the enemy to threaten rail lines connecting North and South Carolina. Valuable farmland could be subjected to Federal depredations and Charleston's northwest flank endangered.[46]

Pemberton's apparent motive was to tighten his defensive lines to be more compatible with the number of troops available to man the works. He was acting on Lee's admonition that holding lines was more important than protecting outlying areas. Pemberton intended to strengthen his James Island and Stono River defenses and to use the Georgetown guns nearer to Charleston. An angry Governor Pickens fired off a letter to Lee complaining that inner defenses were still too incomplete for Pemberton to abandon the exterior line. Lee patiently notified Pemberton of Pickens's concern but left department decisions to Pemberton's discretion.[47]

Pickens also objected to Pemberton's leaving people and property exposed to attack at Georgetown. Lee suggested that Pemberton comply with Pickens's proposal to leave the Georgetown batteries in place until a voluntary evacuation of the area could be completed. Lee gently reminded Pemberton that the ramifications of his decisions must be carefully considered. Through one of his aides, Lee counseled, "It is respectfully submitted to your judgment whether, in order to preserve harmony between the State and Confederate authorities, it would not be better to notify the governor whenever you determine to abandon any position of your defenses, in order that he may give due notice to the inhabitants to look out for their security."[48]

Pemberton responded that it was too late. The Georgetown guns were already either en route to or within the Charleston defenses. Local defense troops were available to protect those who wished to evacuate. He pointed out that, contrary to the arguments of his critics, heavy ships could pass over the sandbar at the Georgetown harbor entrance. In fact, some already had, and he had feared that his big guns might be captured. Regarding his lack of diplomacy, Pemberton gave the lame excuse that he had given notice to S. R. Gist, a member of the council, of his intent to remove the guns. Gist had assured him that the council would be informed. But Gist was not Pickens, and Pemberton had to agree that he must be more careful to give notice of his intentions. He had already conceded to Pickens's demand that the guns on Cole's Island remain in place until new defensive positions were ready. The "perfect harmony" Richmond desired between state officials and himself already existed as far as he could tell from personal talks with the governor.[49] Had Pemberton truly understood Pickens, he would not have been so sanguine.

Satisfying the governor tested the general's unspectacular diplomatic skills. When Pemberton sent reinforcements to Mississippi during the Shiloh campaign, he decided that all except local militia would have to be pulled in from outer areas to plug holes in his interior defensive lines. Pemberton so informed Pickens, who urged that green recruits be sent to protect Georgetown. Pemberton reconsidered, ordered a portion of Georgetown forces to Charleston, and promised to leave the remainder there as long as possible.[50] Though Pemberton was now communicating more effectively with the governor and council, his actions at Cole's and Battery islands and Georgetown set the stage for a series of events that would lead to his being relieved of command.

The fall of Fort Pulaski had fueled an undercurrent of feeling in his department that John Pemberton was not doing a good enough job. Capture of that fort had been inevitable; the Confederacy simply did not have the firepower, manpower, or sea power to prevent it. Lee had expected to lose Pulaski and had devoted his efforts to building strong works closer to Savannah. When Union forces began attacking the fort on April 10, Pemberton informed Lee, warning that the Savannah defenses were still not very strong and that Georgia state troops in the city were being discharged from Confederate service. Pemberton had visited the city on April 10 and was convinced that Pulaski could hold out. The fort fell the next afternoon.[51] This was one of the first examples of his Civil War service in which Pemberton displayed an alarming fault: the failure to read military situations correctly. By not following Lee's example and warning that the fort was vulnerable, thereby preparing the public for the inevitable, Pemberton had undermined trust in his generalship.

Another stain on Pemberton's credibility occurred when the steamer *Planter* was stolen from its moorings in Charleston Harbor on May 13. The boat's captain and all its other officers had gone ashore, a violation of regulations that required the presence of one officer aboard at all times. The vessel's slave crew took the steamer, armed with five cannon, and escaped into Union lines off the coast. The former slaves then informed Federal officers of the imminent abandonment of works on Cole's Island, and gunboats soon entered the Stono and shelled the incomplete Confederate earthworks on James Island. In his report to Richmond, Pemberton railed against the *Planter's* officers for their "inexcusable and gross neglect of duty."[52]

A court-martial resulted in two of the officers being sentenced to imprisonment and fines. Pemberton set aside the ruling on grounds that orders regarding regulations had not been properly communicated nor had the regulations been habitually enforced. The *Charleston Daily Courier* applauded his decision, adding that "General Pemberton has another claim upon our community. His brilliant administration has had many difficulties to overcome, and these have been victoriously met." The praise was deserved as far as it went. But why had regulations not been properly communicated or enforced? The incident did little to convince the public that the commanding general was running a tight ship.[53]

On April 27, 1862, Pemberton moved his headquarters from Pocotaligo to Charleston and the loose organization of troops he found made the *Planter* incident predictable. Popular elections of company and field officers undercut discipline and organization. Worse, and probably as a result, little progress had been made on the city's defenses. He blamed General Ripley for the difficulties in Charleston.[54]

Like others before him, Pemberton had trouble coexisting with Ripley. Pickens reported to Lee that there was bad blood between the two. Lee did his best to sidestep the matter. He thought reassigning Ripley outside South Carolina the best solution but realized that Ripley had expert knowledge of the Charleston area. Ripley also had some supporters in the state who wanted him to have independent command of Charleston, which Lee refused to consider as long as Pemberton commanded a department that included the city. One or the other must go, and Lee was unwilling to make a recommendation to the president. There the matter rested until Ripley was finally reassigned in late May. Though others, including Lee, had had trouble with the departed general, the timing could not have been worse for Pemberton. At a time when public confidence in his ability was already shaky, Pemberton could ill afford dissension with a subordinate.[55]

Confidence in Pemberton continued on a downward trend. After settling in Charleston, he continued to implement his policy to constrict defensive lines. That policy troubled state officials, who feared that any potent Federal threat might convince Pemberton to evacuate the symbolic city. Mayor Charles MacBeth pointedly asked what he would do if enemy gunboats managed to enter Charleston Harbor. Would he abandon the city as General Mansfield Lovell (another Confederate general of Northern birth) had recently abandoned New Orleans, or would he stay and fight it out?[56]

Pemberton refused to commit himself. Such a "calamity may not occur at all," he wrote MacBeth, or "it may be very remote; it is possibly near at hand. The circumstances of to-day may be materially changed. . . . The force at my disposal may be somewhat decreased or much diminished. You will readily perceive how important a bearing these and other conditions . . . must have upon my decision. . . . I do not hesitate to say . . . that women and children should leave the city at once."[57] Though an honest response, these words did not engender public trust and confidence in the general.

Pemberton was equally candid in his reports to Richmond. Construction of new works on James Island had placed eight more guns along the Stono. But, he wrote, "I do not regard Charleston as strong [for] what under the old system of warfare was our strength, is now our greatest weakness." He was more convinced than ever that gunboats made the myriad streams and inlets along the coast a hazard to the Confederacy, not a hindrance to the Union. Batteries too close to the coast could be bypassed and thus were ineffective and vulnerable to capture. Streams could be obstructed, but with so many to obstruct and so little labor to do so, the task was difficult if not impossible. Pemberton concluded "that the most effective defence of the city of Charleston, can & should be made from & around the city itself." The outer batteries and the forts, including Sumter, would certainly fall when the enemy forces increased and made an all-out effort. He proposed the dismantling and destruction of the forts and the construction of ironclad batteries in lieu of mortar and stone.[58]

Pemberton's strategic concepts were no secret. On May 21, the Executive Council passed a three-part resolution, copies of which were sent to Jefferson Davis, the secretary of war, and all generals serving in South Carolina. Part one of the resolution stated that the council preferred a repulse of the enemy at the expense of Charleston being reduced to ruins to an evacuation or surrender. Part two expressed disapproval of a voluntary burning of the city, and part three stated that Confederate authorities alone were responsible for any action that might be taken regarding Charleston's fate.[59]

Two prominent South Carolinians, Confederate Congressman William Porcher Miles and Confederate District Judge A. G. Magrath, sent Pemberton three interrogatories on May 22. The first asked his reaction to a hypothetical situation: if he should decide to give up the defense of Charleston, would he object to the governor and council taking over the city's defense, both under and exclusive of his orders? Second, would he be willing to assist, or advise, or direct defensive operations? Finally, would he be willing to counsel and aid the governor and council in their activities?[60]

Pemberton answered curtly but courteously. He would not object to the first proposal as long as plans were submitted to him and met his approval. Yes, he would be willing to assist in any way possible. He assured Miles and Magrath that their concerns met "with my entire sympathy and concurrence." Circumstances might force the withdrawal of his troops from Charleston, "but this I confidently hope will not be the case."[61]

The next day, May 23, Governor Pickens wrote Pemberton: "I hope and pray that it is well known that the defence [of Charleston] is to be desperate and if they can be repulsed, even with the city in ruins, we would unanimously prefer it. It is due to our cause and our country that we should make a desperate fight in Charleston. We can afford to lose our city, but not our honor. I will stand by you in anything you desire."[62]

A message to Pemberton from Richmond a few days later indicated that Pickens et al. had informed Lee of Pemberton's reluctance to commit to an all-out defense of Charleston. Lee pointed out the importance of defending Savannah and Charleston, especially the latter, to the last extremity. Loss of the city's harbor would cut a vital supply artery to the outside world. Lee urged Pemberton to build the strongest defenses possible and to focus especially on obstruction of waterways. As commander of the department, Pemberton must make clear his intent to fight "street by street and house by house as long as we have a foot of ground to stand upon." Lee refused to support Pemberton's suggestion that forts be dismantled. He insisted that well-manned batteries had had some success in fighting off ironclads. Pickens later claimed that Lee's words "astonished" Pemberton, who had "had no idea of defending" Charleston. Only when he knew Lee's feelings "did he seriously set to work to prepare for defence."[63]

Reaction to Pemberton's strategic thinking indicated a fanatical devotion to the Southern cause that he had trouble grasping. He approached his job from a purely military point of view. He was outnumbered, and if the choice were saving his army by retreating or saving a city, he intended to save his army. Successful generals, like Lee, understood that public support and morale were necessary to favorable military results. John Pemberton never seemed to grasp that concept.

Beyond strategic considerations, the issue of defending Charleston demonstrated a defeatist attitude in the usually confident Pemberton. His thinking focused solely on the defensive, and he seemed to be growing more and more pessimistic. What had happened to the brash, aggressive antebellum Pemberton? Obviously the burden of command had begun to overwhelm him. Governor Pickens was not altogether hyperbolic when he complained to Jefferson Davis that Pemberton seemed "confused and uncertain about everything."[64] Pemberton had never had the scope of responsibilities and pressure that confronted him as a department commander. He knew his nativity made Southerners suspicious of him, and his every move seemed to be under surveillance, both in South Carolina and in Richmond. The lack of confidence in him seemed to drain his own self-confidence. He had begun to fear failure.

Pemberton's anxiety increased when Federal operations along the waterfront increased. On June 2, twenty enemy vessels entered the Stono. Pemberton considered pulling five thousand men away from Savannah to meet the threat. The next day Union troops landed on James and Johns islands but were driven back. An enemy force also landed on Seabrooks Island with the apparent intention of cutting the Charleston-Savannah rail line. An attack never materialized, but Pemberton decided that the Federals planned a general assault on

Charleston. He notified Richmond that he would have to take reinforcements from Savannah and needed any others that could be provided. Two days later he decided that the Yankees were not going to
attack but were merely trying to keep him from sending men to Richmond. He sent four regiments to the Confederate capital, pulling in
more men from Georgetown to replace them in the Charleston defenses.[65]

On June 15, Pemberton wired Pickens that only ten thousand men
were available to defend Charleston. He needed any troops the governor could send.[66] The next day Yankee infantry landed on James
Island and attacked the community of Secessionville. If the Federals
took the place, they would have an avenue to the defenses of
Charleston Harbor.

The Battle of Secessionville was the largest military action in Pemberton's department during his tenure in South Carolina. The village
of Secessionville was a small cluster of summer homes belonging to the
planters of James Island. According to tradition, it got its name because a group of young, married planters "seceded" from the older
planter generation. Whatever its origin, the place had its name before
the secession crisis of 1860–61. The settlement won its place in Civil
War history when sixty-five hundred Federals attacked a Confederate
garrison of five hundred early on the morning of June 16. The Rebel
defenders woke just in time to man their cannon against the invaders.
Assaulting blue columns withered under artillery fire, and nearby
Confederates rushed to reinforce their heavily outnumbered comrades. After two and one-half hours of close-quarter fighting, the
Yankees retreated to their base camp on the Stono. Casualties numbered seven hundred Union and two hundred Confederate soldiers.[67]

General Pemberton issued congratulatory orders to the victorious
troops the day after the battle. He applauded "every officer and soldier" who participated and paid special tribute to the garrison commander. Adhering to his preference for staying behind the lines, Pemberton made no effort to get to Secessionville during the fighting,
although by the time he could have gotten there the battle would
probably have been over.[68]

Pemberton took credit for the results indirectly. In his report to
Richmond, he argued that by abandoning the Cole's and Battery
Island defenses, he had compelled an attack on James Island. The

Secessionville fortifications covered one flank, and newly constructed batteries on the Stono guarded the other. The Federals had fallen into his trap. But after Secessionville, Pemberton displayed considerably more diligence in building up defensive works. The *Charleston Courier* noted that he was "indefatigable in his labors on James' [sic] Island." He visited all positions, giving orders to strengthen works where needed. "Though stern and austere in manner," wrote the editor, "he is ever mindful of his duty to subordinates, and commands the respect of the soldiers under him. Be assured he will do all he can for Charleston."[69]

Governor Pickens was unimpressed. He had begun an active campaign to get Pemberton relieved from command, and he did not let up after the Secessionville victory. The ability of Federal gunboats to enter the Stono convinced Pickens that he was right about the consequences of abandoning the outer line of defense.[70]

Pemberton did not celebrate either. He knew of Pickens's efforts to have him replaced and continued carrying out his duties under a cloud. The persistent pressure put him in a foul humor. He complained to Pickens about the slow progress of harbor obstructions. The railroad bridge across the Ashley River was still unfinished. He argued too that if he had the same strength now as when he had first planned defensive strategy, he could hold off the enemy without the outer works. He argued with the council and with Richmond that putting guns back on Battery and Cole's islands would be impossible with Union gunboats patrolling the Stono. He absolutely refused to send more troops to Georgetown. Those who thought his withdrawal of guns from that place was "a wanton exercise of power" could enjoy their opinions. He had to do what he thought best, and there was no way he could protect the whole coast. So John Pemberton's arguments went as the summer of 1862 drifted by. One thing he and Pickens could agree on: it was time for him to go. Pickens was doing all he could toward that end, and Pemberton was entertaining hopes of returning to Virginia.[71] No doubt Pattie and the children would also welcome a return to Norfolk. Pattie's thoughts are not recorded, but she was very likely furious at those who questioned her husband's ability and loyalty. One can only wonder if she had any second thoughts regarding her part in convincing him to fight for the Confederacy.

Governor Pickens never let up. On June 11 he sent a confidential telegram to Davis: "I fear Charleston is to be sacrificed by a total incompetency in the officer commanding and a total want of knowledge of the country." Davis asked if Pickens had anyone in mind to replace Pemberton. Pickens had several in mind but said that he would be "entirely pleased" with General P. G. T. Beauregard, who had been in command at Charleston at the beginning of the war.[72]

On that same day William Porcher Miles sent a message to Robert E. Lee confiding that Pemberton did "not possess the confidence of his officers, his troops, or the people of Charleston. Whether justly or unjustly, rely upon it the fact is so." Some influential citizens wanted to circulate a petition asking that Pemberton be transferred to another post. Almost anyone would be better, Miles argued, for no matter how solid Pemberton's qualifications were, the lack of confidence in him made all else irrelevant. Lee passed the letter on to Davis with the comment that he did not see how Pemberton's removal could be avoided.[73]

There was merit in Miles's words. Pemberton's strategy had convinced many Carolinians that he would not fight, and the problems in the department reinforced that impression. Too often Pemberton had appeared to lack control. Diarist Mary Boykin Chesnut, wife of council member James Chesnut, wrote on June 11: "Crimination and recrimination. Everybody's hand against everybody else. Pemberton said to have no heart in this business, so the city cannot be defended." The innate bigotry of South Carolinians toward all things Northern further stained John's image, as Mary Chestnut admitted. So did Emma Holmes, who wrote in her diary what others were thinking. Pemberton's behavior, "as he is a Pennsylvanian, engenders suspicion about him." She continued, "Everybody has lost confidence in Pemberton and many even suspect treachery, though it cannot be proved of course."[74]

Disaffection had become widespread, infecting men in the ranks. Some soldiers were angered by a Confederate War Department policy of taking men from regiments involuntarily to form sharpshooter battalions. Pemberton ignored appeals to modify this policy. "He was utterly regardless of the entreaties of the men," wrote one disgruntled officer, who also decried Pemberton's dismantling of coastal defenses. Pemberton "could not be induced to rescind the orders which were working such dissatisfaction among the people and with the army and which were familiarizing them with the idea of defeat."[75] Pemberton's disdain for volunteers dated back to the Mexican War, and the hardening of his personality by years of post duty made it difficult for him to overcome the pall over Charleston. When visiting with troops, he could make a good impression, but he did not visit often enough. His preference for staying behind the lines worked against his establishing good relations with his men.

The problem of choosing a successor to Pemberton initially bogged down Pickens's campaign to have him deposed. Beauregard claimed he was too ill; Braxton Bragg, another general acceptable to the governor, was not available. Pickens composed a list that included William J. Hardee, Earl Van Dorn, James Longstreet, Benjamin Huger, and John B. Magruder. Lee notified Davis that Huger could be spared. Meanwhile, Pickens continued his assault on Pemberton, whom, he said, probably would be a "brave and good officer" at the head of a brigade or division but did not have the "variety of talent" required by the South Carolina situation.[76]

While the search for a replacement went on, Davis sent Samuel Cooper to study the South Carolina dilemma firsthand. Davis urged Pickens to talk with Cooper before continuing his campaign against Pemberton. Pickens, of course, had already made up his mind, and Cooper's findings did little to change it.[77]

After looking over the defensive works and consulting with Pemberton, Cooper concluded that he was doing "all that a zealous, active, and intelligent officer could do with the means at his command." But the negative attitudes about Pemberton were strong enough "to impair his usefulness." Cooper did not think it would be "doing justice" to the general to keep him in his present assignment. "I have great confidence in the zeal and untiring efforts" of Pemberton, Cooper wrote, and "I know that he feels—honestly feels—the weight of responsibility with calmness and a determination to discharge his duty honestly and faithfully, but with such an opposition as constantly surrounds him it would be difficult for any commander situated as he is to effect much."[78]

Pemberton did feel the weight of responsibility, both appreciating it, as Cooper said, and losing his confidence because of it. He was ready and anxious to leave and undoubtedly told Cooper as much.

After returning to Richmond, Cooper notified Pemberton that if the Federals left James Island, some of the outer defenses could be reoccupied and shored up. Then he could come to Virginia with the "residue" of his force (those not needed to man the defenses) and join the Confederate army at Richmond. Cooper asked if daily reconnaissances of James Island were being made. Pemberton replied in the affirmative and reported that the Federals had left the island but had occupied Cole's and Battery islands. The Confederates could not go back to those outer works; thus Cooper's criteria for Pemberton to come to Virginia could not be met.[79]

That Cooper would ask a soldier of Pemberton's experience about daily reconnaissances indicated an air of condescension. This attitude had grown out of Pemberton's uncertainty, indecisiveness, and loss of confidence. An illustrative example in late June resulted from his order that prohibited sailing vessels from taking cotton out of Charleston Harbor. Pemberton felt, rightly, that such boats would be easy targets for Federal steam-powered patrol boats. He notified Richmond of his decision and then proceeded to ask for instructions. An exasperated George Randolph wired that if Pemberton thought sail-powered boats could not exit the harbor without risk, then not to let them go.[80] Pemberton obviously had become so intimidated by Pickens's campaign against him that he did not have enough confidence to issue a simple order without approval. The antebellum Pemberton would not have tolerated the War Department's patronizing attitude. The Charleston Pemberton not only accepted it; he invited it.

In early July, Pemberton's hope of getting away from Pickens and Charleston was renewed. Federal gunboats and troops began departing for Virginia in conjunction with George McClellan's peninsula campaign against Richmond. Cooper notified Pemberton to prepare to come to Virginia. General G. W. Smith would take his place. An exuberant Pemberton responded on July 12: "Shall I go on to Richmond at once? Any troops to be moved can follow me." The next day he received the crushing news that Smith had reported himself unfit for duty. A move to Virginia would have to wait.[81]

July faded into August, Pickens continued to complain, and John Pemberton waited. Davis made clear to Pickens that his confidence in Pemberton was such that he would be pleased to have him anywhere else a capable general might be needed. The president then called

Pemberton to Richmond for consultations on the Charleston situation.[82]

Governor Pickens received a report on the meeting in a letter dated August 16. The president was convinced that Pemberton had made a good start toward building adequate defenses. The general was as determined as the governor to save Charleston, Davis assured. Most differences of opinion seemed related to engineering, and Davis promised that he would send an engineering officer from Richmond to examine Pemberton's works. Meanwhile, Pemberton would meet with the council and governor. Confident that Pemberton met all requirements for the job, Davis ended his letter with the hope that Pickens would develop confidence in him.[83]

On August 20, Pickens responded. Davis seemed to be under the impression, he wrote, that all was going well with construction of harbor defenses. Conversations with Pemberton had convinced Pickens otherwise. The general obviously had little faith in those defenses. Moreover, he had been surprised by the enemy at Secessionville and probably would have evacuated Charleston in May had not Lee intervened. Pickens said he regretted having to speak in such a manner, but the safety of Charleston was at stake.[84]

The president had heard enough by now to convince him that Cooper was right. On August 29, Davis named Beauregard to command the South Carolina and Georgia department. In an August 28 letter, Secretary of War Randolph notified John Pemberton of the action. Randolph explained that Beauregard was being assigned because there was no other commander available with proper rank and the freedom to move without interfering with current operations and because of Pickens's incessant criticism of Pemberton. Randolph assured Pemberton that the president and War Department had confidence that he was doing his job well, but if anything should go wrong he would be blamed regardless of circumstances. With Beauregard in command, the pressure would be off. If the general wished to be assigned to another area, however, Richmond would try to comply.[85]

Pemberton promptly asked for a new assignment. He had done all he could do for South Carolina, he told Randolph, and his defensive arrangements had been made "whether judiciously or not, at least uncontrolled by others." Staying to serve under Beauregard would be humiliating. He had no doubt that Beauregard was "far more capable

of filling satisfactorily the responsible position I have so long held."
His words demonstrated how much his confidence had ebbed. The old
Pemberton would hardly have been so gracious, certainly not to the
point of denigrating himself. Yet his words contained much truth.
Beauregard's engineering expertise and his ability to play to Southern
politicians and to cultivate public opinion certainly made him more
suitable for this particular command. John Pemberton knew that, but
it was a measure of the effect of his South Carolina experience that he
would say as much. All he really wanted now was to go wherever he
might be useful; "I would say to Virginia."[86]

Two Charleston newspapers, the *Courier* and the *Mercury*, editorialized a postmortem on Pemberton's tenure of command. The
Courier had a genuine understanding of the problems he had faced.
That he had come to South Carolina "comparatively a stranger" had
hurt his chances of success. "His efforts and orders and plans have
been too often counteracted by ignorance or prejudice, or by vacillation on the part of those who could and should have aided him."
Obstructionists had kept him from getting the labor he needed to do
the job as he wanted to do it; in spite of this and other problems, he
had "done much and done well." The editor concluded, "We tender
him most cordially and gratefully our thanks and acknowledgements
and our best wishes for his personal welfare and official prosperity and
success in his new field of duty."[87]

The *Mercury* was also laudatory, surprisingly so since a Pemberton
descendant passed down a story years afterward that the general had
offended the powerful Rhett family of Charleston, one of whom
owned the paper. The story is suspect. Supposedly, Pemberton angered
a Doctor Rhett when he consulted another physician to help Pattie
when she was ill after the birth of a child. There is no record that
Pattie had a child in Charleston or at any other time during the Civil
War. Another incident, also rooted in family tradition, had the newspaper Rhett, perhaps seeking revenge for his kinsman's slight, publishing a critical column charging Pemberton with favoritism in ordering
ice, a precious commodity, sent to his home to treat Pattie's fever. The
columns of surviving editions of the paper reveal no such occurrence.
On the occasion of Pemberton's departure, the *Mercury* characterized
his service as "long months of arduous, incessant labor and devoted
energy." Admittedly, he had not been especially popular. "His habitu-

al reserve and occasional brusqueness of manner" would not permit it. Ye he had the confidence and esteem of those who knew him. "His independence and directness are marked characteristics, worthy of appreciation."[88]

General Beauregard did not arrive in Charleston until late September. Pemberton received orders dated September 17 to come to Richmond as soon as Beauregard assumed command. But he delayed departure a few days to give the new commander a tour of the department. Beauregard finally took over officially on September 24.[89]

As the Pembertons prepared to leave for Virginia, John was surprised by a visit to his Charleston Hotel headquarters by the Forty-eighth Georgia Regiment. He was called out to review the troops and asked to say a few words. The *Courier* reported that the general reacted to this tribute "in soldierly style of acknowledgement and advice, and was honored afterwards by calls from the commissioned officers, who lingered to tend him their parting wishes." Obviously Pemberton had not alienated everyone. His ordnance officer, Ambrosio J. Gonzales, would stay behind to serve on Beauregard's staff. Nearly a year later, he wrote his old boss, at a time when Pemberton's spirits needed a boost, applauding his service in South Carolina. He had always defended Pemberton, he said, and the general's arguments regarding strategy were proving to be true. Fort Sumter was being battered down by Federal guns. Charleston was still safe, however, thanks, according to Gonzales, to the defenses Pemberton had ordered built.[90]

As the train steamed out of Charleston with the Pembertons on board, John no doubt felt relieved that his first large-scale command was disappearing in the distance. He had been unable to mobilize public support, had shown an inability to get along with state politicians, had made strategic errors, and had demonstrated confusion and uncertainty about the complexities of the department. One Civil War historian has cited four factors by which to measure a general's performance at high levels of command: technical knowledge, confidence of officers and men under his command, self-confidence, and the confidence of his government.[91] John Pemberton had problems of varying degrees in all four, especially self-confidence. Nor had he gained any useful field or combat experience so whether he would have done better at the division or brigade level, as Pickens suggested, is uncertain. He had done an adequate job of commanding one of Lee's districts, but he had not led large numbers of men in combat. His forte was managing a bureaucracy, and he knew it and felt most comfortable doing it. Even in that area, his lack of confidence had produced mixed results. Still, if he was fortunate, such an assignment would be waiting in Richmond. Without the weight of overall command, he could make positive contributions to the Confederacy.

If he should get a new command similar to the one he was leaving, however, he might have the same problems, and they might be exacerbated by what he had learned in South Carolina. He had learned that he was expected to defend certain positions regardless of the danger to his troops. Charleston had to be held, even if he had to fight street by street and house by house to do it. So Robert E. Lee had said, and John Pemberton would remember. He was destined to pay a high price for the lesson.

CHAPTER 7

Is Anything Going On?

Vicksburg, October 1862–April 1863

The John Pemberton family spent only a few days in Virginia before John received his new orders. He would not be staying in Virginia as he had hoped. Following consultations with Jefferson Davis, he received Special Orders Number 73, issued from the office of Samuel Cooper on October 1, 1862: "The State of Mississippi and that part of Louisiana east of the Mississippi River is constituted a separate military district, the command of which is assigned to Maj. Gen. John C. Pemberton."[1]

Before leaving Virginia, Pemberton delivered verbal messages from Davis to Robert E. Lee regarding operations of Lee's Army of Northern Virginia. There is no written record of their meeting; apparently Davis wanted Pemberton to benefit from Lee's thoughts regarding the Mississippi command. Certainly Davis had any number of couriers who could have delivered messages to Lee.[2]

The day before Special Orders 73 was issued, Secretary of War George Randolph expressed his opinions on Pemberton's new assignment. The "first chief object" should be defending the department. If a "favorable opportunity" to retake New Orleans should be presented, then the city should be retaken. Otherwise, Pemberton must keep in mind that defending his territory was priority number one. These instructions proved to be a great, and sometimes negative, influence on John Pemberton's actions in Mississippi. Another Randolph directive also had much impact on Pemberton's new job; until further notice, "you will report directly to this [War] Department." Even though he would eventually be placed under the orders of two other generals, Pemberton never was told to stop reporting directly to Richmond. This situation created a mind-set that was to cause major command problems in the Confederate western theater.[3]

Pemberton's new assignment brought mixed reactions. Some Southern newspapers printed the strange story that he had led Federal troops against secessionists in Baltimore in early 1861. Apparently such gossip grew out of his delay in joining the Confederacy. Suspicions about him because of his Northern birth refused to go away. The circumstances of his departure from South Carolina had done little to allay such doubts.[4]

Yet prospects in Mississippi seemed brighter for Pemberton personally. Disgust with Generals Earl Van Dorn and Mansfield Lovell made him welcome in the state. It appeared that the "change has given universal satisfaction here." Van Dorn, a native of Mississippi, had angered fellow citizens with too much martial law, and within days after Pemberton received his orders, Van Dorn lost a major battle at Corinth, Mississippi. Lovell, who had been born in Washington, D.C., but was considered by many Southerners to be a Yankee, had been in command at New Orleans when the city fell in April 1862. Lovell had been sent to Mississippi to serve under Van Dorn so now he had two strikes against him. Not only was he a mistrusted soldier with a tainted birthplace, but he was serving under a loser. Little wonder that a new face was welcome.[5]

When Pemberton and his staff arrived in Mississippi on October 9, they found a poorly organized department. His assistant adjutant, Robert W. Memminger, recalled that a thorough reorganization was required. "Confusion reigned equally in the Quartermaster, Commissary, Engineer and Ordnance Departments. No system of any kind prevailed, and the whole department was one Chaos." From this chaos, Memminger remembered, "order began gradually to arise;

chiefs of the various departments were appointed, and through their untiring exertion, aided and directed by the Lieutenant-General commanding, the department was reorganized, remodelled and supplied."[6]

Pemberton assumed command officially on October 14, set up headquarters in Jackson, Mississippi, and named John R. Waddy his chief of staff and adjutant. Memminger was not the only one impressed with the new general's immediate efforts to bring order to the area. Editors of the *Jackson Daily Mississippian* commented glowingly that "already, on every hand, the beneficial efforts of his administration of the affairs of this military district are visible." Pemberton had arrived "in an hour of the greatest gloom and despondency" and had acted quickly, issuing "stringent" orders, restoring discipline, and efficiently organizing departments. "No officer ever devoted himself with greater assiduity to his duties. Late and early he is at his office, laboring incessantly." He examined reports and made sure all departments were functioning well. The *Mississippian* concluded that Pemberton was doing "all that mortal man can do, with the means at his disposal, to strengthen his army and promote its efficiency."[7] In short, Pemberton was doing what he did best, organizing, systematizing, and keeping his finger on the pulse of his department's every activity. He was the consummate bureaucrat; he had performed such activities well almost everywhere he had been assigned during his military career. In ways that he quickly demonstrated, he was, for the moment, just what the Mississippi department needed.

But the department also needed battlefield leadership and military science, and these were needs he could not fill. Given his problems in South Carolina, his selection as the new Mississippi commander is difficult to explain. The Department of Mississippi and East Louisiana was an expansive area riddled with bayous, creeks, and rivers, all of which afforded advantages to Union naval superiority along the Mississippi River, the main avenue of Yankee invasion of the Mississippi-Arkansas-Louisiana region. How to fortify effectively the Mississippi and other rivers without using large numbers of men needed on the battlefield was a problem that perplexed the most gifted of Confederate strategists.

The prime Federal target on the Mississippi at the time Pemberton arrived was Vicksburg, Mississippi, located on the east bank of the river at a bend in the stream where Confederate shore batteries could seriously threaten Union vessels. South of Vicksburg, Confederates would eventually build strong shore batteries on the east bank at Grand Gulf, Mississippi, and Port Hudson, Louisiana. When New Orleans fell in the spring of 1862, the triumvirate of Vicksburg, Grand Gulf, and Port Hudson was destined to become the last obstacle to total Federal control of the Mississippi. Abraham Lincoln thought Vicksburg was "the key," so Vicksburg was the focal point of Union strategy. Following the defeat of Van Dorn at Corinth, Federal General Ulysses S. Grant, hero of Fort Donelson and victor at Shiloh, began planning the capture of the Confederate bastion on the Mississippi.[8]

The Federal emphasis on Vicksburg, combined with the city's geographic location, meant that the new Mississippi department, created by Jefferson Davis and his War Department, presented challenges that surpassed those faced by Pemberton in South Carolina. The new command required defending a plethora of waterways with outnumbered troops. Pemberton's small army was also vulnerable to overland invasion. Losses at Shiloh and Corinth had left west Tennessee and the Tennessee-Mississippi border mostly in Federal hands. The Mississippi-Alabama border was far from secure. Mobile, Alabama, remained under Confederate control, and Braxton Bragg's Confederate Army of Tennessee was a strong presence keeping watch on the rest of Tennessee as well as northern Alabama and Georgia. Yet with so much territory to defend, Bragg could scarcely guarantee the security of Pemberton's eastern and northern flanks. There was potential help across the Mississippi, in the Trans-Mississippi area, but Confederate forces there were occupied with repelling Yankee forays into western Louisiana and Arkansas.

All in all, there was probably not a more difficult, complex command in the entire Confederacy than the one John Pemberton assumed in October 1862. Events in South Carolina had overwhelmed him, drained his confidence, and left him anxious to return to Virginia. Knowing all that he had experienced there, why would Jefferson Davis send him to a place that presented even more formidable problems?

Thomas J. Wharton, attorney general of Mississippi during the war, later claimed that he had asked Davis why Pemberton was appointed during a visit to Richmond in May 1863, shortly after Grant had begun his final, successful campaign against Vicksburg. Davis allegedly responded that he had a high opinion of Pemberton's ability, and he had sought the advice of several military officers, including Robert E. Lee and Samuel Cooper. Lee and Cooper had been consulted separately, and each had named Pemberton his choice for the Mississippi command.[9]

Wharton's is the only known account of the selection process. There is no reason to doubt his veracity, but his story leaves unanswered questions. Why did none of those involved in the decision leave written corroboration? Both Lee and Cooper were intimately aware of Pemberton's difficulties in South Carolina, perhaps more so than Davis, who tended to be blind to the faults of commanders he liked. If Wharton's memory was accurate and Davis was truthful, Lee's and Cooper's endorsement of Pemberton is incredible and difficult to explain. Either both knew that Davis had already made up his mind or they misread the depth and nature of Pemberton's previous difficulties. Perhaps they simply wanted to send a problem general west to get him out of the way. They may have had little understanding or appreciation of the difficulties any general taking the Mississippi command was bound to encounter. Both certainly should have known that Pemberton and the Confederacy would have been better served if a more capable field general had been given the command.

Jefferson Davis did want to give the command to someone he could trust. Sending Pemberton to Mississippi was part of Davis's plan to restructure the command system in the western theater and seemed an answer to the dilemma brought on by Van Dorn's and Lovell's failures. Braxton Bragg was not doing any better; he had lost at Perryville, Kentucky, about the time Pemberton was traveling to Mississippi. Bragg, another Davis favorite, retreated into central Tennessee, and on November 19, 1862, Samuel Cooper informed him that Pemberton was under his command and that he must help save Vicksburg.[10] This was one of several examples of Richmond's distorted approach to the command system in the West. Pemberton kept in touch with Bragg but continued to report directly to Davis. Bragg had so many problems of his own that he had no time to advise Pemberton. Their uncomfortable association was short-lived; just a few days after Cooper's message to Bragg, another general was sent west to command both Bragg and Pemberton.

Joseph E. Johnston, Pemberton's old boss from Virginia, had still not sufficiently recovered from a wound received during the peninsula campaign east of Richmond. His health had improved, but while recuperating he had lost command of his army (later named the Army of Northern Virginia) to Robert E. Lee. Johnston was in a sour mood about that development, had not fully recovered either physically or mentally, and would not welcome just any assignment. Davis, a long-time antagonist of Johnston's, felt compelled to find a place for the general and sent him west, perhaps, as might have been true in the case of Pemberton, to get him far away from Virginia. Johnston's new command included practically all the Confederacy west of a line extending from the Blue Ridge Mountains of North Carolina, through western Georgia, down to the Gulf of Mexico. Significantly, Johnston's domain did not extend beyond the Mississippi so he would not be able to order assistance from the Trans-Mississippi.

Johnston's health and attitude made it impossible for him to put his heart in his new command. Yet he did take a long look at the situation and came up with a logical strategic concept. Success, Johnston argued, depended on concentration of available Confederate forces to attack scattered Federal armies. Standing alone, the troops of Pemberton, Bragg, and the Trans-Mississippi could accomplish little. Concentrated they might have a chance. Coordinating such an operation could be difficult, for the three groups of forces were separated by long distances and geographic barriers, and the problem was compounded because neither of his two subordinates nor Theophilus Hunter Holmes, commanding the Trans-Mississippi Confederacy, ever recognized him as supreme commander of this large expanse. Bragg and Pemberton continued to report directly to Richmond, and Holmes refused to cooperate with Johnston.[11]

Holmes was a fifty-seven-year-old West Pointer, an old friend of Jefferson Davis's, and an irascible personality. He had become increasingly unpopular in Arkansas, where he frequently exhibited jealousy of other commanders. He was miffed because Sterling Price was popular in the Trans-Mississippi and was obviously jealous of John Pemberton's promotion to the Mississippi command, commenting that "Pemberton . . . in my judgement will not mend matters, as . . . [he] has many ways of making people hate him and none to inspire confidence." Whether Pemberton had at some point in the past alienated Holmes or whether Holmes was referring to events in South Carolina

is unclear, but his animosity may have contributed to his frequent
refusal to send much needed troops to Pemberton's aid. In spite of his
attempt to unify the western command, Davis ultimately acquiesced
to Holmes's position that Arkansas would be lost if his forces were
depleted. Both Davis and Holmes conveniently ignored the axiom
that "if Vicksburg fell, Arkansas would be lost anyway."[12]

Pemberton initially busied himself organizing his department. Aside
from assembling a working bureaucracy, he realized that he had a
problem with his own rank. Both Van Dorn and Lovell outranked him
in seniority as major generals. The War Department and Confederate
Senate solved this dilemma by nominating and confirming him in the
rank of lieutenant general to date from October 13, 1862. Pemberton
next addressed the issues of army designation and military districts.
His Mississippi army had been referred to as the Army of West Tennessee and the Army of the West. Pemberton proposed renaming it
the Army of North Mississippi, but the War Department decided that
it should be designated the First and Second Army Corps of the
Department of Mississippi. Van Dorn would lead the First Corps, Price
the Second. Since Lovell had commanded a corps under Van Dorn,
and Van Dorn was now reduced to corps command, the unfortunate
Lovell was left awaiting orders until finally he was relieved.[13]

Acting on his South Carolina experience, Pemberton initially divided his department into three military districts (eventually there
would be five). Headquarters of the districts were at Jackson (First
District), commanded by Daniel Ruggles; Vicksburg (Second District), commanded by Martin L. Smith; and Port Hudson (Third District), commanded by William N. R. Beall. Overall, Pemberton had
better than thirty thousand troops, too few to defend effectively the
large area of his command, especially if the Federals made coordinated
attacks at different points.[14] Time would prove Johnston right about
the necessity of concentrating Confederate forces.

Having set up the department framework, Pemberton began familiarizing himself with his new domain. From the moment he arrived in
Jackson, he realized that Port Hudson, an extensively fortified position
on the Mississippi's east bank above Baton Rouge, was a back door to
Vicksburg that might be the key to future Union operations. He
visited the place soon after assuming command and then wrote detailed orders aimed at improving the network of trenches.[15]

Franklin Gardner took over as commander of Port Hudson in December 1862. Gardner, another Yankee in gray, was a solid soldier, and he and Pemberton worked well together. There never were enough supplies or men to satisfy the needs of both, but Gardner understood that Vicksburg was a higher priority. Though more heavily outnumbered than Pemberton was at Vicksburg, Gardner would hold Port Hudson until the fall of Vicksburg forced his surrender. [16]

Though Pemberton was concerned about Port Hudson, his immediate worry was how to halt a Federal advance into northern Mississippi. Van Dorn had established his headquarters at Holly Springs after retreating from Corinth and rightly suspected that Grant was planning a major overland campaign toward Vicksburg. He asked Pemberton to come to the front for a firsthand look at the situation. "Events are gathering near," he warned. [17]

Pemberton delayed. No doubt he needed to get Pattie and the children settled and to become acquainted with the department's operations, but he still preferred to remain behind the scene, as he had demonstrated in South Carolina. But Van Dorn's ominous messages came in such numbers that he became convinced that Grant indeed was concentrating his forces for an advance southward from west Tennessee. He wired Van Dorn to retire behind the Tallahatchie if Grant applied too much pressure. As in Charleston, Pemberton was expecting to constrict his lines and stay on the defensive. [18]

Meanwhile, Pemberton and his staff worked to gather reinforcements and rebuild morale. He had heard that Arkansas and Missouri troops led by Sterling Price were unhappy because, like their commander, they wanted to go back to the Trans-Mississippi to fight on their home ground. Pemberton decided that he would allow them to leave if Holmes would give him an equal number of troops in exchange. [19]

In early November, the new commanding general boarded a train for northern Mississippi. En route, his train crashed into a southbound engine; there were casualties, but Pemberton escaped unhurt. Looking back at a later date, he must have wondered if this was an omen of things to come. Finally arriving in Holly Springs, he reviewed the troops and immediately changed his mind about Price's men. "I have just witnessed a review and am very much pleased with them," he wired Samuel Cooper. The troops were never transferred; Price would eventually leave without them. [20]

The soldiers also reviewed General Pemberton. Ephraim Anderson described him as "about forty-five, or perhaps a little older—scarcely six feet in height, and of rather slender proportions with dark eyes and hair—a high forehead, thin visage and regular features; his face was considerably furrowed with lines, either of care or age; he appeared well on horseback, and seemed perfectly at ease in the saddle." One sergeant was not impressed and wrote to his wife: "I saw Pemberton and he is the most insignificant 'puke' I ever saw and will be very unpopular as soon as he is known. His head cannot contain sense enough to command a Regt. much less a Corps."[21] Pemberton's problem with men in the ranks was that he never let himself be known. By operating out of sight he gave the men little opportunity to form a learned opinion of him. The few who left written comments almost always based their observations on impressions gained from afar or through camp gossip.

Six days after arriving in northern Mississippi, Pemberton held a council of war with Price, Lovell, and Van Dorn and made the decision to evacuate Holly Springs. He ordered the army to pull back behind the Tallahatchie. Reports from scouts indicated "an immediate and general advance" by Grant's Yankees. Having given the order, Pemberton caught a train back to Jackson. Even an imminent enemy threat could not persuade him to give up his administrative duties for the front line.[22]

Back at his headquarters, Pemberton addressed several challenges, including establishing a relationship with Mississippi Governor John J. Pettus. Pettus had been a fire-eater. He was a grim, quiet man with a fierce temper and an abrupt nature, and he seemed cast in the mold of the independent frontiersman, although he tended to informality and had a tendency to be slow in reacting to the exigencies of war. Despite personality traits that in other circumstances would have created friction between the two, Pettus and Pemberton established a cooperative, if not particularly congenial, working relationship.[23]

As he had in South Carolina, Pemberton requested the state government of Mississippi for help in securing slave labor. Unlike the response in South Carolina, the Mississippi government, or, more particularly, Governor Pettus, issued a large number of orders impressing slaves to work on fortifications. Pettus also impressed supplies for the army. The governor and general communicated with and tolerated each other. As Pemberton stated in a letter to Pettus regarding im-

Martha Thompson (Pattie) Pemberton, wife of John C. Pemberton, in a photo probably taken in the late 1850s. CREDIT: Southern Historical Collection, University of North Carolina Chapel Hill

John C. Pemberton, from a photograph probably taken around the time of the Mexican War. CREDIT: United States Military Academy Archives, West Point, N.Y.

Sword presented to Pemberton by his home city of Philadelphia for his service in the Mexican War, currently on display at the Vicksburg National Military Park. CREDIT: Bowie Lanford

Above: John C. Pemberton, a portrait now on display at the Vicksburg National Military Park. CREDIT: Southern Historical Collection, University of North Carolina - Chapel Hill. *Right:* Statue of John C. Pemberton in the Vicksburg National Military Park. CREDIT: John C. Pemberton [III], *Pemberton: Defender of Vicksburg*

Opposite page, bottom left: U. S. Grant, Pemberton's skilled opponent, in a photograph probably taken in the fall of 1862. *Opposite page, bottom right:* William W. Loring, Pemberton's troublesome subordinate during the Vicksburg campaign. CREDIT: *Miller's Photographic History of the Civil War*

Francis Pickens, South Carolina governor who led a successful campaign to have Pemberton relieved of command of the Department of South Carolina and Georgia. CREDIT: South Caroliniana Library, University of South Carolina

Samuel Cooper, Confederate Adjutant General, who inspected Pemberton's command in South Carolina and recommended his removal. CREDIT: *Miller's Photographic History of the Civil War*

William T. Sherman, defeated by Pemberton's army at the battle of Chickasaw Bayou. CREDIT: *Miller's Photographic History of the Civil War*

Roswell Ripley, who feuded with Pemberton in South Carolina. CREDIT: *Miller's Photographic History of the Civil War*

Carter Stevenson, Pemberton's left wing commander at Champion Hill. CREDIT: *Miller's Photographic History of the Civil War*

Stephen D. Lee, field commander of Pemberton's forces at Chickasaw Bayou. CREDIT: *Miller's Photographic History of the Civil War*

Joseph E. Johnston, who disagreed with Pemberton and Jefferson Davis over Vicksburg strategy and carried on a feud with both after the war. CREDIT: *Miller's Photographic History of the Civil War*

Bottom left: John S. Bowen, Pemberton's best field general and a key figure in the Vicksburg surrender negotiations. CREDIT: *Confederate Veteran. Above:* Lloyd Tilghman, former friend of Pemberton who became the general's enemy during the Vicksburg campaign and was killed at Champion Hill. CREDIT: *Miller's Photographic History of the Civil War*

Above, left to right: Theophilus H. Holmes and Kirby Smith, commanders of the Confederate Trans-Mississippi Department, both of whom did little to aid Pemberton during the Vicksburg Campaign. CREDIT: *Miller's Photographic History of the Civil War*

Franklin Gardner, who cooperated with Pemberton in a failed attempt to save both Vicksburg and Gardner's command at Port Hudson. CREDIT: *Miller's Photographic History of the Civil War*

Jefferson Davis, Confederate president, who erred in sending Pemberton to Vicksburg, but who also stood by the general in the aftermath of surrender. CREDIT: Mississippi Department of Archives and History

Robert E. Lee, famed general of the Confederate Army of Northern Virginia, who had a fateful effect on Pemberton's strategic thinking. CREDIT: *Miller's Photographic History of the Civil War*

John C. Pemberton, a recent portrait by Raymond, Mississippi, artist Jerry McWilliams, that interprets Pemberton's forlorn mood upon receiving a telegram from Jefferson Davis ordering that Vicksburg and Port Hudson must be held. CREDIT: Jerry McWilliams.

Ruins of the railroad bridge across the Big Black River west of Edwards, Mississippi. The bridge was the axis of Pemberton's strategy to defend Vicksburg after Grant moved inland through Port Gibson. CREDIT: Michael Ballard

Left: This cannon in the Vicksburg National Military Park marks the site where Pemberton and Grant first met to discuss the surrender of Vicksburg. CREDIT: Michael Ballard. *Above:* The Rock House in Vicksburg on Jackson Road where Pemberton and his staff rudely received Grant after the surrender. CREDIT: Vicksburg National Military Park. *Below:* Pemberton headquarters house in Vicksburg, privately owned. CREDIT: Michael Ballard

Left: John C. Pemberton, a photograph taken shortly before his death. CREDIT: John C. Pemberton [III], *Pemberton: Defender of Vicksburg. Above:* This marker was placed at the foot of Pemberton's headstone by the Philadelphia, Pennsylvania, chapter of the United Daughters of the Confederacy during the Civil War Centennial. CREDIT: Frank Chressanthis

Pemberton family burial plot, Laurel Hill Cemetery, Philadelphia. To the right of John and Pattie are the graves of Pemberton's brother Israel, his mother Rebecca, and his sister Fanny. CREDIT: Frank Chressanthis

pressment of horses, he wanted to ensure "understanding and agreement between us." Whatever other problems he might encounter in his new post, Pemberton did not have another Francis Pickens to deal with. Apparently he had learned how not to deal with a governor.[24]

Problems did arise involving the Mississippi state militia. Clinging to the militia as vital to the defense of Mississippi, Pettus refused to cooperate with Confederate officials who attempted to weed out eligible conscripts from the state troops. Some Confederate officers charged leaders of state troops with interference in transferring men from state to Confederate service. A fine point of the process was that state troops had to be organized into regiments before being sworn into the Confederate army. State officers had the responsibility of organizing the troops. Correspondence between Pettus and Pemberton straightened out the matter, and Pemberton placated the governor for the loss of men by allowing state officials to enroll conscripts in areas of the state unprotected by the Confederate army. Gradually, Pemberton was beginning to practice the give-and-take of civilian politics.[25]

He also quickly learned that he needed more than Pettus's help to supply his army. Van Dorn had not set up a viable system to collect supplies, and the department commissaries were depleted. Because he had no authority west of the Mississippi, Pemberton first looked to eastern Louisiana for food, and in early 1863 he began purchasing supplies from the Trans-Mississippi. The Mississippi Delta also provided food except when low water and Federal gunboats interfered with shipping. In gathering goods for his own department, Pemberton issued orders that stopped shipments of certain items to other areas, which inevitably led to criticism by buyers and sellers.[26]

The War Department wired both Pemberton and Johnston about "incessant" complaints against the procurement methods of quartermasters in Pemberton's department. Mobile and Ohio Railroad officials were alarmed when he blocked shipments of corn and meat to Mobile. Secretary of War James Seddon reminded Johnston that such measures could be taken only when Pemberton had critical, urgent supply problems. (Seddon had become secretary of war on November 21, 1862, replacing George Randolph.) Assistant Secretary John Campbell lectured Pemberton about procurement abuses by quartermasters and their agents. "Necessity alone," wrote Campbell, excused interference with private property and free commerce. Mere convenience was not sufficient rationale for impressment of supplies. The War Department, Campbell counseled, looked to Pemberton to restore honor and justice to his realm.[27]

Pemberton paid little attention to such complaints, and Johnston, not being on the scene (he established headquarters near Bragg's army), deferred to his subordinate's judgment. There were too many problems, such as what to do about trading regulations regarding commerce with federally occupied Memphis and New Orleans, to worry about hurt feelings. There was also much spoilage of improperly stored food. Lack of funds to purchase supplies was a constant aggravation; most sellers demanded cash. Federal navy dominance of the Mississippi and its tributaries between Port Hudson and Vicksburg forced reliance on "ramshackled" railroads to keep both vital points adequately supplied. Not until April 1863 did Pemberton issue orders stopping impressment of goods from plantations and small farms. Even then, he made it clear that the order could be ignored under special circumstances with permission from his headquarters.[28]

In addition to the governor, state troops, and supplies, Pemberton had to deal with the troubling and sensitive issue of retaliation. Government and civilian pressure on military commanders, North and South, to retaliate against the enemy often followed incidents of violence by either regular troops or partisan guerrillas against noncombatants, prisoners of war, and, in the case of partisans, regular army soldiers. In northern Mississippi Confederate partisans had fired on a Yankee party that was escorting prisoners to Memphis. A private citizen in the area, apparently fearing he would be identified as one of the partisans and probably aware that captured partisans were sometimes executed, panicked and tried to run from the scene. His actions made him appear guilty to Union soldiers, who shot him down. Pemberton informed General William T. Sherman, commanding in Memphis, that he might execute several Federal prisoners unless the killers of the citizen were punished. Sherman refused and promised to kill Confederate prisoners if Pemberton acted. Pemberton also threatened retaliation against Union prisoners if the Union navy persisted in a threat to execute any citizens who interfered with river traffic. Fortunately for each side, extreme cases were the exception rather than the rule. Most incidents resulted in volleys of words and nothing more.[29]

While enmeshed in bureaucratic wranglings, Pemberton kept a wary eye on northern Mississippi. He urged Braxton Bragg to send troops from middle Tennessee to threaten Grant's rear. Bragg responded by ordering the intrepid Confederate cavalryman Nathan Bedford Forrest into west Tennessee.[30]

On November 29, convinced that Grant's push into Mississippi was not a feint, Pemberton journeyed back north, where his army was continuing to fall back slowly under the Federal advance. His force of twenty thousand at Abbeville retired toward Oxford and on to Grenada. He did not have sufficient numbers to meet Grant head-on. Scouts accurately estimated Yankee strength at sixty to seventy thousand along the north Mississippi front. Grant sent detachments to threaten both Rebel flanks so Pemberton had to pull back or risk envelopment. From December 4 to 6, the Confederates entrenched along the Yalobusha River at Grenada. Pemberton wired Bragg for help. Both Vicksburg and Port Hudson were undermanned to meet Grant's threat. Vicksburg had six thousand effectives, Port Hudson some forty-five hundred. Federal activity in the Helena, Arkansas, area concerned Pemberton, who urged Richmond to order Holmes to try to prevent enemy troops from going downriver to attack Vicksburg.[31]

While Pemberton struggled to hold the Yalobusha line, Grant was rethinking his strategy. Grant's army had suffered through miserable weather conditions, which had made the roads south almost impassable, and his lines of communication were becoming more tenuous the deeper he penetrated into Mississippi. On December 4, he proposed to his superior, Henry Halleck, that while he pushed from the north, General Sherman take a force of forty thousand down the Mississippi, land above Vicksburg at the mouth of the Yazoo River, and cut the Mississippi Central Railroad that connected Jackson with the Rebel army facing him in northern Mississippi. Sherman could also cut communications between Jackson and Vicksburg. Grant would keep the Confederates occupied and then cooperate with Sherman as circumstances dictated. The plan was approved.[32]

Grant's plan set the tone for his efforts to take Vicksburg. John Pemberton would be hard-pressed to keep up with Grant's diversions, which would become more numerous and complex in coming months. Even before he learned of Sherman's expedition, Pemberton had to

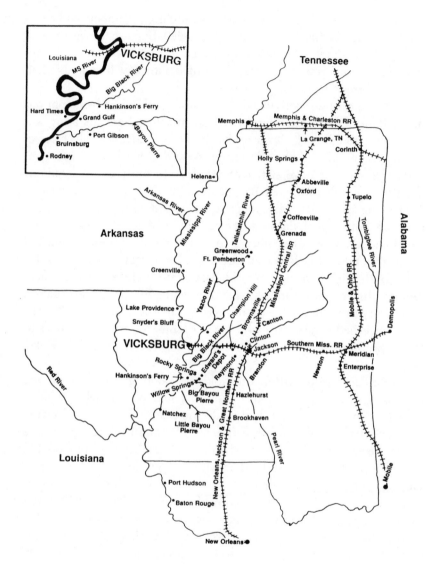

Vicksburg Theater

cope with Union gunboat threats against the Confederate navy yard at Yazoo City. In mid-December he traveled to Jackson, learned that "the situation was not as serious . . . as . . . feared," and returned to the Yalobusha front. En route, he was informed that the Yankee gunboat *Cairo* had sunk in the Yazoo, a victim of a Confederate torpedo (mine). As a result, other enemy boats had retreated back to the Mississippi.[33]

Back in Grenada, where he had established headquarters, Pemberton conferred with one of his colonels, who had suggested a cavalry raid against Grant's rear. Pemberton liked the idea; it might force Grant to pull back to Memphis. Following the colonel's advice, Pemberton gave three cavalry brigades to Earl Van Dorn, a wise move as things turned out. Van Dorn had failed at the head of an army, but as a leader of cavalry he would prove to be an excellent officer. His assault on Grant's supply base at Holly Springs on December 20, 1862, was a brilliant success. Van Dorn's foray, along with Forrest's raids in west Tennessee and unfounded rumors that Bragg was marching on Corinth, forced Grant to retire toward Memphis. Sherman, already on his way to Vicksburg, was on his own.[34]

Van Dorn's raid proved to be the only significant Confederate offensive during Pemberton's tenure in Mississippi. Though the idea was not his, he approved it, and he should have learned from it. When an army was outnumbered, a daring strategic initiative could bring significant results. Doing the unexpected could make the vital difference in a campaign, as Robert E. Lee would prove time and again in Virginia. But with this one exception, Pemberton would conduct affairs in Mississippi much as he had in South Carolina, staying on the defensive and reacting to the opponent's moves. It was true that much of the time he had no choice, but when other opportunities did arise, he let them pass. It was a strategy that had worked in South Carolina; it would not work so well in Mississippi.

Van Dorn's raid helped repair the army's confidence in the commanding general, which had been shaken by his retrograde movement southward. For others, the success confirmed their original judgment of Pemberton. A Jackson reporter wrote two weeks before the raid that he had "too much confidence in the military skill, the acumen and ability" of the general to doubt the wisdom of the retreat to the Yalobusha.

We augur much for the want of fuss and feathers about this man. The Confederate States, more than once disappointed with the great Southwest, looks anxiously to Gen. Pemberton. Public opinion is necessarily sensitive within the jurisdiction of the army of the Mississippi. "A burnt child dreads the fire," yet the people, so swift to condemn, will most graciously fly to the defence and laudation of the man who proves himself the great prop of the South in the terrible ordeal through which she is now passing. The country feels that through some fatality our military success in the Southwest has not been commensurate to the high expectations of the people.[35]

The high expectations seemed on the upswing. Grant had been beaten off, but Sherman remained to be dealt with.

While unaware of Sherman's mission, Pemberton played host to Joe Johnston and Jefferson Davis. Davis had come west to consult with Johnston and while in Tennessee had ordered about nine thousand men, a relatively inexperienced division led by General Carter Stevenson, from Bragg's army to reinforce Pemberton. Davis and Johnston had then proceeded from Chattanooga to Jackson, arriving on December 19. From there the party traveled to Vicksburg to inspect the city's defenses. Johnston did not like what he saw, claiming after the war, with the benefit of hindsight, that the overly extensive works required a large garrison that could be cut off and trapped by an enemy army. After the inspection, president and general traveled by rail to visit with Pemberton.[36]

Pemberton entertained and conferred with his guests until Christmas eve. News had been drifting into his headquarters, beginning on December 21, that a large Federal convoy was moving south from Memphis down the Mississippi. Pemberton put the army on alert and ordered one brigade to Vicksburg. On December 24, the army passed in review for the visitors. Message after message now poured in, some reporting as many as forty-five river transports filled with Federal troops headed for Vicksburg. Pemberton ended the pomp and meetings and ordered another brigade to the threatened city. On Christmas day, Pemberton and guests entrained for Jackson; the president went on to Richmond, Johnston stayed in Pemberton's Jackson headquarters, and Pemberton traveled on to Vicksburg.[37]

Upon his arrival at midnight on December 26 at the headquarters of Vicksburg commander Martin L. Smith, Pemberton learned that Sherman's troops had landed and were advancing on the Walnut Hills north and northeast of Vicksburg. He wired orders to Grenada for a division to rush to Smith's aid and sent word to Jackson urging staff chief Waddy and Johnston to facilitate the routing of reinforcements through the capital city.[38]

During the ensuing Battle of Chickasaw Bayou (December 27–29), the Confederates took advantage of well-defended high bluffs to win a solid victory, forcing Sherman to retreat upriver. Pemberton played his usual behind-the-scenes role, helping maneuver troops to trouble spots and coordinating the placement of incoming reinforcements. In his official report, he gave credit for the victory to Smith and to General Stephen D. Lee, who commanded the troops that bore the brunt of the fighting.[39]

Pemberton once again demonstrated his preference for working behind the lines. He operated as though he were still an aide to General Worth, directing, deploying, and watching over operations. As in South Carolina, he indicated that he viewed his job as that of an administrator, not a combat general. Jefferson Davis and the War Department never seemed to notice that this was his preference and his strength.

So far in his new command, Pemberton's philosophy had not failed him. As 1862 came to an end, he could point with pride to his successful defense of north Mississippi and Vicksburg. Grant had been forced to withdraw from the Yalobusha line, and Sherman, with more than a two-to-one advantage in troop strength, had been battered at Chickasaw Bayou. Pemberton received his share of praise for the successes, praise that had been noticeably absent in South Carolina. The *Memphis Daily Appeal*, publishing in exile in Jackson, editorialized that Pemberton's "foresight" in anticipating enemy movements had brought a victory that would "ensure him the esteem of the troops and the people." The commanding general had "allowed nothing to escape his observation and would permit no laggards in his lines." The editor had confidence that Vicksburg was safe in this general's hands.[40] Of course, foresight had had little to do with it. But Pemberton had used his interior lines well to meet Sherman's threat, and for that he did deserve credit.

Any satisfaction Pemberton enjoyed over the Chickasaw Bayou triumph would have been tempered had he been aware that his hometown newspaper, the *Philadelphia Inquirer,* was for the first time taking notice of the city's most prominent Rebel. The paper's editor commented bitterly:

> In the early days of the Rebellion an officer of the United States Army, by birth and education a Philadelphian, induced by the persuasions of a Southern wife, disgraced the city of his nativity by deserting the flag of his country and uniting his fortunes with those of the other traitors who had taken up arms for the destruction of the Union. John C. Pemberton, from early manhood, had been supported by the United States Government, and no man in the North had less reason to prove recreant to his manly honor, military position and social standing than he who now appears to glory in his appointment to the command of the Rebel army in the Southwest.[41]

One can only imagine the effect of such words on Rebecca Pemberton and the rest of John's family.

The *Inquirer's* tirade was inspired by a story the paper had picked up from the *New Orleans Daily Delta,* a former Confederate paper run by Union soldiers since the fall of New Orleans. According to the *Delta,* Pemberton had delivered an amazing speech in Brookhaven, Mississippi, around November 5. Reportedly he had said:

> Soldiers—In assuming the command of so brave and intelligent an army as that to which President Davis has assigned me, I desire at once to win your confidence by declaring that I am a Northern man by birth; but I have married, raised children, and own negroes in the South, and as such shall never consent to see my daughters eating at the same table or intermarrying with the black race, as the Northern teachers of equality would have them. I take command of you as a soldier, who will not fear to lead where any brave man will follow. I am no *street scavenger*— no General Lovell (Cheers). If any soldier in this command is aggrieved or shall feel himself aggrieved by any act of his superior officer, he must have no hesitation in applying to me personally for redress. The doors of my headquarters shall never be closed against the poorest and humblest soldier in my command. Come to me, if you suffer wrong, as fearlessly as you would charge the enemy's battery, and no Orderly shall turn you off, or tell you, as has been too much the case in our army, that the General cannot see nor hear the complaints of his soldiers. (Applause) In regard to the question of interference by Europe, we want no influence in our private quarrel. (Great Applause) We must settle the question ourselves or fail entirely. The moment England interferes she

will find us a united people, and she will have *to meet with the armies of the South as well as the North.* (Cheers, and cries of "yes, yes, yes" from every quarter—"no interference," "let us settle it between us.") I am glad to see you thus united on this question; and with a reliance on ourselves and a firm trust in the God of battles, in a few days your General will again fling your banners to the breeze and march forward to retrieve the recent disasters we have suffered in this department.[42]

The alleged speech was noticed by the *Inquirer* and other Northern papers with good reason. It provided ample proof, in the words of one high-ranking Confederate general, that the Confederacy was having command problems. Further, the speech contradicted Confederate government policy, which favored England's intervention in the war. Clearly this was not a message that John Pemberton or any other trained career military officer was likely to make. It seemed more plausible that the soldiers running the *Delta* had concocted an elaborate hoax, editorializing in the process. The negative reference to abolitionists was clear enough, as was the attack on England's possible interference in the war.

Southern newspapers ignored or dismissed the speech as blatant Yankee propaganda. They knew that John Pemberton was not by nature a speech maker, and if he had spoken, Brookhaven, located southwest of Jackson on the New Orleans and Jackson Railroad, was not a likely site. Not many soldiers would be there to hear his remarks. If he made such an oration, it would probably have been in Jackson, and certainly the Jackson and Memphis papers would have noticed it. The Yankee ersatz editors seem to have taken ill feelings toward General Lovell, Pemberton's background, common soldiers' complaints, Northern disgust with abolitionists and England, stirred it all together, and produced a detailed speech that was not taken seriously by anybody.[43]

The speech Pemberton likely never delivered became nothing more than a minor, forgotten footnote to his service in Mississippi. Nevertheless, the episode made a curious statement about the status of a Yankee general fighting for the Confederacy. Reaction in the North was predictable. Reaction in the South normally would have been vocal, pro and con, had such a story been printed about Lee, Beauregard, or Davis. In fact, Jefferson Davis did make a speech in 1864 filled with unfortunate remarks about the negative condition of the

Confederacy, and it produced a loud, mixed reaction. Pemberton's alleged remarks were almost completely ignored. No one condemned or defended him. The *Memphis Appeal*, for example, merely dismissed the story as untrue without any further comment. [44] The incident demonstrated that Pemberton was a man without a country *before* he lost Vicksburg. The Union soldiers who printed the story had unintentionally helped delineate his status in the Civil War.

Whatever his personal feelings about being somewhat of an outcast in both North and South, Pemberton did not have time to dwell on such matters. In the early spring of 1863, U. S. Grant began a series of operations aimed at accomplishing what he had thus far failed to do—capture Vicksburg. He created a flurry of activity that thoroughly tested the Confederate intelligence network and found it wanting. Grant would also learn that his opponent had a fatal tendency to become so distracted by diversions that he failed to see major threats.

Grant first tried to complete the canal across De Soto Point opposite Vicksburg. General Thomas Williams, victim of the Battle of Baton Rouge in August 1862, had started the canal in an attempt to divert the Mississippi away from the Vicksburg defenses. Disease among his troops and other problems forced Williams to abandon the project. High water and effective Rebel cannon fire convinced Grant to do likewise. Pemberton was aware of the digging, did not think it would succeed, and was puzzled that the Federals would spend so much time on it. He wrote Johnston that unless the Yankees wanted to land below Vicksburg and try to invest the city or perhaps assault Port Hudson, he could see little to be gained by the business. His speculation, in fact, pinpointed Grant's ultimate plan. [45]

Grant next tried an expedition to Lake Providence. The lake, "a crescent-shaped body of water, just west of the Mississippi some 75-river miles above Vicksburg," could possibly be used as an access to other streams that would give the Federals a route to the Red River. If all went well, the Red could be entered close to where it emptied into the Mississippi south of Vicksburg. If successful, Grant would be able to reinforce Nathaniel Banks's army, take Port Hudson, and then go after Vicksburg. Numerous delays and other problems caused Grant to abandon the attempt, but the flooding his engineers accomplished helped protect his right flank when he later decided to march southward down the west side of the Mississippi to cross below Vicksburg. [46]

The frustrated Union general also had setbacks on the river. On February 13, 1863, the *Indianola* ran past Confederate batteries at Vicksburg but was captured eleven days later. On February 14, the *De Soto* was burned to avoid capture. The *Queen of the West* ran the Vicksburg gauntlet on February 2, was captured by Confederates on the fourteenth, and eventually was sunk as a river obstruction against the Federal navy during the Yazoo Pass expedition.[47]

With a string of failures, Grant had turned to the Yazoo Pass for his next move. The pass was a bayou on the east side of the Mississippi a few miles south of where Helena, Arkansas, stood high on west bank bluffs. A man-made levee helped stem Mississippi floodwaters that periodically threatened rich farmland in the area. Confederate Commodore Isaac Brown had proposed obstructing the pass with trees. Brown realized that the Yankees could use the pass to get to the Coldwater, Tallahatchie, and Yazoo rivers. If that happened, Grant could transport troops to Yazoo City and have an overland route to Vicksburg. John Pemberton agreed, but little was done before Grant's engineers blew the levee. Pemberton had been warned, but, as he tended to do throughout the climactic stages of the campaign, he waited too long.[48]

Even after being informed by Brown of the enemy action, Pemberton did not think the Federals would be successful in getting through to the Coldwater. Meanwhile, Brown selected a strong defensive position near Greenwood, where the Yalobusha emptied into the Tallahatchie to form the Yazoo. Dubbed Fort Pemberton, the place was steadily built up under the direction of William Loring, whom Pemberton sent to take command. The Yankees did indeed get to the Coldwater but were repulsed at Fort Pemberton on March 11 and withdrew on March 16. Another attempt to get to the Yazoo above Vicksburg via Steele's Bayou also met with failure. As March came to an end, Confederate Vicksburg seemed as safe as ever.[49]

Though the Yazoo Pass expedition was successfully repulsed, it resulted in an incident that cast a shadow over Pemberton's future. He had several sharp exchanges with Loring, who continuously asked for more guns and men. Pemberton tried to make it clear that no more were available. Anyway, he argued, Loring could not make good use of additional men in the limited space of the Fort Pemberton defenses. Loring did not agree and openly criticized his commanding general.

Loring, who had practically been run out of Virginia because he could not get along with Stonewall Jackson and Robert E. Lee, made an ally of Lloyd Tilghman, Pemberton's old friend. During the retreat from Abbeville a few months earlier, Tilghman's men had burned some tents, and Tilghman had been arrested as a result. A court of inquiry had cleared Tilghman of any wrongdoing, and Pemberton had approved the court's decision. Nevertheless, according to one witness, the incident left hard feelings between the two. Whatever the case, Loring had found a friend who apparently had a common foe, and the resulting dissension would produce bitter consequences for the Confederate cause in a future battle.[50]

The Yazoo Pass expedition also indicated that Grant's relentless pressure was beginning to have a telling effect on Pemberton. As in South Carolina, he was becoming tentative, uncertain, and slow to react. He had ignored Brown's warnings and endangered the northern approaches to Vicksburg. Worse, the Federal expedition was well under way before he advised Joe Johnston and Richmond of what was going on. Even then, he did so only in response to their inquiries. And as the Federals retreated, he refused to order a pursuit. He did not have a navy to stop the Union boats, but obstructions and harassment from the riverbanks could have had a severe effect. Obviously Van Dorn's raid had been an aberration of aggressiveness on the part of the commanding general.[51]

U. S. Grant had lost none of his daring. He had failed thus far, but he had John Pemberton guessing—guessing that the Federals might land troops below Vicksburg and try siege tactics, guessing that Grant might try to capture Port Hudson, guessing that Yankee gunboats might attack Vicksburg's north and south flanks while Grant sent fifty thousand troops storming the bluffs fronting the river. Grant was determined to keep Pemberton in a state of speculation. On March 29, he made the fateful decision to move his army down the west side of the Mississippi below Vicksburg and then to transport it across the river via boats that would run by the Confederate batteries. Success depended on keeping Pemberton's attention occupied elsewhere. Grant began laying plans to do just that.[52]

Quite by accident, Grant had already made Pemberton think that the Federals were retreating to Memphis. In late March, Grant had ordered several steamers upriver from Vicksburg to relieve traffic congestion on the river. Pemberton jumped to the conclusion that Grant had given up, and he convinced Richmond to the point that Jefferson Davis asked him to send reinforcements to other parts of the Confederacy. Pemberton, not so confident, replied that the enemy presence was still too strong for him to give up troops.[53]

Meanwhile, Grant began implementing his diversionary plans. First, he sent a detachment under Frederick Steele to Greenville. From April 2 to 25, Steele operated along Deer Creek, destroyed Confederate supplies, and further convinced Pemberton that Grant was pulling his main force away from Vicksburg.[54]

On April 8, Pemberton responded to an inquiry from John Bowen, commanding at Grand Gulf. There was some Yankee activity across the river, Bowen reported, and he wanted to know how much resistance his detachment on the west side should offer. Pemberton responded that Bowen's men could contest any enemy advance but that batteries and other important defensive works must not be left unprotected. "I do not regard it of such importance as to risk your capture," he wrote.[55]

The next day, Pemberton wired Samuel Cooper that he was trying to keep Joe Johnston informed of any movement that might affect "his army." Those two words indicated that Pemberton did not think of Johnston as his superior in the chain of command. Johnston was located near the Army of Tennessee and frequently badgered Pemberton for reinforcements for that army. Pemberton's perception explained in part his future reluctance to accept Johnston's advice.[56]

Also included in the message to Cooper was a summary of the Vicksburg situation: "Enemy is constantly in motion in all directions." Pemberton reported the rumor that a Union division of John McClernand's XIII Corps was moving down the west side of the Mississippi, but, illustrating his fatal failure to divine Grant's intentions, he concluded, "Much doubt it."[57]

Despite continual reports from Bowen of heavy skirmishing across the river, Pemberton ignored Grant's march south through the early days of that fateful April. After all, Federal boats had been spotted going toward Memphis. Steele's invasion of Deer Creek had been checked by Stephen D. Lee and his brigade. In an April 11 message to Cooper, Pemberton declared confidently that Steele presented no threat. "So far enemy has gained nothing toward opening the Mis-

sissippi," he assured Richmond. Grant was undoubtedly retreating.
The Confederates were so confident that Carter Stevenson, commanding at Vicksburg, could turn his attention to a pesky raft being
used to obstruct the Yazoo River. Chains holding the raft in place had
broken in several places; now that Grant was no longer a threat,
repairs could be made.[58]

Joe Johnston was also assured that Grant was calling off the campaign. Pemberton, gaining confidence as time passed, offered to send
troops to the Army of Tennessee, which would need them because
Grant was probably going to join William Rosecrans's Union army
facing Bragg. The ever cautious Johnston responded that if there were
any doubt about Grant's intentions Pemberton should not send any of
his army too far away. Perhaps he could post some detachments at
Jackson or Meridian, where they could entrain for Tennessee if
needed. Pemberton immediately offered to send four thousand men;
the next day he doubled that number.[59]

Messages flowing in and out of Pemberton's Jackson headquarters on
April 15 began to change his mind, ever so slowly, about Grant's
intentions. Bowen prophetically wrote that he believed Union troops
on the west side would join forces with gunboats in an effort to drive
him out of Grand Gulf. The infantry would probably be ferried across
the river and come up from the south. If enemy gunboats came south
from Vicksburg, assuming they could get past the batteries, and a few
already had, "our ferriage of the Mississippi would be rendered very
insecure at any point." Carter Stevenson sent reports that Federal
gunboats had attempted to penetrate Bayou Pierre below Grand Gulf.
From northern Mississippi came word that sixty-four Federal steamers
packed with Union troops were moving south toward Vicksburg.
There could no longer be any doubt; Pemberton wired Stevenson that
Grant's retreat toward Memphis had been a ruse.[60]

Confusion clearly reigned in Pemberton's headquarters. On the
same day, orders were issued to a Vicksburg brigade to prepare for
travel to Bragg's Army of Tennessee and in a message to Simon Buckner, commanding at Mobile, Pemberton said he was certain that a
large portion of Grant's army was going to join Rosecrans.[61]

Good sense was finally prevailing, however, and on April 16, Pemberton informed Johnston that he could supply only part of the promised reinforcements. The brigade at Vicksburg was ordered to delay its

departure. Early on April 17, Pemberton received news that several Union vessels had successfully run by the Vicksburg batteries. At 2:30 A.M. he wired Johnston of the situation and advised that he could send no more troops. Pemberton knew that there were enough boats now between Vicksburg and Port Hudson to ferry Grant's troops from the west to the east side of the river. He asked Johnston to send back those men already en route from Vicksburg to Bragg. Johnston agreed and issued the necessary orders.[62]

Bowen, meanwhile, was consulting with Pemberton on whether Confederate troops still contesting Grant's march south on the west side should be withdrawn across the Mississippi. The two agreed that this was the only safe course to take. Pemberton ordered reinforcements to Bowen, but they were only a fraction of the number that would be needed if Grant crossed in force.[63]

Across the Mississippi, Kirby Smith requested troops from Port Hudson to help Richard Taylor fight Yankees in Trans-Mississippi Louisiana. Smith, now commanding the Trans-Mississippi, insisted that because Taylor was occupied by the enemy, he could not help stop McClernand's movement down the Louisiana side. Pemberton replied that lack of transportation, buildup of Union forces around Port Hudson, and Federal dominance of the river made it impossible for him to help Taylor. In any event, he figured that at least part of Nathaniel Banks's army was trying to join a cavalry column that had been cutting its way diagonally through Mississippi. Pemberton was arguing in effect that the real danger was on the east side of the river.[64]

The cavalry raid Pemberton referred to was yet another diversion by Grant, his most effective yet. Grant had ordered numerous cavalry and infantry forays into northern Mississippi, but only one of these would dominate the Confederates' attention. Colonel Benjamin H. Grierson led his horsemen out of LaGrange, Tennessee, on April 17. Grierson's mission was to drive southward and try to cut the Southern Railroad east of Jackson, depriving Vicksburg of a major supply artery, and then to do whatever damage he could without being caught.[65]

The whirlwind of activity in the northern part of the state made it almost impossible for Pemberton's poor communications system to keep track of Grierson. Pemberton had been complaining loudly for months about the transfer of Van Dorn's cavalry to Bragg, and one of his excuses for losing Vicksburg would be that he did not have enough cavalry to track either Grierson or Grant. Because of Grant's many diversions in northern Mississippi, it is difficult to fault Pemberton for refusing to unite all his available cavalry to chase Grierson, but he could have made better use of the cavalry he had; his horsemen were much too scattered among too many unimportant areas to be effective. Without a good intelligence system in place, Pemberton did not hear of Grierson's departure from Tennessee until April 20. Two days later, Pemberton sent his latest of many wires begging Johnston for cavalry. He also sent William Loring and his infantry to Meridian in an attempt to cut off the Yankee riders.[66]

Until the raid ended when Grierson and his exhausted men entered Baton Rouge on May 3, Confederate telegraph wires (except where they had been cut by the Yankees) gave out message after message of rumors and reports of the enemy cavalry's whereabouts. Grierson led his column on a south-southeasterly course before veering to the southwest. Along the way he sent out decoy detachments further to confuse the Rebels. At Newton on April 24, the raiders captured two trains of the Southern Railroad of Mississippi and destroyed much track. With the raid coming so close to Jackson, Pemberton was finally able to get an accurate fix on their location.[67]

Doing something about it was another matter. Broken wires helped Grierson get away while Pemberton's efforts to concentrate detachments on the Yankees' trail were frustrated. He did get word to General John Adams near Newton that assistance should be requested from General Buckner in Mobile. Adams wired Buckner, "All is lost unless you send a regiment or two to Meridian." Adams's words infuriated Pemberton. After seeing a copy of Adams's wire, he informed the general: "You say in your despatch to General Buckner, 'all is lost, unless &c.' Correct it. I never authorized you to use such an expression." The exchange demonstrated how short Pemberton's temper was getting as his frustration in trying to head off Grierson increased. In exasperation, he told one officer, "See if something can be done."[68]

Reports were so confusing that at one point Pemberton was convinced that Grierson had turned back north, and he sent orders to his scattered cavalry to intercept the retreating Yankees. But other intelligence indicated that the Federal column was still moving southwestward. Grierson had thoughts of turning west to join Grant's army after it had crossed over the river, but increasing pursuit by Confederates convinced him that his safest destination was Baton Rouge.[69]

John Pemberton, meanwhile, continued to send out messages trying to locate the elusive raiders. When he heard that they were in the Hazelhurst area, he sent Wirt Adams's cavalry there from Bowen's position at Grand Gulf. Pemberton feared that Grierson might try to destroy the Big Black River Bridge between Jackson and Vicksburg. He sent one wire to Joe Johnston, who had implied that Pemberton had been slow to report the raid's penetration into southern Mississippi. In response, Pemberton correctly pointed out that he had quickly reported the raid, and, furthermore, unless he got cavalry reinforcements, a similar raid could easily be carried out again. As one of Pemberton's staff confided to his diary, the raid had kicked "up a thundering rumpus," and the noise had almost completely drawn Confederate attention away from the real threat about to cross the Mississippi.[70]

Why had Pemberton been so completely engrossed with Grierson while ignoring the Federal thrust down the west side of the Mississippi? One suggestion has been that he wanted an excuse to avoid dealing with Grant's latest scheme across the river. There is certainly an element of truth in that argument. Pemberton was much more comfortable dealing with the known. Grierson posed a real threat. Pemberton had to guess about the raiders' location, but he understood, or at least thought he understood, their intent. Grant's intentions were more abstract and created an air of anxious uncertainty at Pemberton's headquarters. He may well have welcomed the chance to focus on Grierson so as to ignore Grant. Certainly Pemberton had previously displayed his ability to see a situation as he wished it to be, not as it was. Had he exercised better judgment, surely he would have recognized Grierson's raid for the diversion it was.

Evidence to that effect was plentiful. As Grierson rode toward the safety of Union lines in Louisiana, more boats were passing the Vicksburg batteries. Pemberton ordered Carter Stevenson to shift the weight of the Vicksburg garrison to support Bowen if Grant indeed tried to cross. By April 27, Bowen was convinced that Grant would land on the east bank at Rodney, just south of Port Gibson. Bowen toured the area looking for good defensive positions. The next day,

Pemberton wired Davis that Grant was conducting a demonstration in force at Hard Times across the river. His wording indicated that he still had no real appreciation of what Grant was about to do. William T. Sherman's demonstration along the Snyder's Bluff area on April 27 gave Pemberton further doubts that Grant was the real threat. Otherwise, Sherman's movement failed in its attempt to draw attention away from Grand Gulf. Stevenson left the bulk of his troops in position to move south if needed.[71]

On April 28, Bowen reported that an "immense" force was in his front; on the twenty-ninth Federal gunboats shelled his Grand Gulf defenses. Bowen's batteries fought the gunboats to a standstill. The boats then headed downstream to escort the transport vessels that began moving Grant's army to the east bank at Bruinsburg on April 30. John Pemberton was still in Jackson, still trying to keep up with all the activity by telegraph. He funneled more troops toward Bowen's position, but other than reports of cannon fire at Grand Gulf he was unsure of Bowen's situation. Finally, he wired Stevenson, "Is anything going on at Vicksburg or Grand Gulf?"[72]

Much was going on, and Pemberton had lost control of it. From a solid start in his new command, from victory in northern Mississippi and at Chickasaw Bayou, and from frustrating Grant's other attempts to take Vicksburg, he had been reduced to a state of total uncertainty. As in South Carolina, the pressure had finally gotten to him; Grant's diversions had worked beautifully. Of course, poor Confederate communications and a lack of cavalry, no navy, and too little manpower had compounded Pemberton's failure to check Grant's move across the river. Circumstances beyond his control and his own makeup had led to his becoming overwhelmed, as anyone who had witnessed his command in Charleston could have predicted. All was not yet lost, but time would demonstrate that when Grant crossed the Mississippi, he pushed Pemberton across his personal Rubicon.

CHAPTER 8

Indecision, Indecision, Indecision

Vicksburg, the Final Campaign

John Stevens Bowen and his men fought hard at Port Gibson. A native Georgian who had spent most his life in Missouri, Bowen always fought well, and his fiery soldiers reflected their leader's personality. On May 1, 1863, however, they were outnumbered three to one by Grant's Yankees. After hours of hard fighting, Bowen ordered a retreat, and Grant had gained a foothold below Vicksburg. As he led his army across Bayou Pierre, Bowen could be excused if he blamed John Pemberton for not listening to his warnings about Grant's intentions.[1]

Pemberton was listening now but learning little. He had finally moved his headquarters to Vicksburg on May 1, and he kept his telegraph wires humming all day. He notified Jefferson Davis that a battle was raging at Port Gibson and begged for reinforcements. The War Department replied that Beauregard was sending men from South Carolina. But would they arrive in time to help beat Grant? Pemberton knew that Bowen, good as he was, could not hold out for long. Davis contacted Joe Johnston about sending cavalry; later in the day he learned from Pemberton that Bowen was retreating.[2]

At his headquarters in Tullahoma, Tennessee, Johnston received no news of Grant's crossing and the fight at Port Gibson. Based on the intelligence he did have from Pemberton, Johnston wired Vicksburg on May 1 with advice: "If Grant's army lands on this side of the river, the safety of Mississippi depends on beating it. For that object you should unite your whole force." The next day, still unaware of events below Vicksburg, Johnston further advised Pemberton: "If Grant crosses, unite all your troops to beat him. Success will give back what was abandoned to win it."[3]

Johnston's messages would later become a major source of contention between the two generals. Johnston accused Pemberton of disobeying orders by not uniting his "whole force." Pemberton countered that by the time he received the message on May 1, Johnston's instruction were worthless. Later he would expand on that argument and ask rhetorically why Johnston did not issue such an order much earlier after being informed that Federal boats were passing the Vicksburg batteries. The dispute highlighted philosophical differences between the two. Johnston preferred a policy of maneuverability that did not restrict an army to defending a specific area like Vicksburg. Pemberton had learned in South Carolina that when he was entrusted to protect a site (Charleston), he had to fight street by street and house by house to save the place. He brought that dictum to Mississippi, where he hesitated to do anything that might leave Vicksburg vulnerable. Moving south with most of his force to meet Grant would, in his mind, have done just that. Sherman was demonstrating on the Snyder's Bluff flank, making enough noise that Pemberton would keep an eye on him. Federal cavalry was moving through the state with ease. And if Grant indeed was just demonstrating at Grand Gulf, taking the bait would force Pemberton to leave Vicksburg undermanned against a frontal assault, which some of his officers had suggested was Grant's real intent. This was how Pemberton viewed his dilemma, and he was not receptive to presumptuous orders from Johnston, who was too far away to appreciate the situation. But because Johnston was so far away, Pemberton's charge that Johnston's directives should have been given earlier was absurd. Pemberton was the officer on the scene and thus the only one capable of making the decision. He had made the wrong one, but, given his thinking on defending Vicksburg, he could have made no other.[4]

The episode also demonstrated the frailties of the western command system. Johnston was giving long-distance orders, and Pemberton still thought of Jefferson Davis and the War Department as his immediate superiors. The severity of the situation was proven when, by May 6, five days after Grant had won at Port Gibson, Johnston still had not been informed of the results of the battle. On May 7, he finally learned from Pemberton that Bowen had "had to leave his position."[5]

Historians are trained to avoid "what if" scenarios, but it is intriguing to consider what might have happened had Pemberton indeed concentrated his army to meet Grant at the river. One historian has argued convincingly that Grant very likely would have won at Port Gibson anyway. The Confederates could not have mustered enough men to assure victory. Timing was also critical. If Pemberton had acted too quickly, he would have left Vicksburg in a vulnerable position. Yet delays would have created monstrous logistical problems. Troops could not be moved directly to the Port Gibson area by rail, and there was no road directly linking Vicksburg and Grand Gulf. A river, Bayou Pierre, separated Grand Gulf and Port Gibson. If Pemberton had concentrated south of that river, Federal gunboats might have cut him off from Grand Gulf, and, more important, from Vicksburg. So even if Pemberton had anticipated Johnston's orders, success would not have been guaranteed.[6]

Pemberton initially worked to carry out Johnston's suggestion. While trying to gather reinforcements, he wrote Davis that he intended to abandon Port Hudson and Grand Gulf to concentrate more troops to meet Grant. While waiting for a response, he ordered Franklin Gardner to rush to Vicksburg with five thousand infantry. On May 7, Davis responded. The president had been ill, and his judgment may have been clouded, but he ever after applauded Pemberton's strategy in Mississippi so there is little reason to believe he would have given different advice. "To hold both Vicksburg and Port Hudson," he wrote, "is necessary to a connection with the Trans-Mississippi. You may expect whatever is in my power to do." Pemberton immediately wired Gardner to stay in Port Hudson with two thousand men. Davis had spoken, and Pemberton was no doubt delighted to obey instructions that were in line with his own preferences. He would rather remain close to Vicksburg and on the defensive; now he had official sanction to do so.[7]

As events unfolded, Davis's order proved partially beneficial. Grant had envisioned cooperating with Nathaniel Banks's army in Louisiana. He considered turning south after landing on the east bank. After linking with Banks, Grant would take Port Hudson and then move north to Vicksburg. But Grant's success at Port Gibson convinced him to strike north at once rather than risk losing momentum. Banks, meanwhile, knew that Port Hudson was understrength and decided to take the place himself and then join Grant. It should have been easy, but Banks vacillated. Joe Johnston had ordered Gardner to evacuate, but the message came too late, and Gardner found himself invested. Banks, however, was fought to a standstill by the small army holding Port Hudson, and Gardner would surrender only after the fall of Vicksburg gave him no other choice.[8]

While Grant acted decisively and Banks settled in for a siege, Pemberton gathered troops from Meridian, Jackson, and Grenada. He urged Kirby Smith, commanding the Trans-Mississippi, to attack Federals still on the west side of the Mississippi. Communications with Smith were a problem; weeks often passed before messages were delivered. Smith had never been very cooperative with anybody, and by the time he acted, Pemberton's army was trapped in Vicksburg. Jefferson Davis's decision to keep the Trans-Mississippi a separate district had set the stage for a lack of coordinated operations between Confederate forces on either side of the river.[9]

On the east side, Pemberton tried to get more men to Bowen. Pemberton and his staff had never before been severely tested in the heat of military operations. Up to now, enemy movements had been more predictable or less threatening. A straightforward Yankee thrust into northern Mississippi had failed because Van Dorn had been able to sever a vulnerable supply line. Sherman had slammed headlong into impressive entrenchments north of Vicksburg and had failed. Grant's diversions since Chickasaw Bayou had kept Pemberton's headquarters guessing, but good luck and, in the case of Fort Pemberton, good strategy had held off the Federals. But since Grierson's raid, Pemberton and his staff had been off balance, and Grant's crossing created even more confusion. Vicksburg was in more danger than ever before; Pemberton had to take decisive and confident action.

Signs already indicated that the Pemberton regime would have trouble dealing with the crisis. Recalled from his wasted effort to intercept Grierson, William Loring received an urgent message on May 1 to "proceed at once" with several designated detachments. The message ended, "When can you move?" A puzzled Loring wired Vicksburg from Jackson, "Your telegram . . . does not say where we are to go." A reply ordered Loring to proceed to Port Gibson "via Vicksburg." Lloyd Tilgham was directed to start from Edwards Depot, halfway between Jackson and Vicksburg, for Port Gibson. Another wire from headquarters told Tilghman to send his men on ahead but to wait himself for Loring. Loring meanwhile had been told to pick up Tilghman and his brigade before moving on to Port Gibson. Other troops coming westward from Jackson were to be held in reserve in Vicksburg. Though neither Loring nor Tilghman had reputations for alacrity, they were understandably confused by the barrage of vague messages so they hesitated at a time when speed was essential. Pemberton reacted angrily, oblivious that unclear messages from his headquarters had made a major contribution to the problem. He ordered Loring to "obey . . . instructions at once" and told Tilghman that his instructions were "peremptory, and will be obeyed at once." The whole mess widened the schism between Pemberton and the two generals.[10]

Pemberton's fury was not due merely to delays in getting reinforcements to Bowen. While in Jackson, Loring had attempted to issue departmental orders, under his own name, for northern Mississippi. Pemberton's assistant adjutant, Robert W. Memminger, was naturally disturbed by Loring's presumption and wired his boss in Vicksburg. Pemberton responded sharply and to the point: "I command the department from here. All orders [are] to be issued in my name."[11]

Loring had, as usual, overstepped his bounds, but his interference was based on legitimate concerns about reports from the north. While Grant was defeating Bowen on May 1, numerous dispatches from Confederate outposts in northern Mississippi indicated a flurry of Federal activity.[12] John Pemberton was continuing to pay a high price for the loss of Van Dorn's cavalry to Braxton Bragg. He had enough cavalry to get the job done against Grant if he concentrated it all, but to do so would leave too much of northern Mississippi vulnerable. He had not been willing to gamble on a concentration to stop Grierson, and he would not do it now. Criticizing his decision ignores the political realities of leaving much of the northern area without cavalry protection. A good field general, however, would have done whatever was necessary to meet the potentially greatest threat. That threat was at Port Gibson and getting closer. Valuable cavalry was being wasted guarding too many unimportant points in northern Mississippi. Pemberton and other Confederate generals too often sacrificed concentration at the expense of territorial defense. Pemberton needed Van Dorn, but he could have done much better than he did without him.

John Pemberton's problem went beyond flawed strategy. He had become too cautious and had lost too much confidence in his own ability to risk gambling on any of Grant's diversions. In his mind, any of those diversions could become real threats if ignored. With information of Union incursions flowing in from New Albany, Tupelo, Okalona, and other areas to the north, Pemberton had little choice but to leave some cavalry there, although state militia could have taken up much of the slack. True, other reports denied that any emergency existed, but because of the history of uncertainty in his communications network, he never considered abandoning his northern flank. He was promised help from the cavalry of Nathan Bedford Forrest, but it did not materialize. Forrest was incapacitated. Van Dorn would soon be killed by an allegedly jealous husband, and John Pemberton in the end would be left to fend for himself. [13]

John Bowen was still fending for himself, too. Help was on the way, but it was not as much as Pemberton had led him to believe. Pemberton had wired Bowen that Loring was en route with two brigades; in fact, Loring and Tilghman were traveling with two regiments and a battery of artillery. Bowen was certain that he had been defeated by Grant's main army, and he knew from captured Yankees that Grant was aware of Loring's pending arrival. Based on this information, Pemberton decided on May 2 to abandon Grand Gulf rather than risk Bowen's command. Yet on May 1, assuming that two brigades, not two regiments, were on the way, Bowen had already endangered his force by delaying his withdrawal from the Port Gibson–Grand Gulf area. Bowen was convinced that he could guard all crossings of Bayou Pierre with the help of Loring's reinforcements but learned otherwise when Loring arrived. He also learned that the Yankees had crossed Little Bayou Pierre and would soon be in position to cut off potential avenues of retreat. Pemberton's long-distance command system had given Bowen a false impression that almost cost him dearly. Loring took command and ordered a withdrawal toward the Big Black more in compliance with military realities than with Pemberton's May 2 decision. He informed Pemberton that he could communicate via Rocky Springs northeast of Port Gibson. Anxious to communicate, Pemberton responded: "My anxiety to hear is very great, and I hope you will keep me constantly and regularly informed of your position and current events."[14]

Loring began pulling his and Bowen's forces toward the Big Black, which ran northeast to southwest. Once on the west side, the Confederates could use the river as a natural defensive barrier and hope to block any attempt by Grant to approach Vicksburg from the south. While Loring and Bowen retreated, Pemberton made an important strategic decision. He wired Davis: "I shall concentrate all my troops this side of Big Black. The question of subsistence and proximity to base, and necessity of supporting Vicksburg, have determined this." At this juncture, Pemberton was operating on the assumption that Grant's first inland target would be Jackson. He sent word to aides in the capital city to evacuate important records and archives eastward. He also assumed that Grant would turn toward Vicksburg and follow the railroad westward beyond Edwards to the Big Black. If Pemberton posted his army along the high west bank bluff of the river to meet the enemy, Grant might have considerable trouble getting into Vicksburg.[15] Clearly Pemberton's guiding lights in formulating this strategy were his Charleston experience and Davis's admonition. Vicksburg must be saved, street by street, house by house.

Pemberton's defensive state of mind seemingly filtered down the ladder of command. When reinforcements led by Carter Stevenson arrived at Hankinson's Ferry on the Big Black, Loring had an opportunity to strike General James McPherson's corps while it was separated from Grant's main army. Intent on making sure his command was completely safe on the west bank of the Big Black, Loring let the chance go by.[16]

Little by little, Pemberton gathered his army around Edwards and the railroad bridge at the Big Black. Bovina, a community along the rail line west of the Big Black, was fortified. Yet he did not effect the total concentration that would be needed to beat Grant. Pemberton ordered Stevenson to watch the Warrenton approach to Vicksburg from the south. He was still guessing, still unsure of Grant's intent. If he really believed Jackson to be the enemy objective, why bother with Warrenton? In fact, his assumptions had been shaken by Grant's continuing diversions. The wily Union commander sent a detachment toward Hankinson's Ferry in a successful effort to intimidate Pemberton into keeping Confederate forces scattered. To meet these imagined threats, Pemberton made confusing troop dispositions, at times shifting Loring's and Bowen's men without logical regard for their current locations. Grant's diversions kept Rebel troops constantly in motion. Failure to draw cavalry from northern Mississippi to help screen Grant's advance forced a nervous Pemberton to react to every shadow. Scouting reports indicated that the Southern Railroad, not Jackson, was Grant's target. For once the reports were right; Grant indeed had targeted the railroad, aiming to straddle it near Edwards and move westward to Vicksburg. Still Pemberton was not sure; he warned his aides in Jackson that the city might be raided and passed word to Bowen and Loring to be ready for an attack.[17]

Loring had been giving the Confederate situation much thought and decided to express his ideas to Assistant Adjutant Memminger. His failure to wire Pemberton said much about the relationship between the two. As the senior officer in the field, Loring was entitled to an opinion, but he should have given it directly to Pemberton. "The enemy are reported fortifying positions along the road leading to the railroad and toward Jackson," Loring wrote. "They will not attempt to pass the Big Black or move upon the railroad until this is done. Is it not, then, our policy to take the offensive before they can make themselves secure and move either way as it may suit them? . . . I believe if a well concerted plan be adopted, we can drive the enemy into the Mississippi, if it is done in time. They don't expect anything of the kind; they think we are on the defensive."[18]

The Federals were right. Obnoxious as he could often be, Loring had come up with an idea that, if implemented, would certainly surprise Grant. A bold offensive strike had worked in northern Mississippi. It could work again. Certainly it was the kind of maneuver that was the trademark of successful commanders. Outnumbered as he was, Pemberton's best chance was to do the unexpected. Success would not be guaranteed, but it was worth a try.

If Memminger passed the message along to Vicksburg, John Pemberton ignored it. There is no evidence that he ever considered such a move. He may have been miffed at Loring for not contacting him directly, but he would not have acted anyway. He had made up his mind to stay on the defensive, and that was that. In a May 9 letter to Kirby Smith asking for help from the Trans-Mississippi, Pemberton wrote: "Vicksburg, and consequently the navigation of the Mississippi River, is the vital point indispensable to be held. Nothing can be done which might jeopardize it." Complaining about his inadequate cavalry, he concluded: "My force is insufficient for offensive operations. I must stand on the defensive, at all events until reinforcements reach me."[19] Charleston and Davis's order had taken complete control of his strategic thinking. Ironically, if he had remained firm in his resolve, he probably would have fared better. Venturing into another "what if," if Pemberton had entrenched west of the Big Black as he had intended, he might have effectively blocked Grant. With Joe Johnston soon to arrive in Jackson and gathering a force there, Grant would have been caught in a trap. As the campaign developed, Johnston's small army was not a factor. But if he had stayed put behind the Big Black, Pemberton could still have presented the Yankees with a formidable obstacle.

Pemberton did make a decision that reflected one of Loring's ideas. He ordered a brigade led by General John Gregg to Raymond from Jackson to watch for a Federal approach to Jackson from the southwest. With the rest of the army operating in a defensive mode, Gregg was vulnerable; only Wirt Adams's fatigued cavalry could provide support. Pemberton was risking a brigade, but in keeping with his mindset, he ordered Gregg not to fight if outnumbered.[20]

About the time Gregg received his instructions, Pemberton ordered Bowen to "operate against enemy, to capture or repel, as opportunity offers." Bowen inquired, "If the enemy advances in force, shall I give battle at Edwards Depot, or withdraw to the entrenchments [at the Big Black], which will be ready by this evening [May 10]?" The perceptive Bowen probably anticipated his chief's reply: "Withdraw to entrenchments if they advance in heavy force."[21]

Confusion once more reigned when Pemberton attempted to coordinate movements of Loring's and Stevenson's divisions with Bowen's instructions. Misunderstanding his and Stevenson's roles in defending the Big Black line, Loring moved away from where Pemberton intended him to be, within "easy supporting distance" of Bowen. Furious, Pemberton told one of his aides to wire Loring and Stevenson, "The lieutenant-general commanding directs me to say to you that he finds great difficulty in having his views comprehended, and wishes to see you at once personally."[22] Pemberton and his staff were clearly reeling under the pressure of Grant's campaign.

The pressure increased hour by hour. The telegraph at Pemberton's headquarters clicked through another busy day on May 11. Reports continued to indicate that Grant was pushing along the eastern approaches to the Big Black. The news helped dispel lingering doubts; Grant's moves toward Jackson had to be feints. Pemberton wired Bowen, "It is very probable that the movement toward Jackson is in reality on Big Black Bridge." A similar message went to Gregg, again cautioning him to fall back if attacked "too strongly" and to attack Grant's flank and rear if the Yankees indeed came toward Edwards. The message doubtless made Gregg think that any force in his front would not present a serious threat.[23]

Other orders directed Loring and Stevenson to begin shifting their troops currently guarding southwest approaches to Vicksburg between the Big Black and Warrenton. Pemberton wanted to concentrate his strength around the Big Black railroad bridge. He had an aide, James H. Morrison, write Loring reiterating orders to move closer to Bowen. Pemberton feared that Loring "may not have been able to read the communication previously sent," for he had written it "in the dark."[24] This wording must have been delighted Loring; no doubt he thought the commanding general had been in the dark for some time.

Pemberton wired Joe Johnston and Jefferson Davis that he expected to fight Grant at the Big Black. Once more he begged for cavalry, a "positive necessity." His defensive position was weak, he complained, because detachments of troops were guarding all the possible avenues by which Grant might cross below Edwards and flank the Confederates out of their entrenchments. Davis responded that efforts to get cavalry had been unsuccessful. Remembering his general's problems in South Carolina and remarkably underestimating the seriousness of Grant's threat, Davis urged Pemberton to rally the general public. "In your situation," he counseled, "much depends on the good will and support of the people. To secure this, it is necessary to add conciliation to the discharge of duty. Patience in listening to suggestions which may not promise much, is sometimes rewarded by gaining useful information. I earnestly desire that, in addition to success, you should enjoy the full credit of your labors."[25] The hour was late for a lesson in

Southern public relations. Grant was not likely to be impeded by public support of Pemberton.

Pemberton did, however, need the support of his army, and on May 12 he issued a stirring appeal to the "Soldiers of the Army, In and around Vicksburg." He reminded his troops that the "hour of trial" had come. The enemy sought "to control the navigation of the Mississippi River," to gain the "privilege of plunder and oppression." "Your commanding General," he reminded, "believing in . . . this cause, has cast his lot with you, and stands ready to peril his life, and all he holds dear, for the triumph of the right!" God would not allow a cause so just "to be trampled in the dust." If soldiers were "vigilant, brave and active," then "the God of battles will certainly crown our efforts with success." As for Davis's advice, Pemberton wrote the president that he was appreciative, but "little reliance can be placed on the kind of assistance you refer to."[26]

Pemberton's inspirational words to his men seemed to have a positive effect on his own attitude. On May 12, he did what he should have done long before; he moved his headquarters closer to the expected battle front. His staff set up new quarters at Bovina. The day before, he had wired his subsistence officer at the state capital, "If the enemy moves on Jackson, I will advance to meet them." This was the first aggressive statement Pemberton had made since Grant's crossing. He also ordered Bowen to cross to the east side of the Big Black. Loring was delighted with his commander's apparent change of heart. He asked hopefully if Pemberton intended to attack Grant on the thirteenth.[27]

Despite appearances, Pemberton was still in no mood to attack. He made the Jackson statement at a time when he was convinced that Grant's target was the Big Black railroad bridge. He was sure that Grant was coming to him; he would not have to advance. Reports from Bowen and Loring indicated as much. Grant seemed to be still moving toward the area between Edwards and Raymond with the intent of wheeling to his left and striking for the bridge.[28] Incredibly, Grant's army had been in Mississippi for twelve days, and still Pemberton had no concrete information on his enemy's exact whereabouts or intentions.

Another event on this active May 12 forced Pemberton to rethink his strategy. A message from General Gregg said that he had been

"fighting the enemy all day" near Raymond and was falling back to
Jackson. Pemberton had warned Gregg not to fight unless he was sure
Grant's main column was attacking the Big Black. He had further
counseled, "Be careful not to lose your command." Gregg did not lose
his command at the battle of Raymond, but he did suffer five hundred
casualties. Pemberton did not berate Gregg for giving battle; when he
wrote his official campaign report months later, he had not seen
Gregg's report. The prevailing opinion that Grant's main force was
going to attack at the Big Black had given Gregg a false sense of
security. He thought the enemy in his front was a diversion to keep
him from assaulting Grant's rear. Instead, he had found himself fighting James McPherson's entire corps. Gregg had fought well, but in-
ferior numbers made retreat inevitable.[29]

The Raymond battle convinced Grant to change his plans. As of
May 12, his goal had indeed been the Big Black bridge. He knew that
the Confederate government was sending reinforcements to Pemberton and that those reinforcements were being funneled to Vicksburg
via the Southern Railroad. Cutting the railroad would disrupt the flow
of troops. McPherson's victory at Raymond and scouting reports convinced Grant that he could not afford to turn his back on Jackson.
More Rebel soldiers were around the city than he had anticipated, and
if he concentrated on Pemberton at the Big Black, his rear would be
vulnerable. Moreover, reports indicated that Joe Johnston was on his
way to Jackson, or already there, to assume command of Confederate
forces. Yet if Grant turned his attention to Jackson, Pemberton might
move out and attack him from the rear. Months of operations had
proven that the Pennsylvanian preferred the defensive. After all,
Grant and his army had moved mostly unimpeded since disposing of
Bowen at Port Gibson. Diversionary tactics had kept Pemberton off
balance and should continue to do so. So the decision was made:
Grant would attack the Confederate supply and rail center at Jackson.[30]

Joe Johnston did arrive in Jackson on May 13. He had been notified
on May 9 by Richmond that he was to go to Mississippi and "take
command of the forces there, giving to those in the field, as far as
practicable, the encouragement and benefit of your personal direction." He had responded, ominously for the Confederate cause, "I
shall go immediately, although unfit for field service." He complained

that he was too weak from lingering illness to ride.[31] He might have added that he had no desire to get involved in the Vicksburg campaign as his performance there would certainly prove.

For all his avowed confidence in John Pemberton, Jefferson Davis's decision to send Johnston to Mississippi demonstrated his disillusion with the deteriorating military situation there. Johnston, too, knew that he was heading into a potentially disastrous situation. Pemberton had repeatedly sent messages telling of insufficient troop strength at Vicksburg and Port Hudson as well as large numbers of Yankee troops being shipped downstream to join Grant. More bad news awaited Johnston in Jackson. Reports indicated that William T. Sherman's corps, which had left Snyder's Bluff and moved down the Mississippi to cross over and join Grant, was now at Clinton in a position to block the potential junction of Pemberton's and Johnston's forces. Actually, the Federal force at Clinton consisted of two of McPherson's divisions. Undetected by poor Confederate intelligence, Sherman's corps was southwest of Jackson, still en route to join Grant. Of course, it did not matter whose troops they were, they presented a major problem to Johnston and Pemberton. When Johnston learned of the enemy presence at Clinton, he wired Richmond, "*I am too late.*" He had already made up his mind that Vicksburg was lost; all that really mattered was saving the Confederate army. He wired Pemberton to attack the Yankees at Clinton, "if practicable." Johnston would move west in an attempt to trap the Yankees between himself and Pemberton.[32]

John Pemberton would never willingly go along with such a plan. At this point in the campaign he was hesitant to do anything that might result in a debacle for his army. Grant's crossing had cracked the facade of favorable public opinion of this Yankee Confederate and his performance in Mississippi. As Grant drove inland, the editors of the *Jackson Mississippian* had wired President Davis:

> The people with this dept. [,] soldiers and citizens[,] do not repose that confidence in the capacity and loyalty of Genl. Pemberton which is so important at this junction[,] whether justly or not we are certain three fourths of the people in army & out doubt him[.] Send us a man we can trust[,] Beauregard, Hill or Longstreet & confidence will be restored & all will fight to the death for Miss. The *Mississippian* has never encouraged these apprehensions but endeavored on all occasions to allay them & instill perfect confidence in our commanders but fears are daily

expressed by leading influential men that the valley may [not] be saved & this feeling prevails to an alarming extent in army & among our people[,] whether wellfounded or not it must be obvious to you that the prevalence of such doubts at this time is extremely perilous.[33]

Such attitudes doubtless made Pemberton aware of the lack of confidence in his leadership. With Lee's admonition and Davis's directive guiding his thinking, he had no desire to do anything risky that might further fuel public criticism.

Yet he was willing to do something that would not bring on a general engagement with Grant and that, if successful, would leave the Federal general in an awkward situation. Gregg had reported that the enemy was moving toward Jackson from Raymond "in force." Pemberton had ordered Gregg to fall back to Jackson if there was no doubt that the Yankees were going after the state capital. Late in the evening of May 13, Loring informed Pemberton that all sources, "both black and white," indicated that the Federals "are marching on Jackson. I think there can be no doubt of this." If this were true, Pemberton reasoned, it might be possible to destroy Grant's supply line. Much more damage might have been done if Loring had reported his reconnaissance efforts sooner. Union General John McClernand's corps had been isolated as it moved toward Raymond. The Confederates had the opportunity to fall on it and deal Grant a crippling blow. Given Pemberton's reluctance to attack, however, he probably would have allowed McClernand to escape even had he known of the situation in time to act.[34]

As it was, Pemberton did nothing on May 13. The next morning he received Johnston's message about moving out against the enemy at Clinton. He immediately responded, "I move at once with whole available force, about 16,000, from Edwards Depot." Either Pemberton's staff could not calculate very well or he intended to drop off detachments to guard his rear and flanks as he marched. His "whole available force" was almost twenty-three thousand men. He left one brigade to guard the bridge and reported to Johnston that two divisions were holding Vicksburg and vicinity. His experience in beating off Sherman at Chickasaw Bayou, with two-to-one odds favoring the Federals, should have taught Pemberton to have only a token force to guard against Yankees watching the city. Had he been more of a gambler, he would have been willing to run the risk that the enemy along the river watching Vicksburg was not likely to launch an all-out attack without orders from Grant, which probably would not have been forthcoming because Grant was otherwise occupied. Events proved that Pemberton needed all the men he could muster when he moved eastward. But he was not thinking in such terms. Saving Vicksburg was a much higher priority than beating Yankees in the field. He never wanted to risk the latter to effect the former. He warned Johnston that his soldiers were "much fatigued, and, I fear, will straggle very much. In directing this move, I do not think you fully comprehend the position that Vicksburg will be left in, but I comply at once with your order." Pemberton and Johnston, then and in the future, seemed to have ignored that part of Johnston's order that said plainly, "if practicable."[35]

Soon after dictating his message, Pemberton had second thoughts. When he arrived in Edwards from his bridge headquarters, he received scouting reports that indicated a full Union division would threaten his right flank if he moved toward Clinton. Also, the more he thought about attacking the Federals, the less he liked the idea. He would be outnumbered, and if he lost, he might not be able to get back to Vicksburg. Anyway, if there was indeed a Yankee division south of the railroad, he might be attacked in flank and rear before he ever got to Clinton. Then certainly Vicksburg would be doomed. The town must be held, Davis had said. Street by street, house by house, Lee had said. So John Pemberton called a council of war. He made clear "that the leading and great duty" of his army "was to defend Vicksburg." He expected defeat if the army moved forward, he said; but he quickly learned that most of his officers wanted to fight. Pemberton, perhaps fearing that he could not keep a "hold upon the army," as one of his staff officers said later, caved in to the majority opinion to take the offensive.[36]

Pemberton's postcampaign report stated that a majority of his officers voted to do as Johnston had suggested. Two generals, Stevenson and Loring, preferred moving southeast to attack the enemy supply line. Other accounts of the meeting disagree as to how the vote went; one said that only two officers supported Johnston's idea. Though Pemberton had had thoughts similar to Loring's and Stevenson's, he later recalled: "My own views were strongly expressed as unfavorable to any advance which would separate me further from Vicksburg, which was my base. I did not however, see fit to put my own judgment and opinions so far in opposition as to prevent a movement altogether, but believing the only possibility of success to be in the plan of cutting the enemy's communications, it was adopted." Pemberton never made a clearer statement of his loss of confidence in himself. Davis had certainly not helped by sending Johnston to take charge, something Johnston never did or had any desire to do. Contrary to Grant's claim that he abandoned his supply line when he marched inland, the Federal army did indeed have a long supply line of generously loaded wagons coming up from a well-stocked base at Grand Gulf.[37] The Confederate plan to attack the supply line was viable, but Pemberton had waited too long.

Despite its validity, Pemberton's decision to move where he did was a strange one that could have been made only by a defeated and disheartened general. His action proved a Napoleonic maxim which warned that councils of war inevitably led to commanders taking the most timid course available. Johnston later expressed astonishment that Pemberton had "determined to execute a measure which he disapproved, which his council of war opposed, and which was in violation of the orders of his commander." Johnston had decided by the time he wrote those words that his message was an order that gave Pemberton no leeway. Pemberton's chief engineer summed up his commander's dilemma: "He . . . made the capital mistake of trying to harmonize instructions from his superiors [that were] diametrically opposed to each other [Johnston and Davis], and at the same time to bring them into accord with his own judgment, which was adverse to the plans of both."[38] Actually, Pemberton's wishes were not in conflict with Davis's except that Pemberton had been willing to give up Port Hudson to save Vicksburg. The council of war did point out one certainty; Pemberton no longer had the will to do what he thought was best.

Johnston had trouble understanding his subordinate's decision because he never understood that to Pemberton saving Vicksburg was the highest priority. Johnston cared nothing for Vicksburg if it meant losing an army. Pemberton had once felt the same way about Charleston, but Lee and Davis had changed his mind, and his strategic thinking had been muddled ever since. So the decision to move southeast from the Big Black made perfect sense to Pemberton. If he had to move, he would move in the direction of least danger, where he could, if necessary, get back to Vicksburg quickly. Moving in the direction he chose would allow him to attack the alleged Union division if it should materialize. Then Vicksburg would be more secure. If the division was not there, the Confederates could disrupt Grant's supply line and return to the Big Black to block Grant's advance from Jackson. The march toward Raymond was the only offensive John Pemberton could take and still protect Vicksburg. It was the only plan he found palatable. He did not know that when he ordered his army forward, he was setting in motion events that would cost him both his army and Vicksburg.

After the council broke up, Pemberton sent a wire at 5:40 P.M., May 14, to Johnston in Jackson. He said his army would march on May 15 toward Dillon's plantation, on the Raymond–Port Gibson road. "The object," he wrote, "is to cut enemy's communications and to force him to attack me, as I do not consider my force sufficient to justify an attack on enemy in position or to attempt to cut my way to Jackson. At this point, your nearest communication would be through Raymond. I wish very much I could join my reinforcements [at Jackson]." How he thought that could be achieved with Grant's army in the way he did not say.[39]

Johnston had been defeated at Jackson over two and a half hours before Pemberton sent his 5:40 message. By the time he learned of Pemberton's plans, Johnston had ordered the evacuation of the city. He wired Pemberton: "Our being compelled to evacuate Jackson renders your plan impracticable. Therefore, move in the direction of Clinton, and communicate with me, that I may unite with you with about 6,000 troops." At the time, Johnston was retreating toward Canton to the northeast of Jackson, making his own plan impracticable. He should have been moving northwest. By marching to the northeast, Johnston was increasing the time it would take to effect a junction with Pemberton. Grant's task would be easier because he was facing two generals with poor senses of direction.[40]

Despite his May 13 message, the fight at Jackson had demonstrated that Johnston was no more anxious than Pemberton to engage Grant. He had hardly fought at all, leaving so quickly that reinforcements en route to Jackson were cut off from his small army. If he had put up any resistance, there would have been time for those reinforcements to arrive, giving him some ten thousand entrenched troops to face Grant's army on the evening of May 14. If he had managed to hold out for two more days, three thousand additional Confederates would have been on the scene. By stalling Grant, Johnston would have given Pemberton time to come up from Raymond and effect the pincer strategy Johnston had originally envisioned. Such was not to be; Johnston seldom fought if retreat was possible.[41]

At his camp seven miles from Jackson on the night of May 14, Johnston wrote out his thoughts in a message to Pemberton. He hoped that reinforcements on the way to Jackson would halt supplies moving toward the city, which otherwise might fall into enemy hands. Johnston wondered if Grant could still be supplied from the Mississippi; if so, could not Pemberton cut the line and beat Grant? Johnston later conveniently forgot his advocacy of this idea when criticizing Pemberton's decision to move toward Raymond. Johnston still envisioned a concentration of Confederate forces but advised Pemberton that he would be moving toward Canton on the fifteenth. Scouting reports said that only half of Grant's army was at Jackson. Therefore, Pemberton should concentrate his army with reinforcements arriving from the east. Like Pemberton, Johnston did not explain how that could be quickly done with the enemy in between. Ultimately it did not matter. By the time Pemberton received Johnston's rambling essay, his defeated army was retreating from Champion Hill.[42]

After wasting an entire day debating which route to take, Pemberton and his officers finally got his army under way on May 15. Heavy rains on the fourteenth had caused delays and would cause more. The army was supposed to move out at 8 A.M., but nobody moved until midafternoon. Soldiers anxious to be off had to wait while John Forney, commanding the Vicksburg defenses, rushed ammunition and wagons eastward to Edwards. The wait for supplies when the army had been concentrated around the Big Black for so long did not reflect favorably on Pemberton's command system. When the army finally advanced down the Raymond Road, its way was blocked by Bakers Creek, flooded by the previous day's rain. Incredibly, scouts had not been sent ahead to check for such problems nor had any pontoons been brought along to bridge a stream that was very likely to have high water after the heavy downpour of May 14. So the march was delayed again; the army had to swing left to a bridge on the Jackson Road, then veer back to the right to strike the Raymond Road.[43]

The advance soon encountered a crossroads where the Jackson Road turned sharply left and continued over high ground known as Champion Hill. The Middle Road continued straight ahead. Loring's lead division turned right onto the Plantation, or Ratliff, Road and advanced southeastward to a house owned by Sarah Ellison. Generals Pemberton, Loring, and their staffs set up headquarters there. The middle division in the marching order, Bowen's, encamped along the Plantation Road while Stevenson's division, bringing up the rear, stopped in the crossroads area.[44]

Up to this point the march had been pretty much a shambles, a clear indication of the lack of field experience of John Pemberton and his staff and perhaps an indication, too, that Pemberton's heart was not in this aspect of the campaign. As long as he had been in the military, he certainly should have been able to avoid some of the fundamental errors that plagued the army's movement. His bureaucratic background could not excuse all his mistakes. Pemberton had ill-used what cavalry he had; cavalry should have been sent ahead to examine the Bakers Creek bridge on the Raymond Road and also to scout the army's front, where significant evidence of a strong enemy presence to the east would have been found. Pemberton finally did order Wirt Adams to picket all roads and to send out scouting parties, something that should have been done before the army left Edwards. Fortunately, Pemberton had experienced, battle-tested veteran subordinates who helped hold things together. Unfortunately, imminent events would show that Pemberton and his generals were not a team.[45]

Early on the morning of May 16, Pemberton received Johnston's message about the evacuation of Jackson. He penciled a reply, giving his army's location and advising that an "order of countermarch has been issued." The countermarch would be toward Brownsville, north of the railroad, then to Clinton. He added an ominous postscript: "Heavy skirmishing is now going on in my front."[46]

Neither Pemberton nor Johnston knew that a Confederate courier, who was actually a Federal agent, had delivered to James McPherson, who passed it along to Grant, a copy of Johnston's May 13 message suggesting that Pemberton move on Clinton. Grant learned of this intelligence on May 14 after his victory at Jackson. He determined to hit Pemberton before Johnston could effect a concentration. On May 15, Grant set his army in motion. The Federals converged seven divisions, some thirty-two thousand men, toward Edwards. Grant's troops moved along the Jackson, Middle, and Raymond roads. By the morning of the sixteenth, the Yankees were nearly in position to strike Pemberton's line all along its front.[47]

Pemberton had just given the order for a retrograde movement when Federal artillery opened on Loring's advance elements down the Raymond Road. At first Pemberton tried to continue the counter-march, going on the assumption that the cannon were merely evidence of a reconnaissance in force. The intensity of the shelling soon convinced him otherwise, and he agreed with Loring that he had to form a line of battle.[48]

Though his experienced field commanders had warned him that signs indicated the close proximity of the enemy, Pemberton was taken completely by surprise when Grant attacked. A Confederate ordnance officer noticed that Pemberton "looked as if he was confused—and he gave orders in that uncertain manner that implied to me that he had no *matured* plans for the coming battle." A Mississippi infantryman agreed: "It was evident from his movements he had no plan for battle."[49] But he could hardly have been expected to plan for the totally unexpected. An experienced field commander, the kind of general Davis should have sent to Mississippi, would have been better equipped to meet such an emergency.

Dissension among commanders did not help the situation. The day had started with sharp words between Pemberton and Loring. As orders were being given to march back to Edwards, Loring had denied that certain information had been given him the previous night. Pemberton had told him that this was not so and that Loring knew it. "Their manner was warm," an observer later recalled. Their relationship had been warm for some months. Loring was frequently vocal about his dislike of Pemberton, at one point remarking that he "would be willing for Pemberton to lose a battle provided that he would be displaced." Loring and his generals, including Lloyd Tilghman, were overheard the morning of May 16 saying "harsh, ill-natured things" about Pemberton and ridiculing his plans and orders. Such was the atmosphere on the Confederate right flank as the decisive battle of Champion Hill opened in earnest.[50]

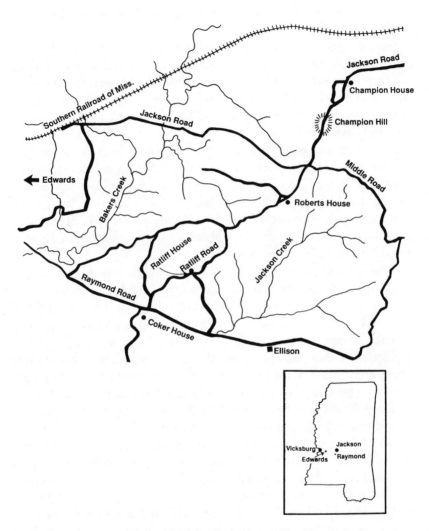

Champion Hill Battlefield

Though shaken, John Pemberton felt optimistic about his defensive line, "a naturally strong one." Yet without proper intelligence of the enemy's strength and location, he was fighting as blindly as when he had marched to the battlefield. At 9 A.M. he established his field headquarters at the Isaac Roberts house, several hundred yards south of the crossroads, just to the left of the midpoint of his three-mile battle line.[51]

From 8:30 to 10:30 A.M. the battle was a process of the opponents gradually making contact. John McClernand's corps advanced along the Raymond and Middle roads. McClernand had been ordered to go slow, and he did. Meanwhile, McPherson's corps was massing on Pemberton's left, which was manned by Stevenson's lone and largely untested division.[52]

Stevenson had by far the largest Confederate division on the battlefield, some 11,700 men, but many of his troops did not fight well when the Federal attack came about 11:15. One Rebel soldier described the Alabamians and Georgians in the division as "very ignorant men" in poor physical condition. Whatever the case, Stevenson's lines were swept back, and after about an hour's fighting his division was decimated with casualties.[53]

When the assault on the left came, Pemberton had been on the right trying to get Bowen and Loring to attack the slow-moving Yankees in their front. Bowen had been willing, but Loring, who had retreated to the area of the Coker House on Raymond Road, insisted that the enemy was too strong to risk an all-out assault. Their two divisions together did not equal Stevenson's in numbers; Bowen had 4,600 and Loring 6,300. Perhaps Loring was justified in being cautious, but his caution would be costly before the day ended.[54]

When Pemberton first learned of the assault on his left, he procrastinated until Stevenson was almost flanked. When he realized the extent of damage, he sent urgent calls for help to Bowen and Loring. He also ordered regiments forward that had been guarding the wagon train and acting as a rear guard in the Edwards area. These men would arrive too late to be of much use to Stevenson. Bowen and Loring both hesitated at first. Bowen finally said he would send men if Loring would agree to help cover the movement by watching the Federal presence in Bowen's front. Loring, as he would do most of the day, refused to help at all. Pemberton became so unnerved and agitated by the delays that an aide had to help him mount his horse. But he did act aggressively, ordering one of Bowen's brigades to hurry to the left. He then changed his mind and sent the brigade to the crossroads, where a gap had opened between Stevenson's right and Bowen's left. A Missouri soldier noticed Pemberton's "excited" manner as Bowen's men marched past and cheered the general. The men were just as cheered by the presence of a group of women in the yard of the Roberts family home, cheering and singing "Dixie." What these women were doing standing out in the open in the midst of a fierce battle has never been determined.[55]

Bowen was soon on hand with more of his men, and he ordered a charge that cleared the crossroads of Yankees. Stephen D. Lee's brigade from Stevenson's division joined the assault as cheering Confederates drove the enemy over the crest of Champion Hill. By 3:15 Bowen had made a deep penetration in Grant's center. Grant ordered reinforcements from his fresh reserves into the breach, and after more hard fighting, Bowen grudgingly retreated.[56]

All the while, Loring ignored calls to rush reinforcements to take advantage of Bowen's initial success. Finally he moved, but he took a little-known road that made it difficult for Pemberton's staff to locate him. Perhaps Loring sensed that he was in a position to make sure that Pemberton did lose a battle. Furious, Pemberton personally rode in search of his cantankerous subordinate. Not until the pressure on Bowen and Stevenson forced a general retreat about 5 P.M. did Loring arrive in the Champion Hill area. In his official report, Pemberton concluded, "Had the movement in support of the left been promptly made when first ordered, it is not improbable that I might have maintained my position, and it is possible the enemy might have been driven back, though his vastly superior and constantly increasing numbers would have rendered it necessary to save my communications with Vicksburg."[57] Of course, he neglected to mention that he did not make effective use of all the forces available to him. His assertion of vastly superior enemy numbers was not totally accurate; Grant had merely done a better job with what he had.

The Confederates retreated across Bakers Creek on the Raymond Road. The ford was shallow now, and engineers had thrown up a bridge. Pemberton at one point was confused about the retreat, wanting to know "where in hell" ordnance wagons were going. When informed that the enemy in Stevenson's rear made the Raymond Road route necessary for escape, Pemberton rode off with his staff. At other times he was seen riding alone, his staff apparently scattered about trying to hold the army together. Little wonder that one dejected Confederate commented: "Today proved to the army and the country, the value of a general[.] Pemberton is either a traitor or the most incompetent officer in the Confederacy. *Indecision, Indecision, Indecision.*"58

Pemberton was neither of those negatives; he simply was an officer who had been given the wrong command. Worse, his first time leading a large army in battle had been under circumstances that would have tested the most able of field generals. It had been a surprise battle, the most difficult kind for a novice. Exacerbating the situation was the lack of help from his division commanders. Only Bowen had fought well. Loring had refused to cooperate, and Stevenson had offered little leadership to his beleaguered division. In fact, Stevenson's activities during the battle, other than calls for help, remain largely a mystery.59

Whatever the unfortunate circumstances, it was certain that Jefferson Davis and the Confederacy were paying a high price for an unfortunate appointment. The results at Champion Hill sealed the fate of Vicksburg, though not necessarily of Pemberton's army. The army could have escaped, but the loss of Vicksburg gave the Federals unlimited control of the Mississippi and severed the Trans-Mississippi from the rest of the Confederacy. Davis and the War Department had gambled on Pemberton at a time when they were well aware of the odds. Now the results were in, and the situation could not be recovered.

Pemberton had lost some 3,800 killed, wounded, and missing. Among the dead was his former friend Lloyd Tilghman, killed instantly by a shell fragment along the Raymond Road. He also lost Loring's division, which got separated, then cut off from the retreating main body of the army. By a circuitous route, Loring managed to get his men away from danger. Eventually they joined Joe Johnston.60

The rest of Pemberton's demoralized force limped back to the Big Black bridge. There the general hurriedly wrote Johnston of the defeat at Champion Hill, informed him that he had about sixty days' provisions in Vicksburg, and asked for instructions. Johnston replied that Pemberton must not get trapped in Vicksburg; "Instead of losing both troops and place . . . save the troops. If it is not too late, evacuate Vicksburg and its dependencies, and march to the northeast."61

Johnston's advice was written on May 17, the day Pemberton suffered another shattering defeat, this time at the Big Black bridge, where he had stopped in the hope Loring would appear. He put a line of men and artillery on the high bluffs west of the river but left Bowen on the east side to protect the bridgehead until Loring could get safely across. Bowen recognized that his position was tenuous at best, but Pemberton seemed more worried about being flanked by the Yankees than about the thinly held lines in his front.[62]

On the seventeenth Grant's energized troops overwhelmed Bowen, crushing his flanks and causing a disorderly retreat of Confederates who got across the Big Black to safety as best they could. Deployed on flat ground, Bowen's battle-weary troops could not hold back the Yankee legions. Pemberton could be criticized for leaving Bowen in such an exposed position. Yet he had no way of knowing that Loring had turned back toward Jackson, and he had done a good job deploying troops to watch the north and south flanks on the west side of the Big Black. These troops could now help cover the retreat. Few were convinced that Pemberton was capable of doing anything good after the Big Black debacle. One soldier characterized the general "as helpless and undecided as a child." But Pemberton was decided enough to have his engineers burn the bridge and a boat that had been used as a bridge. The inferno helped buy time to allow the Confederates to escape.[63]

Pemberton's soldiers, disgruntled as they were, were no doubt guilty of exaggeration in describing his state of mind and his performance at the Big Black. Yet he certainly had been stunned by what had happened. His spirits had been shattered, and he was in somewhat of a daze as he rode westward to Bovina, where he would entrain for Vicksburg. He could have marched his army north-northeast and ordered the evacuation of Vicksburg, but the thought of saving his men at the expense of losing the city never entered his mind. As he mourned what he feared was the disgraceful end to his military career, his chief engineer, Samuel Lockett, tried to provide encouragement. Fresh troops waited in Vicksburg, and President Davis had ordered him to hold Vicksburg and had promised relief if the army were besieged. Pemberton responded that Lockett's "youth and hope were the parents of . . . [his] judgment." Lockett later wrote that Pemberton did not believe "our troops could stand the first shock of an attack."[64]

Upon reaching Vicksburg, Pemberton sent a message to Johnston detailing the Big Black disaster. "The army has fallen back to the line of entrenchments around Vicksburg." The works to the north at

Snyder's Bluff were being abandoned. He had lost contact with Loring, and most of Bowen's artillery had been lost at the Big Black. He concluded with a sentence that infuriated Johnston and fueled the postsiege and postwar dispute over responsibility for the lost campaign: "I greatly regret that I felt compelled to make the advance beyond the Big Black, which has proved so disastrous in its results."[65] His defensiveness ignored the words that had given him an option: "if practicable." He believed, however, that if Johnston had never written the May 13 message, he would not have felt the need to point a finger at someone. Such had always been this way. He had always freely admitted that he found it difficult to fault himself.

On May 18, Pemberton received Johnston's order to abandon Vicksburg. "The evacuation of Vicksburg!" he later wrote. "It meant the loss of valuable stores and munitions of war collected for its defense; the fall of Port Hudson; the surrender of the Mississippi River, and the severance of the Confederacy." He turned once more to a council of war and received a unanimous vote that "it was impossible to withdraw the army from this position with such *morale* and materiel as to be of further service to the Confederacy." While he and his generals discussed their situation, Grant's guns opened on the outer works of Vicksburg. "I have decided to hold Vicksburg as long as possible," he wrote Johnston, "with the firm hope that the Government may yet be able to assist me in keeping this obstruction to the enemy's free navigation of the Mississippi River. I still conceive it to be the most important point in the Confederacy."[66] He had forged all his Mississippi strategy on saving Vicksburg. Could he save it now, or would he lose both the city and his army?

CHAPTER 9

The Saddest Fate

Siege, Surrender, New Duties

Pulling a demoralized army together severely taxed John Pemberton's organizational skills. A Missourian arriving in Vicksburg "found the streets . . . thronged with stragglers, and several hundred slightly wounded men seeking food and hospitalization. There were no sentries, no order. Along in the early afternoon the army came drifting in, footsore, tired, hungry, and dispirited." There had been little order on the march from the Big Black, and many troops cursed Pemberton, saying they would rather desert than serve under him. Some shrieked that their defeats were "all Pem's fault" and accused him of selling Vicksburg. Disgusted Vicksburg women scolded the men telling them that it was their fault for not fighting harder.[1]

Emma Balfour, wife of a Vicksburg physician, noted in her diary, "From twelve o'clock until late in the night the streets and roads were *jammed* with wagons, cannons, horses, men, mules, stock, sheep, everything you can imagine that appertains to an army—being brought hurriedly within the entrenchment." "Nothing like order prevailed," she observed. There was little chance for order at first because most soldiers were convinced that Pemberton had betrayed the army and surrender was imminent. "So firm was this conviction that numbers doffed their dust-begrimed garments and donned their holiday apparel in anticipation of speedy capture." A worried John Bowen sent a message to Pemberton: "I find that the wildest and most absurd rumors are in existence, not only among the men, but the officers of the command." Federal prisoners, perhaps following prearranged instructions, told the Confederates that Grant and Pemberton had an understanding that Vicksburg would be surrendered on May 20. Bowen suggested that Pemberton issue an order stating that all his officers supported him in a "determination not to evacuate or surrender but to hold the place to the bitter end."[2]

Would that be enough to repair morale and convince the soldiers that Pemberton would not surrender without a fight? The storm of criticism continued unabated for several days. Everyone heaped blame on Pemberton, "for whom no language could be too strong. He was freely called a coward and a traitor." His Yankee nativity "was against him in the opinion of all here." Emma Balfour concluded, "Gen. Pemberton has not the confidence of officers, people or men judging from all I am compelled to see and hear."[3]

Recovering his composure somewhat, Pemberton decided to take Bowen's advice. He proclaimed to the army: "You have heard that I was incompetent, and a traitor; and that it was my intention to sell Vicksburg. Follow me, and you will see the cost at which I will sell Vicksburg. When the last pound of beef, bacon, and flour, the last grain of corn, the last cow and hog and horse and dog shall have been consumed, and the last man shall have perished in the trenches, then, and only then will I sell Vicksburg."[4]

His words indicated that Pemberton had regained a fighting spirit that had nearly been destroyed at Champion Hill and the Big Black. The criticism seemed to have struck a prideful nerve and made him determined to show doubters that he was not whipped yet. While still at Bovina, Samuel Lockett had helped him focus on the future by urging that an order be sent to Generals John Forney and Martin L. Smith in Vicksburg "to put the place in a good state of defense." There was no time for dwelling on past disasters. Lockett knew that despite all the work that had been done building Vicksburg's defenses, there was much yet to do. No doubt the words of an acquaintance were on his mind: "After the Lord of Creation had made all the big mountains and ranges of hills, he had left on his hands a large lot of scraps; these were all dumped at Vicksburg in a waste heap."[5]

Pemberton had written the order and Lockett had delivered it. Men worked feverishly shoring up works weakened by winter rains, mounting guns moved from the riverfront to the rear defensive line, and felling trees and throwing out entangled telegraph wire to hold back Grant's invasion. The activity helped morale, perhaps convincing some of the disheartened that so much work would not be necessary if their general had really sold Vicksburg. The men filed into the trenches and toiled hour after hour. Carter Stevenson's division occupied the right of the Confederate Line, Forney's the center, and Smith's the left. Grant's attack was not expected to hit Stevenson's battle-fatigued division. Forney's and Smith's soldiers were fresh and should be ready to fight. Bowen's division and Colonel Thomas Waul's Texas Legion were held in reserve in the rear. The defensive line formed an irregular arc facing Grant's approach from the east. Main roads from that direction approached the Confederate left and center. The Confederate commanders correctly reasoned that these would be the most likely avenues of Grant's attack.[6]

On May 19, while his men continued their digging, John Pemberton sent a report to Jefferson Davis. His words made clear his belief that recent disasters should be laid at the feet of Joe Johnston. "Against my own judgment," he wrote, "but by instructions from superior authority, sustained by the unanimous [sic] voice of my general officers, I felt myself compelled to advance my position beyond Edwards Depot, and to offer or accept battle according to circumstances." Citing the results at Champion Hill and the Big Black, Pemberton informed Davis that his men were now in the Vicksburg trenches awaiting attack. "Our men have considerably recovered their *morale,*" he concluded, "but unless a large force is sent at once to relieve it, Vicksburg must before long fall. I have used every effort to prevent all this, but in vain."[7] The tone of the report was predictable. He was not at fault; Johnston was to blame, and even his own officers had erred in prodding him to advance. John Pemberton against the world; the refrain was familiar.

Though pessimistic in his report, Pemberton continued to work the men and his staff in preparation for Grant's visit. He warned officers to be ready for an attack and ordered Wirt Adams and his cavalry to move out and harass the Federal flanks and rear. Grant's first assault came in the early afternoon of May 19. Safe behind formidable earthworks, Pemberton's army vented its frustrations on the Yankees. As

Siege of Vicksburg

expected, the heaviest attacks came against Forney and Smith, and
the Confederates gained revenge for the past several days by throwing
back their rivals while inflicting some 950 casualties. Pemberton lost
only about 200.[8]

Next day, May 20, Pemberton sent word by courier to Joe Johnston
detailing the repulse of Grant. "At this hour, 8:30 A.M.," he said, the
enemy "is briskly cannonading with long-range guns. That we may
save ammunition, his fire is rarely returned. At present our main
necessity is musket caps. Can you send them to me by hands of
couriers or citizens? An army will be necessary to relieve Vicksburg,
and that quickly. Will it not be sent? Please let me hear from you, if
possible."[9]

Receiving no answer, Pemberton fired off four more messages to
Johnston on May 21. "The enemy kept up incessant sharpshooting all
yesterday," he reported. "The great question is ammunition. The men
credit, and are encouraged by, a report that you are near with a large
force." "Brisk musketry and artillery fire to-day on center." "Incessant
mortar fire from the river." "Our men have replied rarely. Two large
transports came down loaded with troops. They are evidently reen-
forcing their present large force."[10]

Still there was no response from Johnston, and shot and shell continued to pound Vicksburg. On May 22, Grant tried another, more general assault. This time he suffered 3,200 casualties, the Confederates less than 500. In his postsiege report, Pemberton deferred to General Smith's terse summary of action on the Confederate left-center. The first Federal charge "was immediately driven back." The second was "dispersed without great effort and with considerable loss" to the enemy. A third "was promptly repulsed with heavy loss."[11]

Confederate morale soared as the Union army recoiled from its bloody losses, and Grant was convinced that siege, not assault, would be necessary to reduce Vicksburg. One Rebel had previously heard a Missourian declare that if Pemberton surrendered, "his life would pay the forfeit." After Grant was repulsed, the same soldier wrote, "Even the strong prejudices against Pemberton began to soften down." Another Missourian commented in his memoirs that Pemberton's critics had judged him wrongly: "He was incapable of harboring a thought of treason; he may not have been an able commander, but he was brave and true, and they soon found that he would surrender to nothing but starvation."[12]

Pemberton needed local encouragement; he was getting little from Richmond. By courier from Johnston and Loring he finally received a message from Davis. "I made every effort to reenforce you promptly," the president claimed, "which I am grieved was not successful. Hope that General Johnston will join you with enough force to break up the investment and defeat the enemy. Sympathizing with you for the reverses sustained, I pray God may yet give success to you and the brave troops under your command."[13]

Davis offered only encouraging words and sympathy. From Johnston came promises of 200,000 firing caps and aid as soon as a division from Bragg arrived. From the Yankees came storms of iron and lead that drove Vicksburg citizens to seek shelter in caves. Johnston asked Pemberton about the best approach route to Vicksburg, locations of Grant's troops, and the strength of Pemberton's army. Pemberton responded that he had received 38,000 caps and had only about 18,000 men in the trenches. (Actually, he had about 29,500 men, but this total included sick and wounded. Still, he had more than 18,000 fighting men available.) The 200,000 caps had been intercepted by the Yankees. Grant's noose around Vicksburg was tightening. Pemberton urged Johnston to move with 30,000 to 35,000 men toward

Snyder's Bluff behind Grant's right flank. "You may depend on my holding the place as long as possible," he assured.[14]

On May 25, three days after Grant's second assault, Pemberton corresponded with his old Mexican War acquaintance. Summer heat was having a horrible effect on Union dead between the lines, and Pemberton, "in the name of humanity," suggested to Grant "a cessation of hostilities for two hours and a half" so that Federals could remove their dead and severely wounded. Grant agreed, and at 6 P.M. burying parties began recovering decomposing bodies.[15]

The battle lines were comparatively quiet for some time afterward until a fight erupted between Confederate batteries and Federal gunboats. Pemberton's artillerymen fought well, crippling the ironclad *Cincinnati*. A Rebel detachment later managed to set the craft on fire, and, though the Federals eventually salvaged the vessel and put it back in service, Pemberton took "great pleasure in presenting them with the flag captured on the occasion."[16]

As the siege progressed, Pemberton's army enjoyed less success and Vicksburg and its citizens increasingly suffered. Noncombatants learned to walk down the middle of streets so they would have a better view of incoming shells. They felt safe once the missile passed overhead; when it exploded, fragments usually fell forward. Streets were often no more dangerous than caves; solid shot and unexploded shells sometimes burrowed into the ground, causing cave-ins. Yet when cannon boomed, sending a heavy shower of screaming projectiles over the city, people instinctively fled for cover, especially into the caves. The shells intimidated civilians and experienced soldiers alike; John Pemberton was once observed crawling out of a cavern after a Federal barrage.[17]

Citizens and soldiers endured. During lulls in the shelling, Vicksburg miraculously came to life. Pedestrians enjoyed unfettered walks in the sunlight, visited, shopped, and acted as if the siege did not exist. Some collected spent bullets, shell fragments, unexploded shells, and other relics of war. Water was in short supply and sometimes could be found only in ditches and mud holes. Battle lulls also allowed cooks to do their work outside caves without having to be concerned about dodging missiles. When the cannons boomed again, Vicksburg once more turned into a ghost town.[18]

On May 29, the booming was especially loud, shells "seriously damaging many buildings, killing and wounding a large number of soldiers and citizens." Houses converted to hospitals were occasionally hit, rewounding the wounded and wounding the sick. Toward the end of May rations were cut by one-half. To help sustain morale, Pemberton impressed chewing tobacco, ordering it distributed along the trenches. "This had a very beneficial influence," he later noted.[19]

Pemberton suffered privations along with the rest, but he did not have to worry about Pattie and the children. When Grant moved inland, she had packed up her brood and traveled to Alabama, where they would be safe behind Bragg's lines. Letters from friends in the Jackson area assured her that her husband had come through the campaign unscathed. She wrote Samuel Lockett's wife of her hope that there would come a day when the South would realize that its interests had not suffered at the hands of General Pemberton. At least the president had stood by him, and "*his* approval I value beyond all others."[20]

Emma Balfour probably helped fill the void caused by Pattie's absence. The Balfours lived next door to Pemberton's headquarters. She frequently had opportunities for social contact with the general, and a warm friendship developed. Emma was outspoken and blunt and seemed to say what he needed to hear. To her diary, she confided, "I had laughed at Gen. Pemberton the other day for being gloomy and told him the ladies were not despondent, so he told Col. Higgins to tell me he thought things looked brighter now." The Balfours held a lunch to celebrate news of Johnston's alleged march to relieve the city in late May. Pemberton and his staff attended and there was much merrymaking. Of course, the news was false, and the very next day heavy cannonading caused chaos, even among the general and his aides. Such incidents wore on Pemberton. "I think he is inclined to be rather despondent," Emma Balfour recorded, "and very persistent hopefulness cheers him. I hear I am a great favorite with him."[21] No doubt she was right, for her upbeat, strong voice was similar to Pattie's.

Time dragged on, and the siege conditions worsened. Federal reinforcements continued to arrive, artillery barrages made life miserable within Confederate lines, and food rations were cut further. On June 7, Pemberton complained in a note to Johnston that he had heard nothing from the outside since May 29. Couriers were sent out daily but were having more and more difficulty getting through the lines. The men were "still in good spirits." "When may I expect you to move," he queried, "and in what direction? My subsistence may be put down for about twenty days." Johnston responded that he was about ready to move, but he did not know the best route. Cooperation was necessary, and more information was needed regarding the best approach to the city. Obviously Johnston had not received Pemberton's note that included advice to move on Snyder's Bluff. And Pemberton never received Johnston's reply to his June 7 communication. [22]

With no word from Johnston and facing a deteriorating situation, Pemberton sent yet another message on June 10. "The enemy bombards the city day and night from seven mortars on opposite side of peninsula." Artillery and sharpshooters also kept up a constant harassment. Losses were mounting. "I am waiting most anxiously to know your intentions. . . . Can you not send me a verbal message by courier, crossing the river above or below, and swimming across opposite Vicksburg?" On June 12, he sent essentially the same message, adding that he had received more firing caps. [23]

While Pemberton waited, his meat supply dwindled. He ordered Stevenson to impress all available cattle within the Confederate lines. Rice and flour and bred rations were reduced to four ounces per person. At least the caps were getting in; 200,000 more arrived from Jackson via Steele's Bayou. But the men could not eat caps. [24]

Nevertheless, it was good news at a time when any news was rare, and Pemberton so informed Johnston. He also let his procrastinating superior know that more Federal troops were reportedly landing in the area. Too, on the Graveyard Road that penetrated his left-center, Federal sappers had advanced to within twenty-five yards of the outer Rebel works. If Johnston continued to wait, the Federals would have such overwhelming strength that the Confederate lines would begin to give way. Pemberton rightly expected Grant to order his entrenchments mined. Johnston must move at once and let him know how he could best cooperate. [25]

The next day, June 15, additional heavy guns pounded Confederate works and sappers edged ever closer. "Our men have no relief; are becoming much fatigued, but are still in pretty good spirits. I think your movement should be made as soon as possible," he pleaded to Johnston. Though rations were reduced again and again, there seemed to be enough for perhaps twenty more days. Four days later came the "heaviest fire we have yet sustained." The Federals had approached to within twenty-five feet of the powerful Confederate Stockade Redan guarding Graveyard Road. At the center, the Yankees were also moving close to the Third Louisiana Redan and the Great Redoubt, works that blocked the Jackson Road. Fortifications on the Baldwin's Ferry Road were also threatened. Pemberton begged Johnston to advance quickly. "What aid am I to expect from you?"?[26]

Pemberton soon learned that he could expect no aid. On June 20, he received two messages from Johnston. One dated June 14 said all that could be done was to try to save the Vicksburg garrison. "To do this, exact cooperation is indispensable," Johnston said. "By fighting the enemy simultaneously at the same point of his line, you may be extricated. Our joint forces cannot raise the siege of Vicksburg." The other message was more pointed: "I am too weak to save Vicksburg; can do no more than attempt to save you and your garrison." Johnston urged Pemberton to "communicate your plans and suggestions if possible."[27]

The truth was that Johnston never had any intention of trying to save Vicksburg or its defenders. As usual when a bold, offensive maneuver was necessary, Johnston found every excuse not to move. He complained to Richmond that he had too few men and that to draw reinforcements from Tennessee might cause the loss of that state. The government, not Joe Johnston, would have to make the decision to take such a risk. Yet if he tried to save Port Hudson, Mississippi would have to be abandoned. His assignment to the Mississippi command tied his hands; he could not order troops from Tennessee. Jefferson Davis would later bitterly reject Johnston's latter claim, demonstrating forcefully, with evidence, that Johnston's coming to Mississippi had not affected his authority over Bragg.[28] Johnston had never had any enthusiasm for the challenge he faced in Mississippi. John Pemberton, his army, and Vicksburg would have fared no worse if Johnston had remained in Tennessee.

Although Johnston did nothing but point out why he could do nothing, Pemberton composed a reply to his superior's most recent messages on June 21 suggesting that the relief army move north of the Southern Railroad. While Johnston thus gained Grant's attention, the besieged Confederates would try to escape via Warrenton Road and

Hankinson's Ferry to the south and southeast of Vicksburg. "I await your orders," Pemberton concluded.[29]

On the surface this seemed a feasible plan. The Federals were weakest on the Confederate right. Yet even if the Confederates could break through the Union lines in that sector, escape would be difficult, if not impossible. If the Rebels moved south, they would be flanked on the west by the Mississippi and on the east by the Big Black. Thus they would be vulnerable to attacks by Union gunboats on either side. Speed would be essential; the Confederates would have to travel light, without benefit of artillery to defend themselves. The men were fatigued from weeks in the trenches, and Grant was not likely to be diverted enough by Johnston to let Pemberton and his army escape untouched. It was a plan born of desperation and very unlikely to succeed.[30]

On June 22, the day after Pemberton wrote his proposal, Johnston received his messages of June 14 and 15. He responded that Richard Taylor had been ordered by Kirby Smith to assist from the Mississippi's west bank. Taylor would bring supplies and cross over to Vicksburg "if expedient and practicable." Otherwise, Johnston stated, he would be ready to move in "a day or two" and try to make a meaningful diversion.[31]

On June 23, Pemberton, undoubtedly sensing that help was not coming soon or ever, proposed that Johnston contact Grant and convince him that the Vicksburg garrison could hold out a good deal longer and that Johnston himself was gaining strength daily. Grant just might be willing to let the trapped Confederates go in exchange for the city. "If I cut my way out, this important position is lost, and many of my men, too. Can we afford that? If I cannot cut my way out, both position and all my men are lost. This we cannot afford." Finally, though much too late, Pemberton seemed to be recovering from the fog of Lee's admonition and Davis's instructions and was beginning to think in sound strategic terms. But this proposal, even more than the plan to cut through Grant's lines, was totally unrealistic. Grant held all the cards; he had no reason to strike a deal. Pemberton knew as much; perhaps he was just trying to get Johnston to do something. "I will strain every nerve to hold out, if there is hope of our ultimate relief, for fifteen days longer."[32]

On June 25 and July 1, Grant's engineers exploded mines, heavily damaging Confederate works on Jackson Road. In his postsiege report, Pemberton noted, "From this time forward our engineers were kept constantly and busily engaged in countermining against the enemy, who was at work day and night mining on different portions of the line." About the same time, mule meat was issued in place of bacon. "I am gratified to say," Pemberton wrote, "it was found by officers and men not only nutritious, but very palatable, and [in] every way preferable to poor beef."[33]

The use of mule meat was one signal of how low the fortunes of Vicksburg's defenders had sunk; lack of news from Johnston had a similar effect on morale. On June 27, Johnston sent word that Trans-Mississippi troops "had been mismanaged" and forced to retreat. "The determined spirit you manifest," Johnston said, provided encouragement that "something yet may be done to save Vicksburg." Pemberton must conduct negotiations with Grant himself. Johnston correctly pointed out that for him to do so would be an admission of weakness. Pemberton did not receive a copy of the message until August 19, six weeks after he had surrendered. Johnston did not set his army in motion toward Vicksburg until July 1. He wrote a note to Pemberton saying that he hoped to attack by July 7. On July 3, the relief army sat motionless east of the Big Black. On that same day, Pemberton opened surrender negotiations with Grant.[34]

On June 28, Pemberton expressed surprise at the small number of men Johnston reported to be in the relief expedition. (Johnston claimed to have about twenty-three thousand, but the true figure was closer to thirty-one thousand.) He still thought a combined operation might raise the siege but rejected the notion of cooperation with the forces in the Trans-Mississippi. He knew there was little chance that Taylor could get supplies or men across the Mississippi. Though he did not say so, he may have had some inkling that Grant's strength had grown to about eighty thousand men. Having penciled this reply to Johnston's message of June 22, Pemberton had second thoughts and retired the letter to his files. His patience had finally run out.[35]

Pemberton was probably considering surrender when he wrote the message he never sent. That day he had received a letter signed "Many Soldiers"; its origin has never been determined. One historian has speculated that it was dropped into Vicksburg by one of the many kites flown by members of the Union navy. Certainly it sounded like a well-written piece of Yankee propaganda. The letter, supposedly from some of his own men, expressed confidence in the general's leadership and patriotism and pride in the conduct of his army. It complained about reduced rations, suffering in the trenches, and the necessity for immediate relief. "If you can't feed us, you had better surrender us," or witness the soldiers "disgrace themselves by desertion." "This army is ripe for mutiny, unless it can be fed."[36] Pemberton did not comment on the matter, then or ever. Its effect on his thinking can be judged only from his subsequent actions.

On July 1, Pemberton decided to poll his generals on what the trapped Confederates' next move should be. Without Johnston's help and with no immediate hope for smuggling in sufficient supplies, evacuation would soon be essential. In fact, evacuation seemed the only viable option other than surrender. Could the men, he asked their commanders, fight their way out and march to safety?[37]

The gist of the responses was indicated in Carter Stevenson's report: "My men are very cheerful, but from long confinement (more than forty-five days) in the trenches on short rations, are necessarily much enfeebled, and a considerable number would be unable to make the marches and undergo the fatigues which would probably be necessary to a successful evacuation of this city. If pressed by the enemy, and it should be necessary to place the Big Black in our rear in one march, the chances are a large number of them now in the trenches could not succeed." None of the generals had any faith that Johnston would help in time; John Bowen and Martin L. Smith both recommended surrender.[38]

With his commanders unanimously opposed to evacuation, Pemberton penned a note to Grant on July 3. He proposed an armistice "with a view to arranging terms for the capitulation of Vicksburg." Three Confederate commissioners would meet with "a like number, to be named by yourself, at such place and hour to-day as you may find convenient. I make this proposition to save the further effusion of blood, which must otherwise be shed to a frightful extent, feeling myself fully able to maintain my position for a yet indefinite period." Bowen, a friend of Grant's before the war, delivered the communication.

Grant ignored Pemberton's attempted posturing and proposed the terms that had won him fame at Fort Donelson in 1862, "an unconditional surrender of the city and garrison." But, he continued, "Men who have shown so much endurance and courage as those now in Vicksburg will always challenge the respect of an adversary, and I can assure you will be treated with all the respect due to prisoners of war." Grant rejected the idea of commissioners because he considered his terms firm and nonnegotiable.[40]

When Bowen returned to Pemberton's headquarters with Grant's reply, he inferred that Grant wished to meet with Pemberton at 3 P.M. Thinking that perhaps his adversary was not as inflexible as his words indicated, Pemberton agreed to the meeting. Clad in a new uniform, he rode with one of his aides, Louis M. Montgomery, and Bowen to rendezvous with Grant. Upon arriving, he learned to his embarrassment that Grant had not requested the meeting. Bowen, aware that Pemberton would reject Grant's terms, had implied to both commanders that each wished to speak with the other. When Grant reiterated his terms and said they were firm, Pemberton bristled and said the siege would continue. "I can assure you sir," he said to Grant, "you will bury many more of your men before you will enter Vicksburg." He further stated that he had enough provisions "for an indefinite period."[41]

The bluff seemed to work. According to Pemberton's account, Grant suggested that the two step aside and let their respective parties consult on surrender terms. Grant insisted later that this was Bowen's idea. Whatever the case, Grant agreed because he was a pragmatist. He knew that if the Confederates had plenty of food, Pemberton would not have contacted him. Yet the Confederate army was still dangerous, and he would indeed bury more men if he had to fight his way into the city. So while the two commanders chatted about old times in the army, Bowen and Montgomery discussed points of surrender with Union generals Andrew J. Smith and James McPherson.[42]

The officers worked out an agreement, and around 10 P.M. Pemberton received from Grant a written proposal based on the afternoon's negotiations. One Federal division would march into Vicksburg on July 4 at 8 A.M. As soon as the Confederate army was paroled (an arrangement by which captured soldiers agreed not to fight until officially exchanged on a one-to-one basis with prisoners from the opposing army), officers and men would be allowed to leave the city. Officers could retain their "side-arms and clothing, and the field, staff, and cavalry officers one horse each." The rest of the Confederates could retain only their clothing. Rations and cooking utensils from Confederate stores could also be removed, and thirty wagons would be spared for transporting the goods out of Vicksburg. Similar conditions would apply to the Rebel wounded as soon as they were able to travel. The terms were generous, and, though Pemberton was inclined to reject them in an effort to secure even more considerations, his officers voted to accept.[43]

Pemberton finally agreed but proposed that his troops be allowed to march out of the works with colors flying. Arms would be stacked in front of the Confederate lines. Grant's army could then march in and take possession of the works so long beyond its reach. Pemberton also urged that "rights and property of citizens" be respected. Replying early on July 4, Grant said he had no objection to the surrendered troops marching out to stack arms but insisted that they could not leave until paroles were signed. He refused to make any firm promises regarding private citizens and property other than commenting, "I do not propose to cause them any undue annoyance or loss." Tiring of Pemberton's delays, Grant warned that if the proposed terms were not accepted by 9 A.M., he would resume hostilities. Satisfied that he had gotten all the concessions he could, Pemberton accepted and at 10 A.M. formally surrendered his army. With Vicksburg in enemy hands, Franklin Gardner had no choice but to surrender Port Hudson. He did so on July 9.[44]

Though certainly aware that Southern reaction against him would be severe, Pemberton made clear in his report that he had thought ahead to July 4 as his surrender date because he expected to "obtain better terms." His officers concurred in that view, and the strategy appeared to work. Grant had backed away from his original demand for an unconditional surrender. To support his claim that he surrendered to obtain concessions from the enemy, Pemberton pointed out that there were enough supplies left in Vicksburg to keep the garrison going for another week based on rationing formulas in use at the time of capitulation.[45]

Minor victories in the negotiations did little to improve Pemberton's mood, which turned surly in the aftermath of the surrender. He had never accepted personal setbacks gracefully. When, after the formal surrender, Grant and his escort visited the so-called Rock House, north of the Jackson Road and west of the Great Redoubt, they found Pemberton and several of his generals lounging on the porch. The Confederates were not in a hospitable mood, and Grant attempted in vain to engage Pemberton in casual conversation.[46]

Details of the surrender kept Pemberton in Vicksburg for several days. Some 29,500 men were surrendered, including 5,700 hospital patients, so the paperwork was enormous. He refused a suggestion from Martin Smith that Grant be asked about sending Confederates north who refused to accept paroles that required oaths of allegiance to the United States. Pemberton did not think Grant would be impressed with such matters of honor, but he discussed the matter with McPherson, who said that such oaths would not be required. By then it was a moot point. Much of Pemberton's army had left Vicksburg and the men were on their way home. With the rest of his troops disarmed, the forlorn general was powerless to stop them.[47]

Finally, he led the remnants of his force eastward out of the city they had so valiantly defended. On July 12 he notified Johnston that most of the troops, except the disabled, had reached Raymond. "Unless you send me orders to the contrary," he wrote, "I shall move . . . to Brandon [east of Jackson]." Johnston sent orders instructing Pemberton to keep his men well south of the Southern Railroad and Jackson, where Sherman had chased and partially invested Johnston's army. The paroled soldiers were to travel to Enterprise near Meridian and await further instructions. According to a story that is unsupported by documentary evidence, Pemberton reported to Johnston's headquarters as required by the terms of his personal parole. Johnston greeted his subordinate warmly; Pemberton reacted coldly, saluted, and walked away. Certainly he felt betrayed by Johnston; if the incident occurred, it probably happened just as described. Whether Johnston would have welcomed Pemberton warmly is debatable. Johnston had once sworn openly at Pemberton's "stupidity" when he received a dispatch by courier from Vicksburg. Fate had brought the two together under circumstances that could hardly sustain cordial relations.[48]

Setting up temporary headquarters in Brandon before moving on to Enterprise, Pemberton urged Johnston and President Davis to allow his army thirty days' furlough. Davis hesitated, wondering if the demoralized men wanted to "avoid a camp for paroled prisoners" or merely wished to be gone "when [further] service is offered." Pemberton replied that they wanted "to see their families." He had done all he could to prevent it, but of all his force, only sixteen hundred Missourians were willing to stay and go where ordered. Perhaps those hard fighters were making a statement in honor of their revered general, John Bowen, who had died from dysentery on July 13. In any event, Pemberton argued, the only way to keep most of the army in Confederate service was to furlough the men. Davis reluctantly relented and wired Pemberton to "use your discretion." The president still feared that Grant would overwhelm the department if the men were gone for a full thirty days. Of course, it was too late to be concerned about that; the department was already nearly overwhelmed.[49]

While on the march to Enterprise, Pemberton issued a circular granting the furloughs. He urged the men to return to the ranks at the end of thirty days; they were to reassemble at Demopolis, Alabama, where they would receive arms and equipment. Meanwhile, Davis's second thoughts resulted in a new order from Richmond. The government had decided that, "in the present condition of the country," the men could have only ten days' leave. Pemberton had traveled on to Gainesville, Alabama, and from there, using the discretionary power previously given him by Davis, he issued new guidelines that gave Tennesseans thirty days, Georgians twenty, and those from Alabama and Mississippi fifteen. He promised to advise the troops of the new guidelines, but most of them had already gone.[50]

On July 24, Pemberton arrived in Demopolis, where Pattie and the children now resided. Daughter Pattie scarcely recognized her father, so gray and worn had he become from the pressures and privations of the siege. He was also affected by the waves of scorn sweeping down on him as the Yankee who had sold Vicksburg. From friends in Mississippi, Jefferson Davis received warnings that whatever Pemberton's merits as an officer might be, confidence in him had been destroyed. Taking advantage of the situation, one of Johnston's staff officers had already published an account of the campaign which placed the blame for the debacle squarely on Pemberton's shoulders. Davis blasted Johnston for this indiscretion and warned Pemberton to keep the article in mind when writing his own report. "To some men," Davis counseled, "it is given to be commended for what they are expected to do, and to be sheltered when they fail by a transfer of the blame which they may attach; to others it is decreed that their success shall be denied or treated as a necessary result and their failures imputed to incapacity or crime." A court of inquiry would be convened to find the truth.[51]

Pemberton rejoiced at the opportunity to present his side of the story, but the exigencies of war prevented the court from meeting. He had to rely on his official report to state his case, and he stated it extensively and effectively, if not convincingly. Meanwhile, his assistant adjutant at Vicksburg, William H. McCardle, responded to Johnston's officer's article with essays published in a Mobile newspaper. McCardle reiterated the cornerstones of Pemberton's defense: lack of cavalry, orders forcing him to advance beyond the Big Black, and no help from the outside once the siege began. Johnston reacted with a complaint to Richmond, but his protests fell on deaf ears.[52]

During the siege, the *Philadelphia Inquirer* had noted that Pemberton had "all the yelping curs of the Confederacy at his heels, charging him with treachery to their traitorous flag." In the aftermath of the surrender, the *Mobile Advertiser* said that he was the "worst possible selection" to reorganize his paroled army. Among the high-ranking officers who had joined the Confederacy, said the *Inquirer*, "perhaps the saddest fate" had befallen John Pemberton. Having heard a false rumor that Pemberton had been shot in Alabama by a disgruntled Texan, the paper proceeded to analyze the career of the local boy gone bad. He had been known "as a clever and brave officer" but had "rendered himself obnoxious to the old fogies and prudent characters" of the old army "by his arrogance and his severe and sarcastic criticisms." He had a "violent temper and great self-reliance" but was an officer "of good culture, excellent common sense and great bravery." His life in the Confederacy had been turbulent, his "every move scrutinized; every opinion criticized." His death was noted "with sorrow for talent and bravery perverted." Had he lived, he would have "one more glorious opportunity for repentance and amend."[53] Aside from the war propaganda, the paper's analysis was not farfetched and much fairer than any he was likely to get in the Confederacy.

While waiting in Alabama for the court of inquiry that never met, Pemberton hesitated to go out in public. Anonymous faces in the crowd called him a traitor, and he did not wish to subject himself or his family to such heckling. Bill Mackall, his onetime friend from West Point, now a Johnston man and member of Bragg's staff, heard that Pattie "is understood to have said that if she thought he would have no chance to recover that she was ready to kill herself & her children rather than they should grow up to be called the children of a traitor." Mackall thought the outcry against Pemberton "great non-sense" and "rank injustice." The general had done the best he could, but his rapid promotion without reason had caused enmity and envy. Now, noted Mackall, his defenders were few.[54]

Certainly there were none in the Confederate Army of Tennessee. In October 1863, Pemberton, who had been called to Richmond to consult with Davis, accompanied the president on a trip to Bragg's headquarters. Davis had in mind giving Pemberton a corps command in the main western army. The men in the ranks would have none of it. Many said they would desert before they would serve under the traitor Pemberton.

Pemberton made it clear to anyone willing to listen that he would not serve if Johnston was assigned to Bragg's army. As if to make a statement regarding the outcry against him, he showed Mackall a letter of support from Davis. Pemberton also said loudly that if he had the chance to do it over, the only thing he would do differently in the Vicksburg campaign would be to ignore Johnston's orders. He declined an opportunity to speak from a platform that included Davis and Bragg, declaring that he had never made a speech in life. (This would seem to settle the matter of his alleged speech in Brookhaven back in 1862.) A disgusted Mackall, the Johnstonite, said in a letter to his wife, "Has not our Caesar had imperial pap that he has grown so great."[56] Apparently when he spoke of envy, Mackall commented with intimate knowledge of the subject.

John Pemberton returned to Virginia and remained there in limbo into the spring of 1864. Having lost hope of redemption through an official inquiry, he wrote Davis asking for service in the field, "or in any capacity in which you think I may be useful." "You are so thor-oughly acquainted with the circumstances of my position," he con-tinued, "that I need refer neither to them nor to the causes which have brought them about—but I can not help thinking that there is much less prejudice against me now, than there was when you offered me a command (conditionally) in Genl. Bragg's Army." Could not Davis relieve him of the "position of inactivity?"[57]

Davis responded that he still had confidence in his exiled general.

"I thought, and still think," said the president, "that you did right to risk an army for the purpose of keeping command of . . . [a] section of the Mississippi River. Had you succeeded, none would have blamed; had you not made the attempt, few, if any, would have defended your course." Davis's praise was warm, but he considered his hands to be tied. Despite his personal regard for Pemberton, "considerations which I could not control" prevented him from giving the general a new assignment. He had little hope the situation would soon change.[58]

From the town of Boydton, Mecklenburg County, in south-central Virginia, Pemberton composed a remedy to his dilemma on April 19, 1864. In his message to Samuel Cooper, he resigned his lieutenant generalcy and requested assignment as a lieutenant colonel of artillery. He had suggested such a possibility in conversation with Braxton Bragg during his visit with Davis to Bragg's army. Bragg, when asked for his comments on Pemberton's situation, had informed Davis of Pemberton's wishes. So this action was no doubt taken as a result of a prior understanding with Davis and the War Department. This humble act, especially humble given the pride of John Pemberton, quieted some of his critics and gave him what he had always preferred: a command in his beloved Virginia.[59]

For the remainder of 1864, he commanded the Richmond Defense Battalion of Artillery. He drilled his largely inexperienced force and built up artillery positions east of Richmond. He especially concentrated on the Bottoms Bridge area north of the James River as well as Chaffin's Bluff south of Richmond on the James. He consulted with Custis Lee, eldest son of Robert E. Lee, and others to keep defenses viable in assisting General Lee as he fought to keep Pemberton's old nemesis, U. S. Grant, away from Richmond during the bloody 1864 Virginia campaign. Even here Pemberton could not escape controversy. He felt compelled by criticism from unnamed sources at Army of Northern Virginia headquarters to write an extensive defense of his gun emplacements and other work along the Chaffin's Bluff line. He pointed out that there had been considerable problems in the area when he took command, he had done his best to remedy deficiencies, and he had no apologies to make for the results. He argued further that, whatever his "defects of skill, I am not liable to the reproach of indolence or neglect."[60] His words apparently put the matter to rest.

When the center of action in Virginia shifted to Petersburg, Pemberton received a new assignment. In January 1865, he was named general inspector of artillery and ordnance in the armies of the Confederacy. With the Army of Tennessee in shambles after John Bell Hood's Nashville campaign, Pemberton's duties were not as extensive as they might have been earlier in the war. The assignment sent him on journeys that could have resulted in an authoritative, intimate book on dé jà vu. He first traveled to Charleston, where he inspected the artillery defenses of his old department, now commanded by William J. Hardee. His inspection also took him to Fort Sumter, the symbolic structure he had wanted to dismantle. By war's end, the fort would be a shell of its former self, just as he had predicted. He took time to recommend the nomination of his old artillery chief, Ambrosio J. Gonzales, to the rank of brigadier general. Hardee approved, but the war ended before Richmond could make it official.[61]

The tide of war took him to North Carolina in the spring of 1865. Robert E. Lee was about to surrender at Appomattox. Pemberton put together artillery batteries for Joe Johnston, now commanding the remnants of the Army of Tennessee in its final, hopeless campaign against William T. Sherman. During a skirmish against Union General George Stoneman's cavalry near Salisbury, North Carolina, Pemberton watched helplessly as the Yankees captured all his artillery. This brief, final fight ironically took place at a stream called Grant's Creek. Pemberton barely escaped capture.[62]

With Lee out of the war, Johnston about to surrender, and the Confederate government retreating southward, Pemberton tried to join his loyal friend Jefferson Davis. He reached Charlotte the day after the Davis party had moved on into South Carolina. During the hard ride to Charlotte, his horse threw all its shoes. Getting the animal reshod proved impossible in a city in chaos with hordes of surrendered Confederate soldiers passing through. Pemberton gave up the chase and went to Newton, North Carolina, where Pattie and the children were waiting. For John Pemberton, the long Civil War was finally, mercifully over.[63]

Fate and Jefferson Davis had misused a general who could have contributed valuable service to the Confederacy in an administrative capacity. Because he had been given the wrong commands, both Pemberton and the Confederacy suffered. Union naval power and superior numbers would eventually have opened the Mississippi, but perhaps

Pemberton's army would have been saved intact to fight effectively another day. That was history now, nothing could change what had happened, and John Pemberton faced an uncertain future. What would he do now? How would he feed his family? Would his Philadelphia family be willing to reconcile? Did he have a future in the South, and, if so, given the negative feelings about him there, what would it hold? Would he ever be able to escape the shadow of Vicksburg, or would that shadow follow him to his grave?

CHAPTER 10

Not Always to the Strong

Postwar Years

The uncertainty of Pemberton's future was compounded by his having turned his back on Pennsylvania and fought for the Confederacy. His military career was over. The United States Army would not welcome back those who had fought against the Union. The Fourteenth Amendment to the United States Constitution would be adopted in 1868, removing citizenship rights from those Confederates whose positions before the war required oaths of allegiance to the Constitution. Pemberton's options were limited, and those limitations were exacerbated by his perceived status as a traitor to both North and South.

Despite her husband's negative image in the South, Pattie Pemberton's family did not hesitate to help. The Thompsons had also been divided by the war. Pattie's sister Imogene had two sisters-in-law married to Federal naval officers. Imogene's husband had served in the Confederate navy. So Pattie and John could expect, and received, sympathy and material assistance from her relatives.[1]

John's Philadelphia family also came to the rescue. Israel had sympathized with the South and therefore had no ill feelings toward his brother. Rebecca Pemberton had written Israel in August 1864 that she had not forgotten John's birthday. But, she said, "I would not have drank to the prosperity of his *cause,* as you would, because I love my own country & *its* cause." Now all was forgiven; strong antebellum family ties made reconciliation surprisingly easy, especially considering that John's brothers Andrew and Clifford had fought in the Union army.[2]

Rebecca acted quickly on John's behalf, underwriting his purchase of a two-hundred-acre farm in Fauquier County, Virginia, near Warrenton. Israel and Clifford met with their brother early in 1866 to help him with financial planning. The siblings were careful to keep the conference secret; Rebecca warned them that it was too soon for John to be seen in Philadelphia so in a sense they met between the lines.[3]

The former Confederate lieutenant general thus embarked on a farming career. Pemberton's background as an experienced military bureaucrat makes one wonder why he chose farming as a postwar occupation. There are no documented answers, but one logical conclusion is that, probably acting in part on the counsel of Rebecca and his brothers, he decided that he needed low-profile employment. His relatively small farm would allow a degree of anonymity and protect him from public condemnation from either section of the country. The Pemberton country estate and his prewar tours of duty had exposed him to the rudiments of agriculture. Maybe he could support his family until time cooled war passions and opportunities more suited to his talents arose.

Pemberton had the deed to the farm made to Israel, who would hold it in trust for Pattie and the children. Fearing that any obvious association by him with the farm transaction might cause problems, Pemberton left all details to his brothers. Combined with aid from Pattie's family, the Pembertons would get by for a while, living off the land. Eventually, Pemberton would receive his share of family property in Philadelphia, which provided welcome additional income. Though the John Pembertons were never wealthy, the willingness of their families to give support meant that John and Pattie had a much easier time coping with the aftermath of defeat than many Southerners.[4]

Within a year and a half after Appomattox, the Philadelphia Pembertons were visiting their Virginia relatives at Harleigh, John's farm, named by Pattie after some Pemberton ancestral property in Pennsylvania. Rebecca came often, as did Israel, who, at his brother's urging, usually brought a plentiful supply of liquor. Israel and John spent many hours discussing translations of Latin and French; when they were not together they swapped translations by mail. By the early 1870s, Anna and Beck were bringing their youngsters to Virginia for summers at Harleigh. John was more careful, and no doubt frustrated, about visiting his beloved home city. When Anna's husband died in 1872, John followed Israel's advice and did not attend the funeral because his presence might have created an uncomfortable situation for the family.[5]

Rebecca Pemberton, who had played a key role in reuniting her family, died August 17, 1869, having narrowly escaped death during a severe winter illness two years earlier. John spent as much time with her as possible. Perhaps sensing that the end was near, he wrote emotionally to Israel during the summer of 1869, "I yearn to embrace her once more." Rebecca died with the satisfaction of knowing that she had done her part in binding her family's war wounds.[6]

Although he enjoyed being with his Philadelphia family again, Pemberton's most immediate postwar task was to make his farm productive. Despite his relative inexperience, he launched into the agricultural profession with vigor and did tolerably well for a time. With the help of a few black laborers and his sons, he planted grain and dabbled in livestock. Initially farm life seemed to agree with him. A few years after the war, his visiting mother noted, "John looks very hearty & well. . . . I saw him go out in the field this morning with the black man, in his shirt sleeves, & carrying his hoe over his shoulder— his little delicate hands, are now hardened red." At night he was translating Latin and French.[7] His life was a remarkable statement about the fortunes of war. A man who had led thousands in battle and was educated in the classics was now leading a few field hands and experimenting with fertilizer.

Pemberton worked hard and complained bitterly about "the miserable interference of the government in taking away my [black] hands . . . nearly two days . . . off their work for registering" to vote. He cleared land and spread manure in an effort to vitalize poor sections of fields. He took great pride in an "excellent cattle shelter" he built, fifty-two feet long and twelve feet deep, at a cost of seventeen dollars. To Israel he commented, "I don't suppose these matters are very interesting to you, but as I am struggling to do all I can, they and the latin are very principal subjects to think & talk about."[8]

Most farmers periodically experience hard times, and John Pemberton was no exception. Overly wet springs and too dry summers hampered production. Labor problems plagued him as they had during the war. He was disgusted by two black hands who refused to work during a light rain while other farmers all around were getting their fields plowed. Their perceived laziness and taking time off to register to vote caused him to lambaste the Radical Republicans who were running the country. However difficult life might be in the North, conditions there were a paradise compared to the South, he wrote Israel. "A more malignant unprincipled set of villains than are the leaders of the radical party I do not believe ever existed on the face of the earth." Actually, Reconstruction in Virginia was moderate when compared with other areas of the South.[9] This outburst may have been fueled by the adoption of the Fourteenth Amendment, which affected his rights, and the Fifteenth, which gave blacks the right to vote.

Pemberton's moderate farm successes began to wane, and in the winter of 1868–69, he took up schoolteaching to supplement the family income. He enclosed a small room in one of the farm sheds and began instructing his and other local children. Soon he was taking in a limited number of students on a room-and-board basis at twenty dollars each per month. Eventually the part-time occupation was lasting from 9:00 A.M. to 1:30 P.M. each day. His brother Henry placed advertisements in Northern papers to draw more students to Harleigh. John had little faith that the ads would produce results, and apparently they did not. His efforts at making a living drew the attention of a friend, who contacted William T. Sherman, the United States Army's general in chief. Sherman was making recommendations for overseas service in Egypt; would he consider Pemberton, who was having trouble surviving as a farmer and trying to make ends meet by teaching school? Though he recommended other former Confederates, Sherman ignored the request, and there is no evidence that Pemberton ever knew about it.[10]

While he was struggling with farming and teaching, Pemberton's children were growing up and leaving home. The eldest son, Johnny, went to work for Henry in Philadelphia. The parting was not easy on his father, who often longed to see his "dear son." John and Pattie had anxious moments when word came of a storm in the Gulf of St. Lawrence that wrecked several ships, including one that Johnny had been on during a business trip. He survived the wreck without harm. The eldest daughter, Pattie, married a Dr. Baylor. After about five and one-half years of marriage, her husband died following a lengthy illness. She married again and would take care of her invalid mother in later years.[11]

Pemberton gradually underwent personal changes that seemed to produce an older version of the youth at West Point. At first he enjoyed the isolation of Harleigh. He confided to Israel, "I wish we could see more of each other. I lead a very isolated life, but not an unpleasant one."[12]

Isolation began to take a toll, however. "We live so monotonously here," he confessed to his elder brother, "that the correspondence on my part can have very little interest to you." In another letter, he elaborated: "Pattie and I are becoming very weary of the isolated life we are leading here—it will probably become more & more lonesome as we grow older and our children are gone from us."[13] Perhaps the children leaving gave him an excuse to exercise his ever-restless nature. Postwar circumstances had restricted his movements. Now he felt he could get away from Harleigh so he and Pattie gradually began to increase their social activities.

He became fast friends with William Henry Fitzhugh Payne, a former Confederate brigadier, Warrenton lawyer, and unreconstructed Rebel. He exclaimed enthusiastically that on a fishing trip with Payne, "We were most hospitably entertained and I was really quite a big bug. . . . I drank as much as I was disposed to of wine & brandy & thought both delicious." The passage of time had made him less of a pariah, and by the early 1870s he and Pattie were visiting and receiving visitors more than in earlier days at Harleigh. Even in Philadelphia passions were ebbing, and he could go there and appear in public seemingly unnoticed. He visited art galleries and theaters and occasionally had dinner with local politicians.[14]

Such activities indicated that he was becoming accepted in both North and South and reflected his attempts to put the war behind him. By not dwelling on it, he did not draw too much attention to himself. That did not mean he would not defend his war record. He did so at every opportunity, beginning in the latter months of 1865.

A Southerner named Sarah Dorsey contacted Pemberton and Joe Johnston while preparing a biography of her father, Henry Watkins Allen, former Confederate brigadier and governor of Louisiana during the last year of the war. Allen had not participated in the Vicksburg campaign, but Dorsey wanted to know about it so she asked the principals involved. Pemberton responded in great detail, but Johnston was terse and to the point.[15]

Dorsey interspersed quotations from their letters in her narration of the campaign. The result was a book that portrayed Pemberton in a sympathetic light. She was impressed with his arguments, which basically rehashed those in his official report. He restated his position that Johnston should have ordered him to unite his forces to beat Grant weeks before the Federals crossed the Mississippi. Johnston should have said, "It is *my* order, that if Grant lands on this side of the river, you will, *if necessary, abandon* Port Hudson and Vicksburg . . . to beat him." He also reiterated the unjustness of Johnston's claim that Bowen had lost at Port Gibson because of Pemberton's failure to obey the "success will win back what was abandoned to win it" order, which had come too late.[16]

As for Johnston's criticism of Pemberton's assurances in the spring of 1863 that Grant was withdrawing from Vicksburg, he wrote, "I am willing, Madam, to *share* this responsibility, and if there was an error in judgement, to bear my part of the blame, but no more." Not surprisingly, Pemberton insisted that his reports had never misled Johnston; he argued that most of his messages had not indicated that Grant was retreating.

When he wrote to Dorsey, probably in late 1865, over two years had passed since the fall of Vicksburg, but time had not broadened his perspective. His version of events had not changed, yet he was decidedly more bitter. Being forced to resign his high rank in order to stay in the war had hardened his negative views of Johnston. His natural abundance of pride, combined with his post-Vicksburg experiences, had left him in no mood to be objective about any aspect of the campaign. He confessed more than he intended when he blamed his movement to the east of the Big Black on "the clamor of the people" and "the discontent of the army." His error had led to the Battle of Champion Hill, fought "against my own will and convictions." Johnston, in his reports, had "succeeded in maintaining his own reputation, at the expense of mine—I am utterly condemned." Overwhelmed by his anger, Pemberton had acknowledged losing control of the situation at the Big Black by letting forces other than his judgment guide his decisions. It was a rare admission of his own culpability.

Two events brought Pemberton back to the front lines of the postwar refighting of the Vicksburg campaign. War veterans, civil and military, wrote a host of books about their experiences. Some had axes to grind; others merely wanted to protect their reputations. Joe Johnston, who had both motives, published his memoirs in 1874. As might have been expected, especially in light of the Dorsey book, Johnston attacked Pemberton's performance in Mississippi. Also in the 1870s, Jefferson Davis began gathering information for his history of the Confederacy.[17] Davis called on Pemberton for information to clarify certain aspects of the Vicksburg operations. The truth was that he wanted John's version to use against his, and Pemberton's, old enemy Johnston. Pemberton had retained his letterbooks and other papers from Vicksburg and began working on a response to Davis's request. The research seemed to ignite Pemberton's interest, and he even contacted President U. S. Grant about certain campaign and surrender details. He was delighted at Grant's "prompt, polite & very satisfactory" response. Grant confirmed the story Pemberton had heard from one of the president's former officers at Vicksburg that a Confederate courier had indeed been a Union agent and had betrayed his and Johnston's messages to the Federals.[18]

Pemberton not only worked on an answer to Davis's inquiry, he took pen in hand to write a rebuttal to Johnston's tome. He wrote Israel in the summer of 1874: "I have written a great deal but find it very difficult not to be too diffuse and to keep to my text. If I knew how to bring out with the greatest prominence those points which a reader would be most struck by I could hurt Joseph's fictitious reputation a good deal more than he has or can hurt me. Indeed I don't think he has injured me a bit, but rather, so people say in the south, has benefitted me. He has tried his best however, and I am *not* mincing matters in reply. His whole book, so far as I am concerned, is a . . . [series] of false statements and false deductions—without arguments or proofs. I don't intend to say anything I can't prove." An angry Pemberton commented further to his brother Henry, "Johnston's book is a tissue of misrepresentations . . . he is the man who ought to be held responsible for the disasters . . . to the Confederate cause in Mississippi."[19]

Pemberton intended to publish his own account of Vicksburg, but he died before the project was completed. Some of his postwar correspondence regarding Vicksburg operations, including exchanges with Grant about the intercepted Vicksburg messages, was published in volume 3 of *Battles and Leaders of the Civil War* a few years after his death. The same volume also contains his letter to John P. Nicholson, the American editor of the *History of the Civil War* by the Comte de Paris, in which he gave a detailed account of the Vicksburg surrender negotiations (some of which were disputed by Grant). A lengthy manuscript devoted to the campaign, thought to be his reply to Jefferson Davis, was discovered among his papers many years after his death. The edited manuscript, another rendering of familiar points made in official reports, was reproduced in the biography written by his grandson and published in 1942.[20] In that book his personal defense finally appeared in print, though it changed few minds regarding his culpability in the loss of Vicksburg and his army.

Self-defense, not an affinity for the Lost Cause, motivated Pemberton's writings. Though his experiences in South Carolina had changed his strategic thinking, his attitude toward the war never changed. He never accepted the concept of victory at any price. Despite his boastful words at Vicksburg, he had no intention of fighting until every morsel of food was gone, as was proved by the existence of much food in the city when he surrendered. His devotion to the Southern cause had been the matter-of-fact loyalty of a soldier doing his duty. Consequently, his postwar writings concentrated on his personal role. This in itself did not make him unique among Southern generals who wrote of their experiences in the war. Much the same could be said of Johnston. In Pemberton's case, however, his attitude helped ease his transition to private life. He had suffered a great loss in personal esteem and financial stability. But he had no ideological complex about the war's outcome, no hate of all things Northern that typified much Lost Cause thinking. Pemberton carried the burden of wounded pride, not the psychological burden of having lost to the hated North.

By the mid-1870s he considered becoming a Pennsylvanian again, an adjustment that would require little effort on his part. Whether Pennsylvania would easily accept him was a question yet to be answered.

Pemberton took his first step on the road back to permanent residence in his home state while in the midst of his writings. With only one child still at home, he and Pattie decided to put Harleigh up for sale. Thus began another period of wanderings, beginning with a move to Allentown, Pennsylvania, where family connections helped him obtain employment.[21]

Pemberton, the former soldier, farmer, and teacher, became a supervisor with the Iron Storage Department of the Pennsylvania Warehousing and Safe Deposit Company. The arrival of the aging former Confederate officer in Allentown raised some eyebrows, but he made friends quickly.[22]

Perhaps he felt more at ease outside the region where criticism of him had been so vocal after Vicksburg. Time had tempered harsh comments, but an undercurrent of bitterness remained that was expressed in the pages of the *Confederate Veteran* magazine after his death. One Southern veteran made the ridiculous accusation that Grant had paid Pemberton $100,000 to surrender Vicksburg. Other old Rebels defended him, but in qualified terms. Pemberton was not a traitor and was "gallant and loyal," yet he was "unfit" for command, not "great enough" to meet the demands of command, not a "great general."[23] Sensitive as he was to criticism, Pemberton must have been aware of such rumblings. His move north may well have been a deliberate act to get away from the region that had never trusted him and would always be suspicious of his motives.

He delighted new acquaintances in Allentown with his ability to debate the war in a spunky but good-natured style. Pattie joined the town's Episcopal church, which all the Pembertons attended. They lived in a comfortable house in a good neighborhood, and their neighbors did not seem to mind having former Confederates in their midst. As one historian has noted, "Military service frequently provided the necessary ingredient for harmonious relations." Local Union veterans enjoyed the company of the old Philadelphian and helped ease other residents' acceptance of the Pembertons. Prominent families soon were calling on the Pembertons, who did their share of visiting. John's business duties varied, eventually taking him on the road. The roads he traveled soon took him south, even to Mississippi.[24]

Pemberton's charge was to scout the South for possible business opportunities for his company. His employers had warehouses in Philadelphia which they wanted to use to store Southern cotton en route to Europe. They hoped that Pemberton's acquaintances and connections in the South would overshadow any lingering ill feelings about his lack of success in the war. Perhaps he could convince cotton planters to ship their product east rather than to their traditional Gulf Coast markets.

Pemberton traveled to the Deep South in 1875. In Jackson, Mississippi, he lodged at the Edwards House. He turned down an invitation to visit the McCardles in Vicksburg. His excuse sounded legitimate. He told his former aide, William McCardle, that he had to make a business call in Memphis that would take several days and he was in a hurry to finish his travels so he could meet Pattie in Norfolk. Given Pemberton's innate pleasure in meeting with old friends, his more likely reason for not seeing the McCardles was that he could not yet bring himself to visit the site of his great failure. He wanted to see Jefferson Davis but decided that, as in the case of Vicksburg, he did not have time for a trek to Davis's Gulf Coast home. Perhaps seeing the former Confederate president would have evoked painful memories.[25]

In truth, Pemberton was tired of traveling, did not think he could do much to help the Allentown company, and hoped to return soon "to very private life." His stop in Memphis raised his spirits. "I have every where," he wrote Pattie, "been received with the greatest kindness & respect, & have been assured by cotton men of all kinds that they would try to serve me as far as they possibly could." He met with members of the local cotton exchange and with British cotton agents stationed in Memphis. He tried to convince all who would listen that Philadelphia offered better service than New York or Southern ports. Despite the optimistic tone of the meetings, he had little hope of success but remarked to Pattie in an eruption of his old bombast: "I am satisfied that if I, with the multitude of acquaintances, old & new, whom I have met & talked with, cannot induce shipments of cotton to Phila., there is no one they could get who can do it."[26]

Pemberton had often used such cocky talk to shield his insecurities and uncertainties. The fact was that he considered his efforts in the South "useless and a waste of money." In his later written report to his employers, he remarked that his fighting for the South during "'the late unpleasantness'" allowed him to meet with people of all classes connected with the cotton business. He felt it necessary to emphasize his past to assure the company that he had advantages in meeting the right people and getting the facts. He concluded from those meetings that the relationship of local merchants to commission merchants was so deeply ingrained in the Southern cotton market system that a Pennsylvania company could make inroads into the network only if it offered huge incentives. Therefore, the company had to be prepared to make sacrifices to convince Southern merchants that they could make higher profits by shipping to Philadelphia. He also noted that many dealers had asked for a circular or card from the company. Those items should be sent to the names and addresses he had collected, and he should be the one to work with the contacts involved. After all, he had been employed for the purpose of investigating Southern prospects. He would rather follow up as a bona-fide agent than be reduced to writing reports and other clerical duties.[27] His comments contain a hint that he perceived in his employers an air of condescension. Were they using him because they felt sorry for him and because he had influential relatives? He seemed to think so because the company apparently had no intention of following up his suggestions with good faith efforts to make inroads in the South.

Pemberton's observations on the situation in the Southern cotton market, however, demonstrated that he had good business sense. Given the appropriate opportunity, he might have used his bureaucratic training and experience in the military to make a solid contribution to the postbellum business world. But he needed more than a symbolic position because he had too much pride to waste time in a meaningless job. So despite family connections with the business, he soon resigned. He and Pattie moved back to Norfolk for a time to settle myriad business affairs, especially regarding the sale of Harleigh, the disposition of bonds, and the settling of debts.[28]

Eventually the Pembertons returned to Pennsylvania and settled in Philadelphia. They lived off his share of the Pemberton estate, most notably income from rental property. Through both Virginia and

Pennsylvania contacts, he occasionally worked as a representative for other companies, including railroad firms. He also once acted as a gold bullion agent.[29] Though he never could benefit from any war glory, acquaintances North and South had served him well, in varying degrees, during his struggle to find a niche for himself after the war.

Pemberton's cultivation of Pennsylvania contacts produced a special dividend in 1879: his citizenship rights were restored by the United States Congress. The Speaker of the House of Representatives, Samuel J. Randall, a Pennsylvanian, introduced H. R. 1842, a bill to remove Pemberton's "political disabilities." Pemberton's petition to both houses of Congress read: "The undersigned having formerly held the rank of captain and brevet major in the United States Army, and having incurred the political disabilities imposed by the third section of the fourteenth amendment to the Constitution, respectfully petitions your honorable bodies that the same be removed, and that he be reinvested with all the rights of a citizen of the United States." Debate in the House and Senate was brief. Some Pennsylvania lawmakers objected to Pemberton's identification as a Philadelphian. The idea of a Pennsylvanian serving the Confederacy was still not very palatable. One senator ended the discussion abruptly in that body with a simple rejoinder that reverberated with more truth than he realized: "He [Pemberton] had no residence before the war broke out, and he had no residence during the rebellion in all likelihood." Each chamber passed the measure with a majority voice vote, and on June 19, 1879, President Rutherford B. Hayes, a former Union general, signed the measure that restored John Pemberton to full citizenship.[30]

Pemberton spent his last days in Pennsylvania, and those days were mostly quiet ones. He and Pattie lived in Philadelphia and, during the summers, in Penllyn, a suburban community northwest of the city. The aging couple enjoyed "sociable neighbors not more than a stone's throw from us" and socialized with new friends and "old boyhood acquaintances."[31]

His social life had indeed come full circle. The strident strands of his personality, so evident during his long years in the military, were submerged by the congeniality of his youth. In his various military roles, he too often had shown only a part of himself, the egotistical, aloof part that fit the tough, martinet image so many career officers strived for or developed naturally out of their positions of power. Only when his career ended could Pemberton let himself go and become once more the easygoing John of his youth. Many of his military colleagues and most of his soldiers would have been surprised, perhaps shocked, to know the likable man who reemerged after the war.

Though he was more relaxed and at ease, Pemberton still had the urge to be on the move. His greatest disappointment was that he never had the opportunity to travel in Europe with Israel. "I can not conceive," he wrote once to his brother, "that the lives of two brothers, with tastes by no means unlike, could be further asunder. There are no pleasures of travel that you have so long enjoyed that I would not delight in also." To the last, he never gave up hope of traveling the globe.[32]

In the early spring of 1880, Pemberton began to feel the effects of ill health that would doom any chance of crossing the Atlantic. He suffered from the same asthma and consumption disorders that had haunted his family for generations. "I confess that I begin to feel my many years," he wrote Israel. Exposure to the winter of 1879–80 had left him in a state of "lethargy," keeping him indoors for extended periods.[33]

Through 1880 and into 1881 Pemberton's health continued to deteriorate. He spent time in the country and on the Atlantic seacoast in vain attempts to improve his condition. In addition to lung problems, he developed prostate trouble. At times he rebounded, but in early July 1881, he became critically ill. He died on a hot July 13 in the afternoon at his summer home in Penllyn. His death came slightly less than a month before his sixty-seventh birthday. According to family tradition, he commented during his final conscious hours that his only regret was leaving Pattie and their children.[34]

Israel, in Paris, was shocked to learn of his brother's death. Israel had always thought of John as the strong member of the family, full of life and seemingly indestructible. Even though he had been aware of John's declining health, Israel had refused to believe that he might soon die. "Truly the battle is not always to the strong," he wired Henry. "Poor dear John—I hope and think the last years of his life were more tranquil and happy, than the stormy years that preceded them."[35]

The unfortunate legacy of his stormy Civil War years followed him even after death. The Pemberton family hurriedly prepared a lengthy obituary that contained errors about his age and year of birth, errors nobody seemed to notice. Though most major newspapers carried the news, a much more significant headline dominated the press. President James A. Garfield had been shot and eventually would die from an assassin's bullet. Reporters chronicling Garfield's daily fight for life paid little attention to the loss of a man who had once been universally branded a traitor. The comments of his hometown paper, the same paper that had talked about the sad fate of the city's misguided son, indicated that time had softened past rhetoric. The editor noted, "It certainly does appear a hard measure to condemn a self-sacrificing soldier as a perfidious traitor simply because he was unable to defeat and repulse an army of greatly superior numbers."[36]

The South was not so forgiving; most Southerners apparently ignored Pemberton's death, thereby revealing the prevailing attitude toward the man who had lost Vicksburg. Newspapers in Memphis and Atlanta made only brief mention of his death. In Charleston the news got front-page coverage and a comment that was as close to admiration as he was to get in the columns of the press in the old Confederacy: "[Pemberton's] unselfish devotion to the Confederate cause was as marked as his lack of success, and he deserves to be well thought of and remembered in honor by the people for whom he gave up his profession and his State." A Jackson, Mississippi, newspaper noted his death without comment. In Vicksburg he received a front-page notice: "GEN. PEMBERTON, who commanded the Confederate army during the siege here, died at Pennlyn [sic], Penn., on the 13th."[37]

Reactions to the deaths of other Confederate generals who came out of the war with less than scintillating reputations helps put the Southern response to Pemberton's death in perspective. Braxton Bragg died in 1876; his funeral was marked by local militia and Confederate veteran escorts, and many of his former soldiers attended. John Bell Hood's family preferred a quiet funeral when he died in 1879, but the family received many offers for military escorts. Joe Johnston died in 1891; his family declined offers of a veteran escort, but Johnston's funeral was attended by veterans blue and gray. Veterans' groups and newspapers paid him tribute.[38]

If Pemberton's family received such offers, there is no record of it. The only known tribute from Confederate veterans came at the annual reunion of the Virginia division of the Army of Northern Virginia

Association. Jubal Early, "in feeling terms," announced Pemberton's death to those in attendance. Early spoke briefly about his cadet friend, "whom he had intimately known" and "whose devoted patriotism he fittingly eulogized."[39]

Pemberton was buried quietly in the family plot at Laurel Hill Cemetery in Philadelphia.[40] It had been a long trip home, through stormy years, as Israel had said. The proud, arrogant, boastful side of Pemberton would have grieved over the lack of fanfare that accompanied his death. But the other Pemberton, the homesick young cadet, the caring husband and doting father, the congenial, socializing friend, and the ostracized, frustrated soldier whom fate had treated so roughly, would have appreciated the tranquil aftermath of his passing.

Epilogue

In Remembrance

Within two years after her husband's death, Pattie Pemberton made an invaluable contribution to the preservation of Civil War history when she donated his papers to the United States War Department.[1] At the time, that department was gathering war-related documents that would ultimately be published in 128 volumes under the title *War of the Rebellion: A Compilation of the Official Records of the Union and Confederate Armies*. A companion series on the navies would follow. Without the inclusion of Pemberton's records, the Vicksburg story could not have been told.

Pattie lived until 1907. She died on August 14 in New York City at age eighty-two. For the last eight years of her life she was an invalid, cared for by her daughter and namesake. Her body was taken back to Philadelphia and interred by John's side at Laurel Hill.[2] Her years without her husband had been quiet ones. She had carried no torch to salvage his war reputation, but her foresight in preserving his records assured that his side of events would be recorded for posterity.

The Vicksburg National Military Park was established in 1899, eight years before Pattie's death, though her ill health kept her from seeing the place. The formation of the park seemingly assured that General Pemberton's Civil War career would be documented physically, at least regarding his Vicksburg service, as well as in print. But a specific remembrance of him was many years in coming.

As time passed, statues and other markers commemorating campaign and siege participants began to appear throughout the hills and slopes of the park. Noticeably missing was any memorial to Pemberton. The problem was, Who would fund an appropriate marker? State governments and other organizations had taken the lead in planning and funding the honoring of their respective heroes. Because Pemberton fought for the Confederacy, Pennsylvania could not be expected to fund his memorial. Apparently Mississippi refused to do so, and in the end the Federal government finally stepped forward with an appropriation to fund a statue.[3]

At a cost of $2,880, Edmund T. Quinn sculpted Pemberton in uniform. The statue was dedicated in November 1917, not long after a reunion of Civil War veterans, both blue and gray, had been held in Vicksburg. Symbolic of the lingering controversy surrounding Pemberton were street decorations for the veterans' parade. Prominent photographs of Civil War heroes were placed along the parade route. The photographs were of Abraham Lincoln, U. S. Grant, Jefferson Davis, and Robert E. Lee.[4]

Pemberton's grandson John C. Pemberton III did his best to resurrect his ancestor's image from history's scrap heap. Sometime in the 1930s, he began working on a biography of his grandfather. In 1937, he attended an anniversary commemoration of the surrender of Vicksburg, sharing a speaker's platform with the grandson of U. S. Grant. John III challenged historians who criticized his grandfather and in 1942 published a defensive biographical account of the general. *Pemberton: Defender of Vicksburg* was the only book on its subject to that point and for fifty years thereafter. John III's arguments convinced few readers, at the time or since, that John Pemberton was a good general wrongly accused of incompetence. Whatever the merits of the biography (and despite the partisan tone, it is in many ways not a bad study of the Vicksburg campaign), John III followed in his grandmother's steps by taking steps to preserve additional valuable Pemberton documents that were still in family hands.[5]

In 1961 the Philadelphia, Pennsylvania, chapter of the United Daughters of the Confederacy took up the Pemberton torch. The chapter erected a bronze memorial on his grave site in Laurel Hill. The year before, an honor guard of the Hampton Legion, a Civil War reenactment group, had fired a salute over Pemberton's grave.[6] Finally he received recognition in his hometown. These are the only known occasions of such tributes.

The only place that remembers Pemberton in obvious fashion is the city whose newspaper editors had been little moved by his death. In the Vicksburg of the 1990s, one may visit the Pemberton headquarters house, privately owned and, in 1991, in the spirit of the Pemberton legacy, in the midst of a controversy over its preservation. Visitors may also drive their vehicles along Pemberton Boulevard. They may shop in Pemberton Square Mall or Pemberton Plaza, or lunch in Pemberton Cafeteria (where Pemberton and his army would undoubtedly appreciate the "all you can eat" specials). Women may wish to visit Pemberton Hairstylists. In the national park, one can view Pemberton's portrait and his siege and Mexican War swords. A tour of the park eventually leads to Pemberton Avenue, and Quinn's statue of the general stands in Pemberton Circle.

Somehow his remembrance in the place of his greatest disaster provides a fittingly ironic twist to the fate of John C. Pemberton, Confederate general.

Abbreviations

CWM   College of William and Mary, Swem Library, Williamsburg, Virginia

CWP   Conway Whittle Papers, College of William and Mary, Williamsburg, Virginia

HSP   Historical Society of Pennsylvania, Philadelphia

IPP   Israel Pemberton Papers, in Pemberton Family Papers, Collection 484B, Historical Society of Pennsylvania

JCP   John C. Pemberton

JCPP   John C. Pemberton Papers, in Pemberton Family Papers, Collection 484B, Historical Society of Pennsylvania

NA   National Archives

OR   *The War of the Rebellion: A Compilation of the Official Records of the Union and Confederate Armies*, 128 vols. Washington D.C., 1880–1901.

ORN   *Official Records of the Union and Confederate navies in the War of the Rebellion*, 35 vols. Washington, D.C., 1894–1927.

PFP   Pemberton Family Papers, Collection 484B, Historical Society of Pennsylvania

PPP   Pattie Pemberton Papers, in the John C. Pemberton Papers, Pemberton Family Papers, Collection 484B, Historical Society of Pennsylvania

RG   Record Group in the National Archives

RPP   Rebecca Pemberton Papers, in Pemberton Family Papers, Collection 484B, Historical Society of Pennsylvania

SHC   Southern Historical Collection, Wilson Library, University of North Carolina, Chapel Hill

Notes

CHAPTER 1

1. S. H. Lockett, "The Defense of Vicksburg," in Robert Underwood Johnson and Clarence Clough Buel, eds., *Battles and Leaders of the Civil War*, 4 vols. (1887–88; rpt. New York, 1956), 3:488.

2. The foregoing discussion of General Pemberton's ancestry is based on the following: John W. Jordan, ed., *Colonial Families of Philadelphia*, 2 vols. (New York, 1911), 1:276–93; Henry Pemberton, "The Pemberton Family," typescript in John C. Pemberton Papers, SHC, pp. I–IV; Gary B. Nash, *Quakers and Politics: Pennsylvania, 1681–1726* (Princeton, 1968), 170, 295, 323. See also John F. Watson, *Annals of Philadelphia, and Pennsylvania in the Olden Times; Being a Collection of Memoirs, Anecdotes, and Incidents of the City and Its Inhabitants . . .* , 3 vols. (Philadelphia, 1900), 1:47, 56, 72, 282, 287–89, 290, 294, 374, 393–95, 510, 595–96, 607; 2:95, 166–67, 285.

3. John B. Linn and William H. Egle, eds., *Muster Rolls of the Pennsylvania Volunteers in the War of 1812–1814 with Contemporary Papers and Documents*, Pennsylvania Archives, 2d ser. (Harrisburg, 1880), 12:254. John Pemberton's letters home from his army camps are in Rebecca Pemberton Papers, PFP, HSP.

4. Jordan, *Colonial Families of Philadelphia*, 302–3.

5. Rebecca Pemberton to John Pemberton, September 5, 13, October 4, 1814, John Pemberton Papers, PFP, HSP.

6. John Pemberton to Rebecca Pemberton, November? 20, December 6, 1822, January 5, February 2, 23, 1823, October 30, 1818, RPP; Pemberton to Andrew Jackson, April 6, 1829, April 6, 1830, August 9, 1831, Jackson to Pemberton; August 13, 1831, John Pemberton Papers, PFP, HSP.

7. Jordan, *Colonial Families of Philadelphia*, 293.

8. John Pemberton to Rebecca Pemberton, October 30, 1818, RPP, Pemberton to "My Dear Sons," November 26, 1822, IPP, Rebecca to John, November (?)?, 1822, John Pemberton Papers, PFP, HSP.

9. Rebecca Pemberton to John Pemberton, December 15, 1822, John Pemberton Papers, PFP, HSP.

10. Rebecca Pemberton to John Pemberton, December 24, 1822, November 9, 1821?, ibid.

11. Rebecca Pemberton to John Pemberton, January 9, 16, 1823, November 3, 28, December 15, 1822, John Pemberton Papers; Rebecca to John, December 19, 1822, RPP, JCP to John, June 19, 1826, John Pemberton Papers, PFP, HSP.

12. JCP to John and Rebecca Pemberton, September 20, 1833, JCP to Rebecca, May 5, 1835, JCPP, PFP, HSP.

13. Edgar P. Richardson, "The Athens of America, 1800–1825," in Russell F. Weigley, ed., *Philadelphia: A 300-Year History* (New York, 1982), 210, 220, 222–23, 241–42, 245–46; Nicholas B. Wainwright, "The Age of Nicholas Biddle, 1825–1841," ibid., 289–91; Frances Trollope, *Domestic Manners of the Americans* (1832), ed. Donald Smalley (New York, 1949), 275–76.

14. Israel Pemberton to John Pemberton, January 8, 1828, John Pemberton Papers, PFP, HSP.

15. Wainwright, "Age of Biddle," 262–63.

16. Ibid., 289–90; John C. Pemberton [III], *Pemberton: Defender of Vicksburg* (Chapel Hill, 1942), 20.

17. Richardson, "Athens of America," 254–55; Wainwright, "Age of Biddle," 293–96; Michael Feldberg, *The Philadelphia Riots of 1844; A Study of Ethnic Conflict* (Westport, Conn., 1975), 4, 6, 13.

18. S. C. Walker to John Pemberton, June 5, 1830, Walker to "Gentlemen" [Officers of the Collegiate Department of the University of Pennsylvania], July 27, 1830, JCPP, A. D. Bache to John Pemberton, August 4, 1830, John Pemberton Papers, PFP, HSP.

19. Pemberton's desire to be a civil engineer is mentioned in a letter to his mother, October 20, 1836, JCPP, PFP, HSP.

20. Henry Mung? to Lewis Cass, February 20, 1833, J. R.? Barker to Andrew Jackson, April 30, 1833, John Clifford Pemberton File, United States Military Academy Archives, West Point, New York.

21. Rebecca Pemberton to Andrew Jackson, April 30, 1833, ibid.

22. JCP to Andrew Jackson (copy of letter), 1833, in JCPP, PFP, HSP.

23. JCP to Lewis Cass, May 18, 1833, John Pemberton to JCP, June 5, 1834, JCPP, PFP, HSP. A copy of the Cass letter is in Pemberton's file, Military Academy Archives.

24. John Pemberton to Andrew Jackson, May 28, 1833, RPP, PFP, HSP.

25. W. H. Delancey statement, June 7, 1833, Delancey to John Pemberton, June 7, 1833, John Pemberton to Delancey, June 7, 1833, JCPP, PFP, HSP.

26. Pemberton, *Pemberton,* 9; clipping from *Bivouac, An Independent Military Magazine,* Pemberton file, Military Academy Archives.

CHAPTER 2

1. JCP to Rebecca Pemberton, June 17, 1833, JCPP, PFP, HSP.
2. James L. Morrison, Jr., *"The Best School in the World": West Point, the Pre–Civil War Years, 1833–1836* (Kent, Ohio, 1986), 3–4, 21, 40.
3. JCP to John Pemberton, [June 19?], 1833, JCPP, PFP, HSP.
4. Morrison, *"Best School,"* 69; JCP to parents, September 4, 1833, JCP to John Pemberton, July 1, 1833, JCP to Israel Pemberton, July 9, 1833, JCPP, PFP, HSP.
5. JCP to Israel Pemberton, May 8, 1834, JCP to Anna Pemberton, June 28, 1836, August 30, 1834, JCPP, PFP, HSP.
6. JCP to parents, September 4, December 23, 1833, JCP to John Pemberton, January 11, 1834, December 7, 1835, JCPP, PFP, HSP; Cadet Record of John Clifford Pemberton, United States Military Academy, Class of 1837, in John Clifford Pemberton File, United States Military Academy Archives, West Point, New York.
7. JCP to parents, September 20, 1833, March 8, 1834, JCP to John Pemberton, December 7, 1835, JCP to Israel Pemberton, November 19, 1834, JCP to Rebecca Pemberton, May 3, [1834], JCPP, PFP, HSP; Cadet Record of Pemberton, Military Academy Archives.
8. JCP to Rebecca Pemberton, October 10, 1836, JCPP, PFP, HSP; Cadet Record of Pemberton, Military Academy Archives.
9. Cadet Record of Pemberton, Military Academy Archives.
10. Ibid.; JCP to Israel Pemberton, April 3, 1836, JCP to parents, June 20?, 1836, JCP to John Pemberton, June 21, 1836, JCPP, JCP to Israel, June 23, 1836, IPP, PFP, HSP.
11. JCP to John Pemberton, May 31, 1834, John Pemberton to JCP, June 5, 1834, JCPP, PFP, HSP.
12. JCP to parents, March 8, 1834, JCP to John Pemberton, September 20, 1835, May 20, 1836, JCPP, PFP, HSP.
13. JCP to Israel Pemberton, August 4, 1833, JCP to Rebecca Pemberton, August 23, 1835, JCP to Anna Pemberton, April 20, 1837, JCPP, PFP, HSP.
14. John Pemberton to JCP, September 7, 1833, JCPP, PFP, HSP.
15. JCP to Rebecca Pemberton, May 21, 1834, JCPP, PFP, HSP.
16. Ibid., JCP to John Pemberton, December 27, 1835, November 3, 1836, JCP to Rebecca Pemberton, March 31, 1836, JCPP, PFP, HSP.
17. JCP to Israel Pemberton, November 19, 1834, July 9, 1833, JCP to parents, November 25, 1834, JCP to John Pemberton, March 21, December

27, 1835, May 20, 1836, JCP to Rebecca Pemberton, May 5, 1835, JCP to Anna Pemberton, December 14, 1835, John Pemberton to JCP, September 7, 1833, JCPP, PFP, HSP.

18. JCP to Anna Pemberton, December 14, 1835, JCP to Israel Pemberton, May 8, 1834, JCPP, PFP, HSP; U.S. Military Academy Battalion Order No. 101, November 27, 1833, Military Academy Archives.

19. JCP to Israel Pemberton, November 20, 1833, JCP to Anna Pemberton, November 24, 1833, JCPP, PFP, HSP.

20. JCP to Rebecca Pemberton, September 18, October 24, 1835, JCP to parents, November 8, 1835, JCPP, PFP, HSP.

21. JCP to John Pemberton, March 21, 1835, JCP to Israel Pemberton, June 23, 1835, August 4, 1833, JCP to parents, August 3, 1833, JCP to Rebecca Pemberton, April 22, 1835, JCPP, PFP, HSP.

22. JCP to parents, September 20, 1833, JCP to Israel Pemberton, August 4, 1833, November 19, 1834, JCPP, PFP, HSP.

23. JCP to Anna Pemberton, November 24, 1833, August 30, 1834, JCPP, PFP, HSP; Judith A. Sibley, West Point Manuscripts Librarian, to the author, June 21, 1989.

24. JCP to Anna Pemberton, December 14, 1835, JCP to John Pemberton, January 11, 1834, January 25, December 7, 1835, JCP to parents, November 5, 1833, JCP to Israel Pemberton, May 8, 1834, JCPP, PFP, HSP. Pemberton's name does not appear in the circulation records of the academy's library archives (Sibley to author, June 21, 1989).

25. JCP to John Pemberton, December 15, 1833, December 27, 1835, January 19, 1836, JCP to Anna Pemberton, December 27, 1836, JCPP, PFP, HSP.

26. JCP to Israel Pemberton, November 20, 1833, JCP to John Pemberton, January 25, 1835, JCP to parents, November 25, 1834, JCPP, PFP, HSP; Rebecca Pemberton to Israel Pemberton, April 8, 1837, IPP, PFP, HSP.

27. JCP to John Pemberton, December 15, 1833, JCP to Rebecca Pemberton, April 22, 1835, JCPP, PFP, HSP. The story of Pemberton's Southern sentiments, in conversation and in the company he kept, is based on a postwar letter written by Jubal Early to the editor of the *Lynchburg* (Virginia) *News*, May 6, 1879. Pemberton's West Point letters do not support Early's contentions. Early's letter is in a clipping in the John C. Pemberton Papers, SHC.

28. JCP to Rebecca Pemberton, October 20, 1834, October 25, 1835, February 14, December 6, 1836, JCP to John Pemberton, November 3, 1836, JCPP, PFP, HSP.

29. JCP to Anna (?) Pemberton, November 22, 1835, JCP to parents, November 29, 1835, JCPP, PFP, HSP.

30. *1953 Register of Graduates and Former Cadets, 1802–1953, of the United States Military Academy* (New York, 1953), 167–171; JCP to Rebecca Pemberton, June 17, 1836, JCPP, PFP, HSP.

31. Jubal Early to *Lynchburg* (Virginia) *News* editor, May 6, 1879, clipping in Pemberton Papers, SHC; JCP to parents, March 21, 1834, September 4, 1833, JCP to Anna Pemberton, November 24, 1833, JCP to John Pemberton, December 27, 1835, January 19, 1836, March 21, 1835, JCP to Israel Pemberton, June 23, 1835, JCPP, PFP, HSP. See also JCP to Israel, May 8, 1834, and JCP to John Pemberton, January 25, 1835, ibid. Pemberton's namesake and grandson claimed that William Mackall was John's best friend, but Mackall, though certainly a friend during the pre–Civil War years, is not mentioned in any of John's West Point letters. See John C. Pemberton [III], *Pemberton: Defender of Vicksburg* (Chapel Hill, 1942), 10.

32. JCP to John Pemberton, August 5, 1836, JCPP, PFP, HSP. The nickname Jack is mentioned in Pemberton, *Pemberton,* 9. The origin of the name is not given and probably is not known, but West Point gave birth to many nicknames, and Pemberton more than likely received his there.

33. JCP to parents, November 25, 1834, JCPP, PFP, HSP. All the various literary and debate societies merged to become the Dialectic Society in 1837 (Morrison, "Best School," 75).

34. JCP to John Pemberton, February 28, 1836, JCP to Anna Pemberton, June 28, 1836, JCPP, PFP, HSP; Morrison, "Best School," 70.

35. Rebecca Pemberton to Israel Pemberton, September 16, 1836, Anna Pemberton to Israel, September 21, 1836, IPP, JCP to Rebecca, October 20, 1836, JCP to Israel, October 20, 1836, JCP to John Pemberton, November 3, 1836, JCPP, PFP, HSP.

36. JCP to Anna Pemberton, December 13, 27, 1836, April 20, 1837, JCPP, Rebecca Pemberton to Israel Pemberton, March 27, April 8, 1837, IPP, PFP, HSP.

37. JCP to John Pemberton, November 30, 1836, JCPP, PFP, HSP. Included in the JCP Papers with the letter is a copy of the statement of charges against Pemberton.

38. JCP to John Pemberton, December 7, 1836, JCPP, PFP, HSP.

39. Ibid.

40. JCP to John Pemberton, December 11, 1836, JCPP, PFP, HSP.

41. JCP to Anna Pemberton, December 13, 1836, JCPP, PFP, HSP; Morrison, "Best School," 78.

42. John Pemberton to JCP, December ?, 1836, JCP to John Pemberton, December 20, 1836, JCPP, PFP, HSP.

43. Rebecca Pemberton to Israel Pemberton, January 29, February 5, 1837, IPP, PFP, HSP.

44. Cadet Record of Pemberton, Military Academy Archives; JCP to "My Dear Aunt," September 29, 1833, JCP to Anna Pemberton, October 9, 1835, June 28, 1836, JCP to Israel Pemberton, October 20, 1836, JCP to John Pemberton, January 19, February 28, 1836, JCPP, PFP, HSP.

45. Morrison, *"Best School,"* 15; John Pemberton to Henry Gilpin, June 27, 1837, John Pemberton Papers, PFP, HSP; H. D. Gilpin to John Pemberton, July 11, 1837, Adjutant General's Office to JCP, June 29, 1837, "General Orders No. 46, Head Quarters of the Army Adjutant General's Office, Washington, D.C., July 12, 1837" (copy), JCPP, PFP, HSP.

46. JCP to Israel Pemberton, October 20, 1836, JCPP, PFP, HSP.

CHAPTER 3

1. *Niles' Weekly Register* 52 (July 22, 1837): 324, (June 3, 1837): 212–13; Douglas Southall Freeman, *R. E. Lee: A Biography,* 4 vols. (New York, 1934–35), 1:186–87.

2. JCP to John Pemberton, July 3, 1837, JCPP, Anna Pemberton to Israel Pemberton, July 8, 1837, IPP, all in PFP, HSP.

3. Rebecca Pemberton to Israel Pemberton, July 24, August 27, September 3, 6, October 25, 1837, IPP, PFP, HSP.

4. John K. Mahon, *History of the Second Seminole War, 1835–1842* (Gainesville, 1967), 129. The First Seminole War had been touched off in 1816 when the United States invaded Florida to protect Georgia's border from Indian raids and to pressure Spain into ceding Florida to the United States.

5. Ibid., 323.

6. Rebecca Pemberton to Israel Pemberton, November 14, 1837, January 8, 1838, IPP, JCP to parents, January 27, 1838, JCPP, PFP, HSP; Mahon, *Second Seminole War,* 232–35.

7. JCP to John Pemberton, April 22, 1838, JCPP, PFP, HSP.

8. Ibid., JCP to parents, April 21, 1838, JCPP, PFP, HSP.

9. JCP to John Pemberton, April 22, 1838, JCP to parents, April 21, 1838, JCPP, PFP, HSP.

10. JCP to John Pemberton, June 17, 1838, JCPP, PFP, HSP.

11. Ibid.; Angeline Stebbins to Rebecca Pemberton, June 20, 1838, RPP, PFP, HSP. In one letter to his parents, John did ask that Anna occasionally write to Angeline. JCP to parents, January 27, 1838, JCPP, PFP, HSP.

12. JCP to John Pemberton, August 29, 1838, JCPP, PFP, HSP.

13. John Y. Simon, ed., *The Papers of Ulysses S. Grant,* 16 vols. to date (Carbondale, 1967–), 1:235; JCP to Rebecca Pemberton, September 20, 1838, JCPP, Rebecca Pemberton to Israel Pemberton, October 18, 1838, IPP,

Israel Pemberton to Rebecca Pemberton, September 2, 1838, RPP, PFP, HSP.

14. Rebecca Pemberton to Israel Pemberton, October 18, 1838, IPP, Angeline Stebbins to Rebecca Pemberton, January 5, 1838, Israel Pemberton to Rebecca Pemberton, September 23, 1838, RPP, JCP to Rebecca Pemberton, September 20, 1838, JCPP, PFP, HSP.

15. JCP to Rebecca Pemberton, September 20, October 4, 1838, JCP to John Pemberton, October 15, 1838, JCP to Anna Pemberton, January 5, 1839, JCPP, PFP, HSP; Mahon, *Second Seminole War*, 131–32.

16. JCP to John Pemberton, October 15, 1838, JCPP, PFP, HSP.

17. Rebecca Pemberton to Israel Pemberton, November 16, 1838, IPP, PFP, HSP.

18. JCP to John Pemberton, December 6, 1838, JCPP, PFP, HSP.

19. Ibid.

20. JCP to John Pemberton, January 26, 1838, JCPP, PFP, HSP.

21. Ibid., JCP to John Pemberton, January 13, 15, 1839, JCP to Anna Pemberton, January 23, 1839, JCP to Rebecca Pemberton, February 12, 1839, JCPP, PFP, HSP.

22. JCP to Rebecca Pemberton, March 2, 1839, JCP to Anna Pemberton, January 23, 1839, H. G. Stebbins to JCP, April 12, 30, 1839, JCPP, PFP, HSP.

23. JCP to Rebecca Pemberton, March 2, 12, April 16, 1839, JCPP, PFP, HSP.

24. JCP to John Pemberton, January 15, 1839, December 6, 1838, JCP to Rebecca Pemberton, December 12, 1839, JCPP, PFP, HSP.

25. JCP to Anna Pemberton, January 23, 1839, JCPP, PFP, HSP.

26. JCP to Rebecca Pemberton, February 12, 1839, JCPP, PFP, HSP.

27. Ibid., JCP to Israel Pemberton, December 13, 1839, JCPP, PFP, HSP.

28. JCP to Rebecca Pemberton, April 16, 1839, JCP to Israel Pemberton, February 13, 1839, JCPP, PFP, HSP; Mahon, *Second Seminole War*, 290–93, 323.

29. JCP to Rebecca Pemberton, March 2, April 16, July 3, 1839, JCP to Israel Pemberton, May 21, 1839, JCPP, PFP, HSP.

30. *Niles' National Register* 57 (September 21, 1839): 55.

31. JCP to Rebecca Pemberton, July 3, August 31, October 7, 1839, JCPP, PFP, HSP.

32. JCP to Israel Pemberton, January 5, 1840, JCP to Rebecca Pemberton, May 13, 1840, JCPP, Sarah Ward to Rebecca Pemberton, March 10, 1840, RPP, PFP, HSP.

33. Francis Paul Prucha, ed., *Army Life on the Western Frontier: Selections*

from Official Reports Made between 1826 and 1845 by Colonel George Cooghan (Norman, 1958), 40–41; Walter Havighurst, *Three Flags at the Straits: The Forts of Mackinac* (Englewood Cliffs, 1966), 100–101; JCP to Rebecca Pemberton, May 13, 1840, JCPP, PFP, HSP.

34. JCP to Israel Pemberton, November 16, 1840, JCPP, PFP, HSP.

35. Ibid., April 27, 1841. For an examination of the nose-pulling tradition see Kenneth S. Greenburg, "The Nose, the Lie, and the Duel in the Antebellum South," *American Historical Review* 95 (February 1990): 57–74.

36. JCP to Israel Pemberton, April 27, 1841, JCPP, PFP, HSP.

37. JCP to Rebecca Pemberton, August 15, 1841, JCPP, PFP, HSP; F. Clever Bald, *Michigan in Four Centuries* (1954; rpt. New York, 1961), 151.

38. JCP to Rebecca Pemberton, January 22, 1842, JCPP, PFP, HSP.

39. Ibid.

40. Ibid.

41. Richard Taylor, *Destruction and Reconstruction: Personal Experiences of the Late War* (New York, 1879), 116. Taylor thought Pemberton incompetent in independent command during the Vicksburg campaign but defended him against personal attacks by Southerners (p. 117). See also Chapter 2, note 31.

42. G. W. Cullum, *Biographical Register of Officers and Graduates, U.S. Military Academy*, 3 vols. (West Point, 1891), 1:684, excerpt in Pemberton Papers, SHC; Adjutant General's Office, Special Orders 119, November 14, 1843, document in JCPP, PFP, HSP.

43. JCP to Israel Pemberton, March 31, 1844, JCP to Rebecca Pemberton, May 15?, 1844, JCPP, PFP, HSP.

44. Ibid.

45. JCP to Israel Pemberton, August 11, 1844, JCPP, PFP, HSP.

46. Rowland Baylor to John C. Pemberton III, April 23, 1936, August 10, 1939, Pemberton Papers, SHC; John C. Pemberton [III], *Pemberton: Defender of Vicksburg* (Chapel Hill, 1942), 11–12; JCP to Rebecca Pemberton, July 29, 1845, JCPP, Anna Pemberton to Israel Pemberton, January 15, 1845, IPP, PFP, HSP. Pemberton's grandson claims that John and Pattie met in 1842. Family correspondence indicates otherwise, as I have stated in the text.

47. JCP to Rebecca Pemberton, July 29, 1845, JCPP, PFP, HSP.

48. JCP to Rebecca Pemberton, August 11, 1845, JCPP, PFP, HSP.

49. JCP to Rebecca Pemberton, August 30, 1845, JCPP, PFP, HSP.

CHAPTER 4

1. Anna Pemberton to Israel Pemberton, October 27, 1845, IPP, PFP, HSP.

2. Gerald S. Pierce, *Texas under Arms: The Camps, Posts, Forts, and Military Towns of the Republic of Texas, 1836–1846* (Austin, 1969), 39–40.

3. For the background, political aspects, and military campaigns of the Mexican War I have relied almost exclusively on John S. D. Eisenhower, *So Far from God: The U.S. War with Mexico, 1846–1848* (New York, 1989). Other studies of the war that were consulted include K. Jack Bauer, *The Mexican War, 1846–1848* (New York, 1974); Justin H. Smith, *The War with Mexico*, 2 vols. (New York, 1919); Otis A. Singletary, *The Mexican War* (Chicago, 1960); and John Edward Weems, *To Conquer a Peace: The War between the United States and Mexico* (1974, rpt. College Station, Texas, 1988).

4. JCP to Rebecca Pemberton, November 16, 1845, JCPP, PFP, HSP.

5. Pierce, *Texas under Arms*, 40; JCP to Rebecca Pemberton, November 16, 1845, JCPP, George Meade to Israel Pemberton, December 16, 1845, IPP, PFP, HSP.

6. JCP to Rebecca Pemberton, November 16, 1845, JCPP, George Meade to Israel Pemberton, December 16, 1845, IPP, PFP, HSP.

7. John Pemberton to Israel Pemberton, February 23, 1846, IPP, JCP to Anna Pemberton, January 28, 1846, JCP to Rebecca Pemberton, November 16, 1845, JCPP, PFP, HSP.

8. JCP to Rebecca Pemberton, November 16, 1845, March 6, 1846, JCP to Anna Pemberton, January 28, 1846, JCPP, PFP, HSP.

9. JCP to Rebecca Pemberton, November 16, 1845, March 6, 1846, JCP to Anna Pemberton, January 28, 1846, JCPP, PFP, HSP.

10. *Niles' National Register* 70 (May 16, 1846): 163; JCP to Rebecca Pemberton, March 6, 1846, JCPP, PFP, HSP.

11. Eisenhower, *So Far from God*, 49–50.

12. Ibid., 54–57, 60–64.

13. Ibid., 71, 75–76.

14. JCP to Israel Pemberton, May 28, 1846, JCP to John Pemberton, June 9, 1846, JCPP, PFP, HSP; George Meade, *The Life and Letters of George Gordon Meade*, ed. George Gordon Meade [grandson], 2 vols. (New York, 1913), 1:95.

15. JCP to Israel Pemberton, May 28, 1846, JCPP, PFP, HSP. For details of the Matamoras campaign, including battles at Palo Alto and Resaca de la Palma, see Eisenhower, *So Far from God*, 71–85.

16. Ibid., JCP to John Pemberton, June 9, 1846, JCPP, PFP, HSP.

17. JCP to Israel Pemberton, May 28, 1846; JCP to John Pemberton, June 9, 1846, JCPP, PFP, HSP.

18. JCP to John Pemberton, June 9, 1846, JCPP, George Meade to Israel Pemberton, June 10, 1846, IPP, PFP, HSP.

19. JCP to John Pemberton, June 9, 1846, JCPP, PFP, HSP.

20. Ibid., May 10, 1846.

21. Ibid., June 9, 1846.

22. Ibid.

23. Ibid.

24. JCP to Israel Pemberton, May 28, 1846, JCP to John Pemberton, June 9, 1846, JCPP, George Meade to Israel Pemberton, June 10, 1846, IPP, PFP, HSP. See also Eisenhower, *So Far from God,* 72.

25. JCP to John Pemberton, June 9, 1846, JCPP, PFP, HSP.

26. Ibid.

27. Eisenhower, *So Far from God,* 105, 167.

28. Ibid.; G. W. Cullum, *Biographical Register of Officers and Graduates, U.S. Military Academy* (West Point, 1891), 1:684, excerpt in John Clifford Pemberton Papers, SHC; JCP to Rebecca Pemberton, August 5, 1846, JCPP, PFP, HSP.

29. Edward S. Wallace, "General William Jenkins Worth and Texas," *Southwestern Historical Quarterly* 54 (October 1950) 159–160; John K. Mahon, *History of the Second Seminole War, 1835–1842* (Gainesville, 1967), 294–95. The only biography of Worth is Edward S. Wallace, *General William Jenkins Worth: Monterey's Forgotten Hero* (Dallas, 1953). Pemberton is not mentioned in this book.

30. Eisenhower, *So Far from God,* 109–10; Weems, *To Conquer a Peace,* 211–12.

31. JCP to Rebecca Pemberton, August 5, 1846, JCPP, PFP, HSP.

32. For a summary of the Monterrey campaign see Eisenhower, *So Far from God,* 111–43.

33. Cullum, *Biographical Register,* excerpt in Pemberton Papers, SHC; *Niles' National Register* 71 (February 20, 1847): 396.

34. *Niles' National Register* 71 (November 21, 1846): 180–81; *Charleston Mercury* quoted ibid., p. 180. See also *Niles' National Register* 71 (December 5, 1846): 223.

35. JCP to John Pemberton, December 21, 1846, JCPP, PFP, HSP. On the Saltillo situation see Eisenhower, *So Far from God,* 167–68, 171.

36. JCP to John Pemberton, December 21, 1846, JCPP, PFP, HSP.

37. JCP to Israel Pemberton, January 28, 1847, JCPP, PFP, HSP.

38. Anna Pemberton to JCP, January 31, 1847, Pemberton Papers, SHC.

39. The story of the Mexico City campaign is in Eisenhower, *So Far from God,* 266–342.

40. Rebecca Pemberton to Israel Pemberton, October 25, 1846, IPP, Israel Pemberton to Rebecca Pemberton, September 8, 1846, RPP, PFP, HSP. Pemberton did resign once after an argument with Worth, but the general

talked him out of it. See Anna Pemberton to Israel Pemberton, May 5, 1847, IPP, ibid.

41. JCP to Israel Pemberton, January 28, 1847, JCPP, PFP, HSP.

42. *Niles' National Register* 72 (March 6, 1847): 16; Eisenhower, *So Far from God*, 259–64.

43. *Niles' National Register* 72 (March 6, 1847): 1, (April 17, 1847): 100; JCP to Rebecca Pemberton, March 31, 1847, JCPP, PFP, HSP.

44. Newspaper clipping, ca. 1877, in John C. Pemberton III Collection, Mississippi Department of Archives and History, Jackson.

45. JCP to Rebecca Pemberton, August 27, 1847, JCPP, PFP, HSP.

46. Cullum, *Biographical Register*, excerpt in Pemberton Papers, SHC.

47. U. S. Grant, *Personal Memoirs of U. S. Grant*, 2 vols. (New York, 1885–86), 1:96–97.

48. JCP to Rebecca Pemberton, September 16, 1847, JCPP, PFP, HSP.

49. Rebecca Pemberton, to Israel Pemberton, July 22, 1847, IPP, JCP to Rebecca, September 16, 1847, JCPP, PFP, HSP.

50. Rebecca Pemberton to Israel Pemberton, October 31, 1847, IPP, PFP, HSP.

51. For example, see Worth to Scott, Generals of the Civil War, Confederate, vol. 3, John C. Pemberton, in F. J. Dreer Collection, HSP. See also Wallace, *General William Jenkins Worth*, 172–84.

52. Rebecca Pemberton to Israel Pemberton, August 20, December 30, 1847, Anna Pemberton to Israel, September 19, 1847, IPP, PFP, HSP; John C. Pemberton [III], *Pemberton: Defender of Vicksburg* (Chapel Hill, 1942), 15. The sword presented by the city of Philadelphia is on display in the visitors center of the Vicksburg National Military Park.

CHAPTER 5

1. Marriage Record of John Clifford Pemberton and Martha Thompson, Notes by Ms. Rowland Baylor, both in John C. Pemberton Papers, SHC; Rebecca Pemberton to Israel Pemberton, August 20, 1847, IPP, PFP, HSP.

2. Rebecca Pemberton to Israel Pemberton, April 23, May 15, 20, 28, 1848, IPP, PFP, HSP.

3. Ibid., March 29, April 11, 23, May 28, 1848, Anna Pemberton to Israel Pemberton, March 19, 1848, IPP, Israel to Rebecca Pemberton, April 4, 1848, RPP, PFP, HSP.

4. Rebecca Pemberton to Israel Pemberton, June 18, 1848, IPP, PFP, HSP.

5. Ibid., July 9, 1848.

6. Ibid., August 8, 1848.

7. Ibid., August 20, 1848.

8. Pattie Pemberton to Rebecca Pemberton, October 31, December 21, 1848, PPP, JCPP, Rebecca Pemberton to Israel Pemberton, September 10, October 15, December 24, 1848, IPP, PFP, HSP.

9. Pattie Pemberton to Rebecca Pemberton, October 31, 1848, PPP in JCPP, PFP, HSP; Mary Thompson to "My Dear Friend," December 2, 1848, CWP, Manuscripts Department, Swem Library, CWM.

10. Mary Thompson to "My Dear Friend," December 2, 1848, CWP, CWM; JCP to Rebecca Pemberton, November 17, 22, 1848, JCPP, PFP, HSP.

11. JCP to Anna Pemberton Hollingsworth, January 2, 1849, JCP to Rebecca Pemberton, January 8, 1849, JCPP, PFP, HSP; Mary Thompson to "My Dear Friend," December 2, 1848, CWP, CWM.

12. JCP to Rebecca Pemberton, January 8, 1849, JCPP, PFP, HSP.

13. Rebecca Pemberton to Israel Pemberton, March 6, 1849, IPP, Israel to Rebecca, February 5, 1849, RPP, JCP to Rebecca, February 14, 1849, JCPP, Pattie Pemberton to Rebecca, February 17, 1849, PPP in JCPP, PFP, HSP.

14. Rebecca Pemberton to Israel Pemberton, April 25, May 20, 1849, IPP, Pattie and JCP to Rebecca, April 20, 1849, PPP in JCPP, PFP, HSP; Edwin C. McReynolds, *The Seminoles* (Norman, 1957), 264–65.

15. Israel Pemberton, June 3, 1849, RPP, JCP to Israel, May 27, 1849, JCPP, PFP, HSP.

16. JCP to Israel Pemberton, May 27, 1849, JCPP, Rebecca Pemberton to Israel, June 19, 1849, JCPP, PFP, HSP.

17. JCP to Rebecca Pemberton, July 5?, 1849, JCPP, PFP, HSP.

18. Pattie Pemberton to Rebecca Pemberton, July 19, 1849, PPP in JCPP, JCP to Rebecca, October 26, 1849, JCPP, PFP, HSP.

19. JCP to Rebecca Pemberton, September 21, 1849, JCPP, PFP, HSP.

20. Pattie Pemberton to Rebecca Pemberton, December 12, 1849, PPP in JCPP, JCP to Rebecca, January 21, February 11, 1850, JCPP, PFP, HSP.

21. JCP to Rebecca Pemberton, January 21, 1850, JCP to Israel Pemberton, November 19, 1849, JCPP, Pattie Pemberton to Rebecca, December 12, 1849, PPP in JCPP, PFP, HSP.

22. JCP to Israel Pemberton, November 19, 1849, JCP to Rebecca Pemberton, January 21, February 11, 1850, JCPP, Rebecca to Israel, February 26, 1850, IPP, PFP, HSP; Mary Thompson to "My Dear Fanny" [not JCP's sister], February 25, 1850, CWP, CWM.

23. McReynolds, *Seminoles*, 267; Pattie Pemberton to Rebecca Pemberton, March 26, 1850, PPP in JCPP, PFP, HSP.

24. Powell A. Casey, *Encyclopedia of Forts, Posts, Named Camps, and Other Military Installations in Louisiana, 1700–1981* (Baton Rouge, 1983), 84–86, 88.

25. Pattie Pemberton to Rebecca Pemberton, March 26, 1850, Pattie to Israel Pemberton, May 8, 1850, PPP in JCPP, PFP, HSP; Mary Thompson to "My Dear Fanny," May 4, 1850, CWP, CWM.

26. Pattie Pemberton to Rebecca Pemberton, March 26, 1850, PPP in JCPP, PFP, HSP.

27. Ibid.; JCP to Rebecca Pemberton, April 7, 1850, JCPP, Pattie Pemberton to Israel Pemberton, May 8, 1850, PPP in JCPP, PFP, HSP; Mary Thompson to "My Dear Fanny," May 4, 1850, CWP, CWM.

28. Pattie Pemberton to Israel Pemberton, May 8, 1850, PPP in JCPP, JCP to Israel, June 1, 1850, JCPP, PFP, HSP.

29. Pattie Pemberton to Israel Pemberton, May 8, 1850, PPP in JCPP, PFP, HSP.

30. JCP to Rebecca Pemberton, July 13, 1850, JCPP, PFP, HSP.

31. Pattie Pemberton to Rebecca Pemberton, July 21, September 22, 1850, PPP in JCPP, PFP, HSP.

32. Rebecca Pemberton to Israel Pemberton, October 7, 1850, IPP, JCP to Rebecca, October 25, 1850, JCPP, PFP, HSP; Certificate of Promotion, Pemberton Papers, SHC.

33. Pattie Pemberton to Rebecca Pemberton, December 14, 1850, January 7, 1851, PPP in JCPP, Rebecca to Israel Pemberton, January 10, 1851, IPP, PFP, HSP.

34. JCP and Pattie Pemberton to Rebecca and Fanny (Frances) Pemberton, February 1, 1851, PPP in JCPP, Fanny to Israel Pemberton, March 14, 1851, Rebecca to Israel, April 15, 1851, IPP, JCP to Rebecca, April 14, 1851, JCPP, PFP, HSP.

35. Rebecca Pemberton to Israel Pemberton, November 2, 1851, IPP, PFP, HSP.

36. Ibid.

37. JCP to Rebecca Pemberton, February 27, 1851, JCPP, PFP, HSP; Mary Thompson to "My Dear Fanny," February 26, 1851, CWP, CWM.

38. JCP to Rebecca Pemberton, August 9, 1851, JCPP, Israel Pemberton to Rebecca, August 12, 18, 1851, RPP, Rebecca to Israel, August 12, 1851, IPP, PFP, HSP.

39. JCP to Israel Pemberton, January 3, 1852, Pattie Pemberton and JCP to Rebecca Pemberton, January 18, 1852, JCPP, Rebecca to Israel, January 26, 1852, IPP, PFP, HSP.

40. JCP to Israel Pemberton, January 3, 1852, JCPP, PFP, HSP.

41. Rebecca Pemberton to Israel Pemberton, March 25, April 11, May 3, 11, 1852, IPP, Israel to Rebecca, May 11, 1852, RPP, PFP, HSP.

42. Pattie Pemberton to Rebecca Pemberton, March 10, June 10, July 28, September 29, October 21, November 8, 17, 1852, PPP in JCPP, PFP, HSP.

43. JCP to Israel Pemberton, March 5, May 30, 1851, JCPP, Israel to Rebecca Pemberton, February 8, 1850, RPP, PFP, HSP.

44. Mary Thompson to "My Dear Fanny," December 20, 1852, CWP, CWM; JCP to Rebecca Pemberton, September 15, 1852, JCPP, Rebecca to Israel Pemberton, December 17, 26, 1852, IPP, PFP, HSP.

45. Rebecca Pemberton to Israel Pemberton, January 11, 1853, IPP, PFP, HSP.

46. Ibid., and February 3, 1853, Israel to Rebecca, December 25, 1852, February 13, 1853, RPP, PFP, HSP.

47. Fanny Pemberton to Rebecca Pemberton, March 3, 1853, RPP, PFP, HSP.

48. Rebecca Pemberton to Israel Pemberton, March 26, 1853, IPP, PFP, HSP. Rebecca's letter contains Fanny's account of the incident.

49. Rebecca Pemberton to Israel Pemberton, April 14, 1853, including two newspaper clippings (newspapers not identified), March, May 1853, IPP, Israel to Rebecca, June 2, 1853, RPP, PFP, HSP; Mary Thompson to "My Dear Mary," April 8, 1853, and to "My Dear Fanny," May 17, 1853, CWP, CWM; Lynda Lasswell Christ et al., eds., *The Papers of Jefferson Davis*, 6 vols. to date (Baton Rouge, 1971–), 5;187–88.

50. Mary Thompson to "My Dear Fanny," May 17, 1853, CWP, CWM; Pattie Pemberton and JCP to Rebecca Pemberton, April 21, 1853, Pattie to Caroline Pemberton, April 24, 1853, PPP in JCPP, PFP, HSP.

51. Mary Thompson to "My Dear Fanny," July 22, 1853, and to "My Dear Mary," September 19, 1853, CWP, CWM.

52. Pattie Pemberton to Israel Pemberton, September 15, 18, 1853, Pattie to Rebecca Pemberton, May 3, 19, 1853, PPP in JCPP, PFP, HSP; Mary Thompson to "My Dear Mary," September 19, 1853, CWP, CWM; JCP to Lt. Col. L. Thomas, September 14, 1853, Simon Gratz Autograph Collection, HSP.

53. Pattie Pemberton to Israel Pemberton, September 15, 1853, Pattie to Rebecca Pemberton, May 3, 19, 27, 1853, PPP in JCPP, PFP, HSP; Mary Thompson to "My Dear Fanny," May 17, July 22, 1853, CWP, CWM.

54. JCP to Israel Pemberton, March 25, 1854, May 13, 1856, JCP to Charles Newbold, March 2?, 1854, JCPP, Rebecca Pemberton to Israel, May 4, 1854, IPP, PFP, HSP.

55. Rebecca Pemberton to Israel Pemberton, December 22, 1854, IPP, JCP to Israel, May 13, 1856, JCPP, PFP, HSP; Mary Thompson to Mary Whittle, October 3, 1855, and to "My Dear Fanny," May 16, 1856, CWP, CWM.

56. McReynolds, *Seminoles*, 266–67, 286–88; Rebecca Pemberton to Israel Pemberton, December 27, 1856, IPP, PFP, HSP.

57. JCP to Israel Pemberton, June 8, 1857, JCPP, PFP, HSP; Mary Thompson to "My Dear Fanny," April 1, 1857, and to Mary Whittle, March 2, August 11, 1857, CWP, CWM.

58. G. W. Cullum, *Biographical Register of Officers and Graduates, U.S. Military Academy* (West Point, 1891), 1:684, excerpt in Pemberton Papers, SHC.

59. Mary Thompson to "My Dear Fanny," March 25, June 18, 1858, CWP, CWM; Pattie (JCP's daughter) Pemberton's reminiscences, Pemberton Papers, SHC.

60. Mary Thompson to "My Dear Fanny," November 2, 1858, CWP, CWM.

61. Kenneth Lee Walsh, "A Biography of a Frontier Outpost—Fort Ridgely," M.A. paper, University of Minnesota-Duluth, 7, 21, 31, Minnesota State Historical Society, St. Paul; Richard W. Musgrove, *Autobiography of Captain Richard W. Musgrove* (n. p., 1921), 161–162; Pattie Pemberton reminiscences, Pemberton Papers, SHC.

CHAPTER 6

1. Israel Pemberton to JCP, April 15, 1861, JCPP, PFP, HSP.

2. Ibid.

3. OR, ser. 1, vol. 2, p. 580. See also ser. 1, vol. 51, pt. 1, p. 329.

4. Rebecca Pemberton to Caroline Hollingsworth Pemberton, April 23, 1861, John C. Pemberton Papers, SHC.

5. Ibid.

6. Ibid.; *Twelfth Annual Reunion of the Association of the Graduates of the U.S. Military Academy at West Point, New York, June 9, 1881* (East Saginaw, Mich., 1881), 19, copy in Pemberton Papers, SHC.

7. John C. Pemberton, *Pemberton: Defender of Vicksburg* (Chapel Hill, 1942), 20–22; *Twelfth Annual Reunion*, 17; *Vicksburg Daily Herald*, April 19, 1874, clipping in Pemberton Papers, SHC.

8. OR, ser. 1, vol. 51, pt. 2, p. 50; Certificates of Rank, *Vicksburg Daily Herald*, April 19, 1874, clipping, all in Pemberton Papers, SHC; Joseph E. Johnston, *Narrative of Military Operations, Directed, during the Late War between the States* (New York, 1874), 12.

9. OR, ser. 1, vol. 2, pp. 856, 963; Certificates of Rank, Pemberton Papers, SHC.

10. John M. Daniel, *The Richmond Examiner during the Civil War, or the Writings of John M. Daniel* (1868; rpt. New York, 1970), 16–17; *Daily Richmond Enquirer*, May 14, 1861.

11. OR, ser. 1, vol. 2, pp. 982–83, ser. 1, vol. 4, p. 666; Douglas Southall

Freeman, *Lee's Lieutenants: A Study in Command*, 3 vols. (New York, 1942–44), 1:204.

12. Douglas Southall Freeman, *R. E. Lee: A Biography*, 4 vols. (New York, 1934–35), 1:606; Charles E. Cauthen, *South Carolina Goes to War, 1860–1865* (Chapel Hill, 1950), 136–37.

13. *OR*, ser. 1, vol. 6, p. 334.

14. Ibid., 344–45.

15. Freeman, *R. E. Lee*, 1:613, 630–31.

16. *OR*, ser. 1, vol. 6, pp. 44–46, 66–68, 344.

17. Ibid., 366.

18. *Ibid.*, 374–75, 395, 398; *ORN*, ser. 1, vol. 12, pp. 495, 560.

19. Certificates of Rank, Pemberton Papers, SHC.

20. *OR*, ser. 1, vol. 6, pp. 402, 407.

21. Ibid., 414, 523.

22. Ibid., 309, 407, 428, 430, 432.

23. Ibid., 414; JCP to Samuel Cooper, September 6, 1862, JCP to Judah P. Benjamin, March 24, 1862, Letters Sent and Received by Gen. J. C. Pemberton, March–September 1862, RG 109, Chap. II, vol. 21, NA; General Orders 23, June 3, 1862, Orders, Department of South Carolina and Georgia, November 1861–September 1862, RG 109, Chap. II, vol. 42, NA.

24. JCP to Judah P. Benjamin, March 25, 1862, JCP to George Randolph, May 18, 1862, Robert E. Lee to JCP, May 31, 1862, JCP to W. H. Taylor, April 28, 1862, JCP to Lee, April 26, 1862, JCP to Samuel Cooper, May 5, 1862, JCP to Lee, May 31, 1862, Randolph to JCP, April 3, 1862, JCP to Randolph, March 27, 1862, JCP to Frances Pickens, June 26, 1862, RG 109, Chap. II, vol. 21, NA.

25. JCP to Samuel Cooper, July 28, 1862, George Randolph to JCP, July 8, 1862, JCP to Robert E. Lee, May 31, 1862, JCP to Francis Pickens, June 25, 1862, JCP to C. G. Memminger, July 5, 1862, Ibid.

26. JCP to I. W. Hayne, March 9, 1862, Ibid.; Charles E. Cauthen, ed., *Journals of the South Carolina Executive Councils of 1861 and 1862* (Columbia, 1956), 114–15; Cauthen, *South Carolina Goes to War*, 142, 144, 161.

27. JCP to I. W. Hayne, March 22, 1862, RG 109, Chap. II, vol. 21, NA.

28. JCP to I. W. Hayne, June 7, 1862, JCP to Francis Pickens, June 15, 26, 1862, JCP to James Chesnut, August 13, 1862, JCP to W. W. Harllee, August 30, 1862, Chesnut to JCP, August 5, 1862, ibid.; Cauthen, ed., *Journals of Councils*, 164, 169, 233.

29. Cauthen, ed., *Journals of Councils*, 240–41, 256–57.

30. See Cauthen, *South Carolina Goes to War*, 147–49.

31. JCP to Samuel Cooper, June 12, 1862, RG 109, Chap. II, vol. 21, NA; Alfred Roman, *The Military Operations of General Beauregard in the War between the States, 1861 to 1865*, 2 vols. (New York, 1883), 2:4–5.

32. JCP to Robert E. Lee, April 10, 19, 1862, Lee to JCP, April 10, 1862, JCP to T. A. Washington, April 23, 1862, RG 109, Chap. II, vol. 21, NA.

33. JCP to Jefferson Davis, June 4, 5, 1862, Davis to JCP, June 4, 1862, George Randolph to JCP, June 11, 1862, JCP to Randolph, June 18, 1862, Robert E. Lee to JCP, April 21, May 23, 1862, ibid.; OR, ser. 1, vol. 14, pp. 568, 575, 591.

34. JCP to Samuel Cooper, April 9, 1862, JCP to Robert E. Lee, April 10, 1862, RG 109, Chap. II, vol. 21, NA; OR, ser. 1, vol. 14, pp. 471–72.

35. JCP to George Randolph, April 19, 1862, RG 109, Chap. II, vol. 21, NA.

36. George Randolph to JCP, May 7, 1862, ibid.; OR, ser. 1, vol. 14, pp. 502, 547–48.

37. JCP to I. W. Hayne, March 18, 27, April 2, 21, 1862, R. W. Memminger to Hayne, April 16, 1862, JCP to W. W. Harllee, April 26, 28, 1862, Harllee to JCP, April 23, 1862, JCP to Francis Pickens, June 26, 1862, JCP to Samuel Cooper, April 9, 1862, JCP to T. A. Washington, April 23, 1862, R. H. Chilton to JCP, May 13, 1862, RG 109, Chap. II, vol. 21, NA; Cauthen, ed., *Journals of Councils*, 165; OR., ser. 1, vol. 14, pp. 428, 503.

38. JCP to Robert E. Lee, April 11, 1862, RG 109, Chap. II, vol. 21, NA.

39. JCP to Francis Pickens, April 28, May 1, 1862, Pickens to JCP, April 28, 1862, ibid.; Cauthen, ed., *Journals of Councils*, 161–62, 165; OR, ser. 1, vol. 14, pp. 491–92.

40. OR, ser. 1, vol. 14, pp. 492, 495, 497; Robert E. Lee to JCP, May 7, 1862, JCP to Lee, May 8, 9, 1862, RG 109, chap. II, vol. 21, NA.

41. OR, ser. 1, vol. 14, pp. 593–94, 596–94, 596–99; Jefferson Davis to JCP, August 6, 1862, JCP to Francis Pickens, August 15, 1862, RG 109, Chap. II, vol. 21, NA.

42. OR, ser. 1, vol. 14, p. 477; JCP to Samuel Cooper, March 18, 1862, RG 109, Chap. II, vol. 21, NA.

43. John B. Edmunds, Jr., *Francis W. Pickens and the Politics of Destruction* (Chapel Hill, 1986), 10, 167–69.

44. R. W. Memminger to Francis Pickens, May 10, 1862, JCP to Pickens, May 28, 1862, Pickens to JCP, May 16, 26, 1862, F. J. Moses to JCP, May 20, 1862, RG 109, Chap. II, vol. 21, NA.

45. James Chesnut to JCP, May 20, 1862, Francis Pickens to JCP, May 23, 1862, JCP to Chesnut, May 23, 1862, ibid.; OR, ser. 1, vol. 14, 515–18, 524, 527–28.

46. JCP to Samuel Cooper, March 27, 1862, RG 109, Chap. II, vol. 21, NA.

47. OR, ser. 1, vol. 14, pp. 423–24.

48. Ibid., 424–25.

49. Ibid., 429–30.

50. Ibid., 433–34, 476; JCP to Francis Pickens, April 10, 1862, RG 109, Chap. II, vol. 21, NA.

51. Freeman, *R. E. Lee*, 1:627; JCP to Robert E. Lee, April 10, 1862, RG 109, Chap. II, vol. 21, NA; OR, ser. 1, vol. 6, p. 166.

52. OR, ser. 1, vol. 14, pp. 13–15; JCP to A. L. Long, May 21, 1862, RG 109, Chap. II, vol. 21, NA.

53. *Charleston Daily Courier*, July 31, 1862.

54. OR, ser. 1, vol. 14, p. 483; JCP to W. H. Taylor, May 14, 1862, RG 109, Chap. II, vol. 21; NA.

55. JCP to A. L. Long, May 21, 1862, RG 109, Chap. II, vol. 21, NA; OR, ser. 1, vol. 14, pp. 503–4, 524.

56. OR, ser. 1, vol. 14, pp. 490–91.

57. Ibid.

58. JCP to A. L. Long, May 21, 1862, RG 109, Chap. II, vol. 21, NA.

59. OR, ser. 1, vol. 14, pp. 510–11.

60. Ibid., 513.

61. Ibid., 514.

62. Francis Pickens to JCP, May 23, 1862, RG 109, Chap. II, vol. 21, NA.

63. OR, ser. 1, vol. 14, pp. 523–24; Dunbar Rowland, ed., *Jefferson Davis, Constitutionalist: His Letters, Papers, and Speeches*, 10 vols. (Jackson, Miss., 1923), 5:327.

64. Francis Pickens to Jefferson Davis, June 12, 1862, in Letterbook, vol. 6, January 1861–May 1862, Samuel Wylie Crawford Papers, Library of Congress.

65. JCP to Jefferson Davis, June 2, 5, 1862, JCP to George Randolph, June 3, 1862 (three messages), JCP to James Chesnut, June 6, 1862, RG 109, Chap. II, vol. 21, NA.

66. OR, ser. 1, vol. 14, p. 567.

67. E. Milby Burton, *The Siege of Charleston, 1861–1865* (Columbia, S.C., 1970), 99, 105–9.

68. OR, ser. 1, vol. 14, pp. 89–90.

69. Ibid., pp. 85–88; *Charleston Daily Courier*, June 26, 1862.

70. Burton, *Siege of Charleston*, 114.

71. OR, ser. 1, vol. 14, pp. 573, 579, 588–89; JCP to Samuel Cooper, July 10, 1862, RG 109, Chap. II, vol. 21, NA.

72. OR, ser. 1, vol. 53, p. 247.

73. Ibid., ser. 1, vol. 14, p. 560.

74. C. Vann Woodward, ed., *Mary Chesnut's Civil War* (New Haven, 1981), 332, 375; John F. Marszalek, ed., *The Diary of Miss Emma Holmes, 1861–1866* (Baton Rouge, 1979), 174, 177.

75. John G. Pressley, "Extracts from the Diary of Lieutenant-Colonel John G. Pressley, of the Twenty-Fifth South Carolina Volunteers," *Southern Historical Society Papers* 14 (January–December 1886): 36–37; Pressley, "The Wee Nee Volunteers of Williamsburg District, South Carolina, in the First (Hagood's) Regiment, *Southern Historical Society Papers* 16 (January–December 1888): 131.

76. OR, ser. 1, vol. 14, pp. 560–61, 567, 569; Rowland, *Jefferson Davis*, 5:275.

77. Burton, *Siege of Charleston*, 114.

78. OR, ser. 1, vol. 14, pp. 569–70.

79. Ibid., 579.

80. JCP to George Randolph, June 24, 1862, Randolph to JCP, June 25, 1862, RG 109, Chap. II, vol. 21, NA.

81. OR, ser. 1, vol. 14, pp. 581–82, 584–85.

82. Ibid., 594.

83. Ibid., 597–98.

84. Francis Pickens to Jefferson Davis, August 20, 1862, vol. 2, Crawford Papers, Library of Congress.

85. OR, ser. 1, vol. 14, p. 601; George Randolph to JCP, August 28, 1862, Pemberton Papers, SHC.

86. OR, ser. 1, vol. 14, p. 601.

87. *Charleston Daily Courier*, September 26, 1862.

88. *Charleston Mercury*, September 29, 1862, clipping in Pemberton Papers, SHC; Pemberton, *Pemberton*, 29–30.

89. OR, ser. 1, vol. 14, pp. 603–4, 608–9, 613.

90. *Charleston Daily Courier*, September 26, 1862; A. J. Gonzales to JCP, September 17, 1863, Pemberton Papers, SHC.

91. Richard M. McMurry, *Two Great Rebel Armies: An Essay in Confederate Military History* (Chapel Hill, 1989), 35.

Chapter 7

1. OR, ser. 1, vol. 15, p. 820.

2. Ibid., ser. 1, vol. 51, pt. 2, p. 638.

3. Ibid., ser. 1, vol. 17, pt. 2, pp. 726–17.

4. *Columbus* (Georgia) *Sun*, quoted in *Charleston Daily Courier*, October 16, 1862; *Richmond Examiner* quoted in *Memphis Daily Appeal*, October 25, 1862.

5. *Mobile Advertiser and Register* quoted in *Charleston Daily Courier*, October 18, 1862; Edwin Cole Bearss, *Vicksburg Is the Key*, vol. 1 of *The Campaign for Vicksburg*, 3 vols. (Dayton, Ohio, 1985–86), 43; Ezra J. Warner,

Generals in Gray: Lives of the Confederate Commanders (Baton Rouge, 1970), 314–15, 194–95.

6. R. W. Memminger, "The Surrender of Vicksburg—A Defence of General Pemberton," *Southern Historical Society Papers* 12 (July–August–September 1884): 353.

7. *Jackson Daily Mississippian* quoted in *Memphis Daily Appeal* (published in Grenada, Mississippi, at the time), November 28 [29], 1862.

8. Earl Schenck Miers, *The Web of Victory: Grant at Vicksburg* (1955; rpt. Baton Rouge, 1984), 38–39; David D. Porter, *Incidents and Anecdotes of the Civil War* (New York, 1885), 95–96.

9. *New York Herald*, August 17, 1881, clipping in John Clifford Pemberton Papers, Library of Congress.

10. *OR*, ser. 1, vol. 17, pt. 2, p. 752.

11. Ibid., 157–58.

12. Warner, *Generals in Gray*, 141; Albert Castel, *General Sterling Price and the Civil War in the West* (Baton Rouge, 1968), 141; *OR*, ser. 1, vol. 13, p. 888; Steven E. Woodworth, *Jefferson Davis and His Generals: The Failure of Confederate Command in the West* (Lawrence, Kan., 1990), 182. On Holmes's resistance to cooperation, see *OR*, ser. 1, vol. 17, pt. 2, pp. 754, 757, 763, 767–68, 771, 786.

13. *OR*, ser. 1, vol. 17, pt. 2, pp. 757, 787.

14. *OR*, ser. 1, vol. 15, p. 840, ser. 1, vol. 17, pt. 2, p. 814. The paper strength of the entire department as of December 1862 was over seventy thousand, but the "aggregate present" strength at that time was only forty-eight thousand, which, when scattered over a wide area, was not sufficient. When he first assumed command it was much less.

15. John C. Pemberton [III], *Pemberton: Defender of Vicksburg* (Chapel Hill, 1942), 290; *OR*, ser. 1, vol. 15, p. 841.

16. Warner, *Generals in Gray*, 97; *OR*, ser. 1, vol. 15, p. 913.

17. *OR*, ser. 1, vol. 17, pt. 2, p. 728.

18. Ibid., 735.

19. Ibid., 739, 759–61; Castel, *General Sterling Price*, 128.

20. "Capt. J. T. Cobbs—Ranger, Soldier, Scout," *Confederate Veteran* 5 (October 1897): 526; *OR*, ser. 1, vol. 17, pt. 2, p. 740.

21. Ephraim McD. Anderson, *Memoirs: Historical and Personal, Including the Campaigns of the First Missouri Confederate Brigade* (1868), ed. Edwin C. Bearss (Dayton, Ohio, 1972), 245; Bell Irvin Wiley and Lucy E. Fay, eds., *"This Infernal War": The Confederate Letters of Sgt. Edwin H. Fay* (Austin, 1958), 179.

22. *OR*, ser. 1, vol. 17, pt. 2, p. 745; *Memphis Daily Appeal* [Grenada], November 15, 1862.

23. John K. Bettersworth, *Confederate Mississippi: The People and Policies of a Cotton State in Wartime* (1943; rpt. Philadelphia, 1978), 46–47.

24. JCP to John J. Pettus, February 3, 14, April 1, 25, 1863, microfilm reels MF-39, MF-40, and Military Orders Issued, December 23, 1862–November 17, 1863, pp. 20–59, 81–104, 128, 156, 168–217, box 58, all in Governors' Papers, GG 27, Mississippi Department of Archives and History, Jackson.

25. Bettersworth, *Confederate Mississippi*, 48–49, 66–68; OR, ser. 1, vol. 24, pt. 3, pp. 737–38, 740–41, 745–46, 758.

26. Bearss, *Vicksburg Is the Key*, 599–604; JCP to Daniel Ruggles, January 30, February 15, March 2, 1863, John Clifford Pemberton Papers, United States Naval Academy Archives, Annapolis, Maryland; OR, ser. 1, vol. 24, pt. 3, pp. 625, 634–35.

27. OR, ser. 1, vol. 24, pt. 3, p. 635, ser. 1, vol. 15, p. 864.

28. "An Interesting Batch of Telegrams," *Confederate Veteran* 2 (April 1894): 110–11; Bearss, *Vicksburg Is the Key*, 607, 704; OR, ser. 1, vol. 17, pt. 2, pp. 839–40, ser. 1, vol. 24, pt. 3, pp. 594–95, 610–11, 634–35, 743, ser. 1, vol. 52, pt. 2, p. 412; Jefferson Davis to JCP, January 14, 1863, Samuel Richey Collection, Walter Havighurst Special Collections, Miami University Library, Oxford, Ohio.

29. OR, ser. 1, vol. 17, pt. 2, pp. 870–73, ser. 1, vol. 24, pt. 3, pp. 636–37. Sherman did have the Tennessee town of Randolph leveled in September 1862 as retaliation against guerrilla activity.

30. OR, ser. 1, vol. 17, pt. 2, pp. 754–55.

31. OR, ser. 1, vol. 17, pt. 2, pp. 763, 765–66, 771–72, 778–79, 785–86; Bearss, *Vicksburg Is the Key*, 22, 57, 86.

32. OR, ser. 1, vol. 17, pt. 1, pp. 472, 474.

33. Bearss, *Vicksburg Is the Key*, 289–90.

34. Robert G. Hartje, *Van Dorn: The Life and Times of a Confederate General* (Nashville, 1967), 254–69; OR, ser. 1, vol. 17, pt. 2, p. 451.

35. R. S. Bevier, *History of the First and Second Missouri Confederate Brigades, 1861–1865* . . . (1879; rpt. St. Louis, 1985), 175; *Jackson Daily Mississippian*, December 7, 1862, quoted in *New Orleans Daily Picayune*, December 12, 1862.

36. Bearss, *Vicksburg Is the Key*, 143–46.

37. Ibid., 148–50; Bevier, *History of First and Second Missouri*, 166–67.

38. Bearss, *Vicksburg Is the Key*, 154.

39. Ibid., 172, 190, 200, 208–9; OR, ser. 1, vol. 17, pt. 1, p. 669.

40. *Memphis Daily Appeal* (Jackson), January 5, 6, 1863.

41. *Philadelphia Inquirer*, November 27, 1862.

42. *New Orleans Daily Delta*, November 12, 1862.

43. For reaction within the region of Pemberton's command see the *New Orleans Daily Picayune*, December 24, 1862.

44. *Memphis Daily Appeal* (Jackson), December 16, 1862. The *Appeal* reaction is noted by the *Picayune*, December 24, 1862.

45. Bearss, *Vicksburg Is the Key*, 437, 448–49; OR, ser. 1, vol. 24, pt. 3, p. 618.

46. Bearss, *Vicksburg Is the Key*, 467, 478.

47. River warfare in the campaign is discussed at length in ibid., 597–704.

48. Ibid., 482–83.

49. The Yazoo Pass expedition and the Steele's Bayou episode are discussed in ibid., 479–595. On Pemberton's role during the Yazoo Pass operations see pages 483, 485, 497–507, 539–41, 547. See also ORN, ser. 1, vol. 23, p. 709, ser. 1, vol. 24, p. 294.

50. Bearss, *Vicksburg Is the Key*, 503, 539; Warner, *Generals in Gray*, 194; William A. Drennon Diary, May 30–July 4, 1863, p. 6, Mississippi Department of Archives and History, Jackson; F.W.M., "Career and Fate of Gen. Lloyd Tilghman," *Confederate Veteran* 9 (September 1893): 274–75; JCP, General Orders No. 33, February 1, 1863, Orders and Circulars, 1862–65, Records of the Department of Mississippi and East Louisiana and of the Department of Alabama, Mississippi, and East Louisiana, Entry 94, Lloyd Tilghman to John Waddy, January 27, 1863, Gen. J. C. Pemberton Papers, 1862–64, Entry 131, all in RG 109, NA.

51. Bearss, *Vicksburg Is the Key*, 504–5, 547, 717.

52. OR, ser. 1, vol. 24, pt. 3, pp. 618, 650, 151–52.

53. Ibid., vol. 24, pt. 1, p. 24, pt. 3, pp. 714, 719.

54. Edwin Cole Bearss, *Grant Strikes a Fatal Blow*, vol. 2 of *The Campaign for Vicksburg*, 3 vols. (Dayton, Ohio, 1985–86), 107–26.

55. OR, ser. 1, vol. 24, pt. 3, p. 724.

56. Ibid., 730.

57. Ibid.

58. Ibid., 731–33, 749, 751; Bearss, *Grant Strikes a Fatal Blow*, 88, 90.

59. OR, ser. 1, vol. 24, pt. 3, pp. 734, 738.

60. Ibid., 743–44.

61. Ibid., 744–45.

62. Ibid., 747, 749, 751–53, 760–61.

63. Ibid., 754–55.

64. Ibid., vol. 15, pp. 1046–47, 1049–50, 1058.

65. D. Alexander Brown, *Grierson's Raid* (Urbana, Ill. 1962), 8–9.

66. Ibid., 17; JCP to Daniel Ruggles, April 20, 1863, Pemberton papers, Naval Academy Archives; OR, ser. 1, vol. 24, pt. 3, p. 776.

67. OR, ser. 1, vol. 24, pt. 3, pp. 783–87; Brown, *Grierson's Raid*, 62, 108–13.

68. *OR*, ser. 1, vol. 24, pt. 1, p. 532, pt. 3, pp. 785, 791.

69. Brown, *Grierson's Raid*, 144, 185.

70. *OR*, ser. 1, vol. 24, pt. 3, pp. 792, 794, 798, 802–3; John C. Taylor Diary, April 2–July 7, 1863, April 27 entry, Harry Baylor Taylor Papers, University of Virginia Library, Charlottesville.

71. *OR*, ser. 1, vol. 24, pt. 3, pp. 792–93, 797; Bearss, *Grant Strikes a Fatal Blow*, 253, 258–59, 267.

72. *OR*, ser. 1, vol. 24, pt. 3, pp. 797, 804. On the bombardment of Grand Gulf, see Bearss, *Grant Strikes a Fatal Blow*, 291–316.

CHAPTER 8

1. For an account of the battle at Port Gibson see Bearss, *Grant Strikes a Fatal Blow*, vol. 2 of *The Campaign for Vicksburg*, 3 vols. (Dayton, Ohio, 1985–86), 317–407.

2. *OR*, ser. 1, vol. 24, p. 3, pp. 807–8, 844.

3. Ibid., 808, 815.

4. For recent comments about the conflict between the two generals see Larry J. Daniel, "Bruinsburg: Missed Opportunity or Postwar Rhetoric?" *Civil War History* 33 (September 1986): 264–65; Lawrence Lee Hewitt, *Port Hudson: Confederate Bastion on the Mississippi* (Baton Rouge, 1987), 44, 124, 127.

5. *OR*, ser. 1, vol. 24, pt. 3, pp. 839, 842.

6. Daniel, "Bruinsburg," 256–67, esp. 265–67.

7. *OR*, ser. 1, vol. 24, pt. 3, pp. 814–15, 828, 835, 840, 842, 845.

8. Bearss, *Grant Strikes a Blow*, 22–23, 434–35; Hewitt, *Port Hudson*, 108–9, 125,127.

9. *OR*, ser. 1, vol. 234, pt. 3, pp. 808–9, 846, 935–36; Edwin Cole Bearss, *Unvexed to the Sea*, vol. 3 of *The Campaign for Vicksburg* (Dayton, Ohio, 1985–86), 1153–1241.

10. *OR*, ser. 1, vol. 24, pt. 3, pp. 810–13.

11. Ibid., 809.

12. Ibid., 808, 813, 820, 826–27, 831–33, 845, 858, 875.

13. For a critical view of Pemberton's handling of his cavalry see Daniel, "Bruinsburg," 259. Forrest had been wounded by an unhappy soldier. See John Allan Wyeth, *That Devil Forrest: Life of General Nathan Bedford Forrest* (1899; rpt. New York, 1959), 200–202. On the Van Dorn incident see Robert G. Hartje, *Van Dorn: The Life and Times of a Confederate General* (Nashville, 1967), 307–27.

14. *OR*, ser. 1, vol. 24, pt. 3, pp. 815–16, 818.

15. Ibid., 821.

16. Bearss, *Grant Strikes a Fatal Blow*, 423.

17. Ibid., 441, 443, 453–54; *OR*, ser. 1, vol. 24, pt. 3, pp. 823, 828, 835–36, 843.

18. *OR*, ser. 1, vol. 24, pt. 3, p. 849.

19. Ibid., 846.

20. Ibid., 851, 853.

21. Ibid., 851.

22. Ibid., 852.

23. Ibid., 852–56.

24. Ibid., 856–58.

25. Ibid., 859.

26. Bearss, *Grant Strikes a Fatal Blow*, 482.

27. *OR*, ser. 1, vol. 24, pt. 3, pp. 858, 863–64.

28. Ibid., 861, 863, 865.

29. Ibid., 862, 864, pt. 1, pp. 260, 737.

30. Bearss, *Grant Strikes a Fatal Blow*, 480, 512–14.

31. Joseph E. Johnston, *Narrative of Military Operations, Directed, during the Late War between the States* (New York, 1874), 172–73, 187.

32. Ibid., 506; *OR*, ser. 1, vol. 24, pt. 3, pp. 870, 872.

33. Cooper and Kimball, editors of the *Mississippian*, to Jefferson Davis, May 8, 1863, Jefferson Davis Papers, Louisiana Historical Collection, Howard-Tilton Memorial Library, Tulane University, New Orleans. Davis was surprised at the criticism and hoped the editors could "correct" the situation. See *OR*, ser. 1, vol. 52, pt. 2, p. 469.

34. *OR*, ser. 1, vol. 24, pt. 3, pp. 873, 875; Bearss, *Grant Strikes a Blow*, 561.

35. *OR*, ser. 1, vol. 24, pt. 3, p. 877.

36. Ibid., pt. 1, p. 261, pt. 2, p. 125.

37. Ibid., pt. 1, pp. 261–62; Bearss, *Grant Strikes a Blow*, 480–81.

38. Thomas R. Phillips, ed., *Roots of Strategy* (Harrisburg, Pa., 1955), 427; Johnston, *Narrative of Military Operations*, 181; S. H. Lockett, "The Defense of Vicksburg," in Robert Underwood Johnson and Clarence Clough Buel, eds., *Battles and Leaders of the Civil War*, 4 vols. (1887–88; rpt. New York, 1956), 3:487.

39. *OR*, ser. 1, vol. 24, pt. 3, p. 876. The time is on a copy of the original document. See JCP to Johnston, May 14, 1863, JCP Letterbook in Benjamin S. Ewell Collection, Swem Library, CWM.

40. *OR*, ser. 1, vol. 24, pt. 3, pp. 876, 882, pt. 1, p. 240.

41. Bearss, *Grant Strikes a Blow*, 554.

42. *OR*, ser. 1, vol. 24, pt. 3, pp. 877–78.

43. Ibid., pt. 2, p. 74, pt. 1, p. 262, pt. 3, p. 883.

44. Bearss, *Grant Strikes a Blow*, 575–76.

45. *OR*, ser. 1, vol. 24, pt. 2, p. 75, pt. 1, p. 263.

46. Ibid., pt. 1, pp. 241, 263.

47. Bearss, *Grant Strikes a Blow*, 562–63, 568, 571.

48. *OR*, ser. 1, vol. 24, pt. 1, p. 263, pt. 2, p. 75.

49. William A. Drennan Diary, May 30–July 4, 1863, p. 4, and James R. Binford, "Recollections of the Fifteenth Regiment of Mississippi Infantry, C.S.A.," in Patrick Henry Papers, p. 41, both in Mississippi Department of Archives and History, Jackson.

50. Drennan Diary, pp. 6–7.

51. *OR*, ser. 1, vol. 24, pt. 1, p. 263, pt. 2, p. 126; Bearss, *Grant Strikes a Blow*, 586.

52. Bearss, *Grant Strikes a Blow*, 592–93.

53. Ibid., 563, 605–6; Drennan Diary, p. 2.

54. Bearss, *Grant Strikes a Blow*, 563–64, 607.

55. *OR*, ser. 1, vol. 24, pt. 2, pp. 94–95, 110, 120–21, pt. 1, p. 264; Ephraim McD. Anderson, *Memoirs: Historical and Personal, Including the Campaigns of the First Missouri Confederate Brigade* (1868), ed. Edwin C. Bearss (Dayton, Ohio, 1972), 311–12; James E. Payne, "Missouri Troops in the Vicksburg Campaign," *Confederate Veteran* 36 (September 1928): 340. In his memoirs, Anderson mistakenly places the women singing "Dixie" in the yard of the Champion house.

56. Bearss, *Grant Strikes a Blow*, 609–14, 621.

57. *OR*, ser. 1, vol. 24, pt. 2, p. 126, pt. 1, pp. 264–65. For an analysis of Pemberton's misuse of troops available to him, see Bearss, *Grant Strikes a Blow*, 641–42.

58. *OR*, ser. 1, vol. 24, pt. 1, pp. 241, 265; Drennan Diary, pp. 9–10; Francis G. Obenchain to William F. Rigby, July 4, 1903, General Correspondence Files, and John A. Leavy Diary, May 16, 1863, both in Vicksburg National Military Park Collection, Vicksburg, Mississippi.

59. I am indebted to Terrence J. Winschel, historian of the Vicksburg National Military Park, for pointing out the mystery of Stevenson's activities during the battle.

60. Bearss, *Grant Strikes a Blow*, 627, 636–37, 642.

61. *OR*, ser. 1, vol. 24, pt. 1, p. 241, pt. 3, p. 887.

62. Bearss, *Grant Strikes a Blow*, 653–58.

63. Ibid., 669, 673–76; B. E. Houston, "History of Vaughn's Confederate Brigade," quoted in Bearss, *Grant Strikes a Blow*, 669; Lockett, "Defense of Vicksburg," 488.

64. Lockett, "Defense of Vicksburg," 488.

65. *OR*, ser. 1, vol. 24, pt. 3, p. 887.

66. Ibid., pt. 1, p. 272.

Chapter 9

1. James E. Payne, "Missouri Troops in the Vicksburg Campaign," *Confederate Veteran* 36 (October 1928): 377; Edwin C. Bearss, *Unvexed to the Sea*, vol. 3 of *The Vicksburg Campaign*, 3 vols. (Dayton, Ohio, 1985–86), 735; Mary Ann Loughborough, *My Cave Life in Vicksburg* (New York, 1864), 43.

2. Emma Balfour Diary, May 16–31, 1863, p. 3, Mississippi Department of Archives and History, Jackson; R. S. Bevier, *History of the First and Second Missouri Confederate Missouri Brigades, 1861–1865* . . . (1879; rpt. St. Louis, 1985), 200; OR, ser. 1, vol. 24, p. 3, p. 890.

3. Lieut.-Col. [James A. L.] Fremantle, *Three Months in the Southern States, April–June, 1863* (New York, 1864), 116; Balfour Diary, p. 3.

4. John S. C. Abbott, *The History of the Civil War in America . . .* , 2 vols. (New York, 1873), 2:292.

5. S. H. Lockett, "The Defense of Vicksburg," in Robert Underwood Johnson and Clarence Clough Buel. eds., *Battles and Leaders of the Civil War*, 4 vols. (1887–88; rpt. New York, 1956), 3:488; Lockett, "The Defense of Vicksburg—Notes and Sketches from an Engineering Point of View," manuscript in Samuel Henry Lockett Papers, SHC.

6. Lockett, "Defense of Vicksburg," 488.

7. OR, ser. 1, vol. 24 pt. 3, pp. 891–92.

8. Ibid., pp. 890, 893–94; Bearss, *Unvexed to the Sea*, 773.

9. OR, ser. 1, vol. 24, pt. 3, p. 899.

10. Ibid., 903.

11. Ibid., pt. 1, p. 276; Bearss, *Unvexed to the Sea*, 858, 869.

12. Kenneth Trist Urquhart, ed., *Vicksburg: Southern City under Siege, William Lovelace Foster's Letters Describing the Defense and Surrender of the Confederate Fortress on the Mississippi* (New Orleans, 1980), 3, 20; Bevier, *First and Second Missouri*, 200.

13. OR, ser. 1, vol. 24, pt. 3, pp. 909, 916.

14. Ibid., pp. 917, 930–31, pt. 1, p. 278.

15. Ibid., pt. 1, pp. 276–77.

16. Ibid., p. 277, pt. 3, pp. 933, 937.

17. A. A. Hoehling et al., eds. *Vicksburg: 47 Days of Siege, May 18–July 4, 1863* (Englewood Cliffs, 1969), 43–44, 50, 267.

18. Ibid., 44, 103, 117, 157.

19. OR, ser. 1, vol. 24, pt. 1, pp. 277–78, pt. 3, p. 913.

20. Pattie Pemberton to Nelie Lockett, May 28, 1863, Lockett Papers, SHC.

21. Balfour Diary, pp. 16, 18–19.

22. OR, ser. 1, vol. 24, pt. 1, p. 278, pt. 3, p. 953.

23. Ibid., pt. 1, p. 278, pt. 3, p. 958.

24. Ibid., pt. 1, p. 279.

25. Ibid., pt. 3, p. 963.

26. Ibid., pp. 964, 967.

27. Ibid., pp. 963, 965–66, pt. 1, 279–80.

28. Ibid., pt. 3, pp. 970–71; Bearss, *Unvexed to the Sea*, 1063–65; Dunbar Rowland, ed., *Jefferson Davis, Constitutionalist: His Letters, Papers, and Speeches*, 10 vols. (Jackson, Miss., 1923), 5:556–63; Lawrence Lee Hewitt, *Port Hudson: Confederate Bastion on the Mississippi* (Baton Rouge, 1987), 127.

29. *OR*, ser. 1, vol. 24, pt. 3, p. 969.

30. I am indebted to Vicksburg National Park historian Terrence J. Winschel for strategic insights regarding the breakout plan. Discussion of some of those potential problems by Pemberton's generals are in *OR*, ser. 1, vol. 24, pt. 1, pp. 281–83.

31. *OR*, ser. 1, vol. 24, pt. 3, p. 971.

32. Ibid., 974.

33. Ibid., pt. 1, pp. 280–81.

34. Ibid., pt. 3, pp. 980, 987; Bearss, *Unvexed to the Sea*, 1131, 1134.

35. *OR*, ser. 1, vol. 24, pt. 3, pp. 971, 981; Bearss, *Unvexed to the Sea*, 1063.

36. *OR*, ser. 1, vol. 24, pt. 3, pp. 982–83; Bearss, *Unvexed to the Sea*, 1281.

37. *OR*, ser. 1, vol. 24, pt. 1, p. 281.

38. Ibid., 281–83.

39. Ibid., 283.

40. Ibid., 283–84.

41. Ibid., 284; John C. Pemberton, "The Terms of Surrender," in Johnson and Buel, eds., *Battles and Leaders of the Civil War*, 3:544; Bearss, *Unvexed to the Sea*, 1287n.

42. Pemberton, "Terms of Surrender," 544–45; *OR*, ser. 1, vol. 24, pt. 1, p. 284.

43. *OR*, ser. 1, vol. 24, pt. 1, p. 284.

44. Ibid. 284–85; Edward Cunningham, *The Port Hudson Campaign, 1862–1863* (Baton Rouge, 1963), 117–18.

45. *OR*, ser. 1, vol. 24, pt. 1, pp. 285, 292; Battle McCardle to John C. Pemberton III, May 27, 1937, John C. Pemberton III Collection, Mississippi Department of Archives and History, Jackson; Bearss, *Unvexed to the Sea*, 1301.

46. Bearss, *Unvexed to the Sea*, pp. 1293–94; "Fred Grant as a Boy with the Army," *Confederate Veteran* 16 (January 1908): 14.

47. *OR*, ser. 1, vol. 24, pt. 3, pp. 993, 1000.

48. Ibid., 1001–2; Bearss, *Unvexed to the Sea*, 1305; John C. Pemberton [III], *Pemberton: Defender of Vicksburg* (Chapel Hill, 1942), 241; "Capture of a Soldier and What Followed," *Confederate Veteran* 15 (May 1907): 234.

49. OR, ser. 1, vol. 24, pt. 3, pp. 1002, 1005, 1007, 1010.

50. Ibid., 1015, 1018, 1025.

51. Ibid., 1025, 1044–45, 1070; Pemberton, *Pemberton*, 249; Rowland, *Jefferson Davis*, 5:581–82, 587–88.

52. OR, ser. 1, vol. 24, pt. 1, pp. 249–95, pt. 3, pp. 1057, 1061–65.

53. *Philadelphia Inquirer*, May 27, August 21, September 1, 1863.

54. William Mackall to Minie Mackall, October 3, 1863, William Whann Mackall Papers, SHC.

55. Ibid., October 9, 1863; OR, ser. 1, vol. 30, pt. 4, pp. 727, 735, 742.

56. William Mackall to Minie Mackall, October 10, 12, Mackall Papers, SHC.

57. JCP to Jefferson Davis, March 9, 1864, John C. Pemberton Papers, SHC.

58. OR, ser. 1, vol. 52, pt. 2, pp. 833–34.

59. JCP to Jefferson Davis, March 9, 1864, including Bragg's endorsement, Pemberton Papers, SHC; OR, ser. 1, vol. 33, p. 1296.

60. OR, ser. 1, vol. 36, pt. 1, p. 1051, pt. 2, pp. 993–94, pt. 3, p. 810, ser. 1, vol. 42, pt. 2, p. 1164, pt. 3, p. 1131; R. H. Fitzhugh to Mr. Sims, September 12, 1864, William Bailey Papers, University of Virginia Library, Charlottesville.

61. OR, ser. 1, vol. 47, pt. 2, p. 1020, 1153–54, 1159.

62. Ibid., pt. 3, p. 720, ser. 1, vol. 49, pt. 1, pp. 324, 334.

63. Rowland, *Jefferson Davis*, 7:74–75.

CHAPTER 10

1. John C. Pemberton [III], *Pemberton: Defender of Vicksburg* (Chapel Hill, 1942), 21–22.

2. Ibid., 21; Rebecca Pemberton to Israel Pemberton, August 15, 1864, IPP, PFP, HSP.

3. Dunbar Rowland, ed., *Jefferson Davis, Constitutionalist: His Letters, Papers, and Speeches*, 10 vols. (Jackson, Miss., 1923), 7:75; Rebecca Pemberton to Israel Pemberton, January 21, 1866, IPP, JCP to Israel, March 26, 1866, JCPP, PFP, HSP.

4. JCP to Israel Pemberton, April 3, December 9, 24, 1866, February 13, September 1?, 1873, JCPP, PFP, HSP. For examples of assistance the Pembertons received from their families, see JCP and Israel, correspondence of January 8, 11, 15, 1867, October 3, 1869, August 18, 1870, May 7, 1871, in JCPP.

5. Pemberton, *Pemberton*, 267; JCP to Israel Pemberton, December 9, 1866, June 7, July 7, 1867, December 16, 1872, April 27, 1873, JCPP, PFP, HSP.

6. JCP to Israel Pemberton, December 11, 24, 1867, August 9, 1869, JCPP, PFP, HSP.

7. Rebecca Pemberton to Israel Pemberton, June 25, July 4, 17, 1868, JCPP, PFP, HSP.

8. JCP to Israel Pemberton, July 7, 1867, February 6, 1868, JCPP, PFP, HSP.

9. Ibid., April 12, 1868, September 21, 1869, October 27, 1870; Jack P. Maddex, Jr., *The Virginia Conservatives, 1867–1879: A Study in Reconstruction Politics* (Chapel Hill, 1970), 47.

10. JCP to Rebecca Pemberton, September 1, 1868, November 17, December 30, 1869, February 12, August 18, December 7, 1870, JCPP, PFP, HSP; R. H. Chilton to William T. Sherman, October 31, 1872, William T. Sherman Papers, Library of Congress.

11. JCP to Israel Pemberton, February 12, 1870, September 1, October 8, 24, 1873, June 14, 1879, JCPP, PFP, HSP.

12. Ibid., December 7, 1870.

13. Ibid., May 7, 1871, February 13, 1873.

14. Ezra J. Warner, *Generals in Gray: Lives of the Confederate Commanders* (Baton Rouge, 1970), 230–31; Maddex, *Virginia Conservatives*, 113; JCP to Israel Pemberton, May 13, 27, 1872, JCPP, PFP, HSP.

15. Sarah A. Dorsey, *Recollections of Henry Watkins Allen, Brigadier General, C.S.A., Ex-Governor of Louisiana* (New Orleans, 1866), 183ff. (This citation refers to the page on which Dorsey begins quoting from Pemberton's postwar letters to her.)

16. The quotations here and in the next two paragraphs are from ibid., 183, 188, 194–95, 198, 213, 219–20, 222.

17. Joseph E. Johnston, *Narrative of Military Operations, Directed, during the Late War between the States* (New York, 1874); Jefferson Davis, *The Rise and Fall of the Confederate Government*, 2 vols. (New York, 1881).

18. JCP to William McCardle, May 6, 1877, William McCardle Papers, Mississippi Department of Archives and History, Jackson; JCP to Israel Pemberton, February 13, 1874, JCPP PFP, HSP.

19. JCP to Israel Pemberton, June 12, 1874, JCP to Henry Pemberton, June 16, 1874, JCPP, PFP, HSP.

20. Robert Underwood Johnson and Clarence Clough Buel, eds., *Battles and Leaders of the Civil War*, 4 vols. (1887–88; rpt. New York, 1956), 3:543–46; Pemberton, *Pemberton*, 289–319.

21. JCP to Israel Pemberton, April 27, 1873, June 12, 1874, JCPP, PFP, HSP.

22. Ibid., January 18, 1875.

23. James E. Payne, "General Pemberton and Vicksburg," *Confederate Veteran* 36 (July 1928): 247; "Vicksburg: Some New History in the Experience of Gen. Francis A. Shoup," ibid. 2 (June 1894): 174; T. L. Lanier, "The Surrender of Vicksburg," ibid. 2 (August 1894): 248.

24. Allentown, Pa., newspaper clipping in John C. Pemberton Papers, SHC; JCP to Henry Pemberton, August 17, 1875, JCPP, PFP, HSP; Daniel E. Sutherland, *The Confederate Carpetbaggers* (Baton Rouge, 1988), 243.

25. JCP to William McCardle, November 5, 1875, McCardle Papers, Mississippi Department of Archives and History, Jackson.

26. Ibid., Anna Pemberton (JCP's daughter) to Henry Pemberton, November 11, 1875, Henry Pemberton Papers, PFP, HSP.

27. Pattie Pemberton to Henry Pemberton, November 25, 1875, ibid., JCP to Messrs. Pemberton, Sloan, and Andenreid(?), December 7, 1875, JCPP, PFP, HSP.

28. JCP to Henry Pemberton, March 7, 1876, JCP to Israel Pemberton, March 16, 1876, September 10, 12, 1876, JCPP, PFP, HSP.

29. JCP to Israel, march 12, June 14, 1879, March 15, 1880, August ?, 1878?, ibid.

30. *Congressional Record*, 46th Cong. 1st sess. vol. 9, pt. 1, pp. 1042, 1190–91, pt. 2, pp. 1889, 2195.

31. JCP to Israel Pemberton, July 1, 1877, August ?, 1878, March 15, 1880.

32. Ibid., August ?, 1878? March 15, 1880.

33. Ibid., March 15, 1880.

34. J.H.A.? to Israel Pemberton, September 16, 1881, IPP, Henry Pemberton, Jr., to Henry Pemberton, July 2, 13, 1881, Henry Pemberton Papers, PFP, HSP; *Philadelphia Public Ledger*, July 14, 1881, clipping in Pemberton Papers, SHC; Pemberton, *Pemberton*, 277.

35. Israel Pemberton to Henry Pemberton, July 15, 1881, Henry Pemberton Papers, PFP, HSP.

36. *New York Times*, July 14, 1881; *Philadelphia Inquirer*, July 15, 1881.

37. *Atlanta Daily Constitution*, July 16, 1881; *Memphis Daily Appeal*, July 19, 1881; *Charleston News and Courier*, July 14, 1881; *Jackson Comet*, July 23, 1881; *Vicksburg Daily Herald*, July 16, 1881.

38. Don C. Seitz, *Braxton Bragg: General of the Confederacy* (Columbia, S.C., 1924), 543–44; Richard M. McMurry, *John Bell Hood and the War for Southern Independence* (Lexington, Ky., 1982), 203; Gilbert E. Govan and James W. Livingood, *A Different Valor: The Story of General Joseph E. Johnston, C.S.A.* (Indianapolis, 1956), 398.

39. "Annual Reunion of the Virginia Division A. N. Va. Association—

Address of Col. Archer Anderson on the Campaign and Battle of Chickamauga," *Southern Historical Society Papers* 9 (September 1881): 418.

40. Interment Permit No. 7918 for Gen. John C. Pemberton, July 15, 1881, Pemberton Family File, Laurel Hill Cemetery Company, Philadelphia.

EPILOGUE

1. Marcus J. Wright to R. V. Scott, January 13, 1883, RG 109, Entry 131, John C. Pemberton Papers, NA.

2. *New York Times*, October 15, 1907; Pemberton file, Laurel Hill Cemetery Company, Philadelphia.

3. Terrence J. Winschel, Vicksburg National Military Park historian, to the author, [November 1990]; John C. Pemberton statue record, Vicksburg National Military Park.

4. Colonel Willard D. Newbill, *General Report of National Memorial Celebration and Peace Jubilee* (Washington, D.C., 1917), 21.

5. A scrapbook detailing the 1937 commemoration is in the John C. Pemberton III Collection, Mississippi Department of Archives and History, Jackson. For an example of John III's debates with historians see his correspondence with Matthew Steele in the John C. Pemberton Collection, Museum of the Confederacy, Richmond. John III donated a large number of Pemberton items to the Southern Historical Collection, University of North Carolina, Chapel Hill.

6. *Philadelphia Sunday Bulletin*, October 8, 1961.

Bibliographical Notes

Significant collections of John C. Pemberton's papers are in three archival repositories: the Historical Society of Pennsylvania, National Archives, and Southern Historical Collection, University of North Carolina at Chapel Hill. Other material directly and indirectly related to Pemberton is scattered among several repositories. The best guide to these items is *The National Union Catalog of Manuscript Collections*.

The Historical Society of Pennsylvania has the largest number of known Pemberton letters from the antebellum and postbellum periods. There are large gaps in the correspondence, especially in the late 1830s and early 1840s and in the mid to late 1850s. Gaps also exist, though not as severely, in the postwar period letters. The general's papers are part of the Pemberton Family Papers, Collection 484B, which also contain the correspondence of his parents, wife, and siblings. These series of papers are most valuable in complementing Pemberton's papers. Interestingly and unfortunately, all these sets of papers contain practically no items from the Civil War years.

The National Archives has large collections of Pemberton's official Civil War papers in its Confederate Record series, Record Group 109. The major collection of items related to Pemberton's service in South Carolina is in Chapter II, volume 21, which contains copies of letters sent and received, Department of South Carolina and Georgia, for the period March to September 1862. Copies of outgoing correspondence for the department from February to July 1862 are in Chapter II, volume 28. Chapter II, volumes 22, 31, 32, 42, 183, and 184 contains additional records falling within the time period of Pemberton's service in the department.

Vicksburg materials are in the records of the Department of Mississippi and East Louisiana. Outgoing correspondence is in Chapter II, volumes 57 and 60, incoming correspondence in Entry 93. Other Vicksburg materials are in Chapter II, volumes 56, 1 3/4, 7 1/2, Chapter VIII, volume 370, Chapter V, volume 235, and Entries 94 and 95. A large collection of John C. Pemberton papers is assembled as Entry 131. Other papers of generals pertinent to operations in South Carolina and Mississippi are collected as separate entries. See *Preliminary Inventories, Number 101, War Department Collection of Confederate Records*, compiled by Elizabeth Bethel (Washington, D.C., 1957), for further information. An 1863 Pemberton order book from his service in the Department of Mississippi and East Louisiana is in the manuscript collections of the Virginia Historical Society.

The best access to most of the National Archives collections, as well as to the order book in the Virginia Historical Society and scattered materials in other locations, is in *War of the Rebellion: A compilation of the Official Records of the Union and Confederate Armies*, 128 vols. (Washington, D.C., 1880–1901), and *Official Records of the Union and Confederate Navies in the War of the Rebellion*, 35 vols. (Washington, D.C., 1894–1927).

The John C. Pemberton Papers in the Southern Historical Collection contain records and correspondence from all periods of his life. These items were collected and used by his grandson, John C. Pemberton III, in his book, *Pemberton: Defender of Vicksburg* (Chapel Hill, 1942). Some of the items included in the collection are photocopies and typescripts. The originals are apparently still in the hands of family members.

Pemberton: Defender of Vicksburg, despite its partisan tone, is a useful volume because it contains data derived from oral tradition within the Pemberton family. Because until now it was the only book available on Pemberton, it has had great influence on historians' interpretations of the general. For a contrasting view, see Joseph E. Johnston, *Narrative of Military Operations, Directed, during the Late War between the States* (New York, 1874). Other published autobiographies and biographies of Pemberton's contemporaries offer few insights into his Civil War career.

On the Vicksburg campaign, see the massive three-volume *Campaign for Vicksburg* (volume 1: *Vicksburg Is the Key*; volume 2: *Grant Strikes a Fatal Blow*; volume 3: *Unvexed to the Sea*), by Edwin Cole Bearss (Dayton, Ohio, 1985–86). Bearss's massive bibliography in volume 3 is especially useful. There is no comparable study of South Carolina operations. A provocative recent volume on Confederate politics and strategy that includes Vicksburg in its discussions is Steven E. Woodworth's *Jefferson Davis and His Generals: The Failure of Confederate Command in the West* (Lawrence, Kan. 1990).

Finally, a taste of contemporary reaction to Pemberton's Civil War years may be found in the volumes of the *Confederate Veteran* and the *Southern Historical Society Papers*. Fortunately for researchers, both these works have recently published, very thorough indexes.

Index